GOOD
MORMON
GIRL

GOOD
MORMON
GIRL

A MEMOIR

From a World of Sexual Shame

To a Life of Self-Love

JENNIFER JOY WILSON

For more information, email jennifer@goodmormongirl.com

ISBN: 979-8-89694-331-0 - Ebook

ISBN: 979-8-89694-332-7 - Paperback

ACKNOWLEDGEMENTS

I am forever indebted to Alan Fishleder for his patience through multiple revisions of this book as he took this creative venture with me. I'm especially grateful to him for helping me become more diligent in matters related to clear, concise writing. He so graciously offered his years of experience as a reporter, writer, and editor to make me a better storyteller. As an invaluable source of writing wisdom, Alan helped bring my book to life.

A special holler of appreciation to my big sister and her best friend—my literary editors. I appreciate their remarkable attention to detail, but even more, their loyal, intuitive, deep thinking, and openminded support over the years of this project. Thank you, ladies, for your hours and hours of work and for always cheering me on.

And last, special thanks and much love goes out to my husband, Charlie for his extraordinary support, helpful input, spiritual insights, and encouragement while writing this book. I also applaud him for his willingness to take over the household chores for the past seven and a half years while I pounded away at my computer to complete this book.

DOWNLOAD THE AUDIOBOOK FREE!

READ THIS FIRST

To say thanks for downloading my book, I would like to

Give you the Audiobook version 100% FREE!

I know you're more likely to finish this
book if you have the audiobook.

I even narrated the book myself so it will feel
like we are having a conversation.

Instead of paying $10-20 for the audiobook,
I'd like to give it to you for free …

http://www.goodmormongirl.com/

Free Audible Chapters of my Book

DEDICATION

To all of you who feel lost in your faith, whether you are struggling alone or in a relationship, I hope my story will inspire you to never give up. When life feels impossible, when the storm seems endless, remember you are your best keeper, you are your best friend.

For within each of us is a fighter. And to break free from the madness, we must know and trust that still small voice within, for here is where we find the answers that lead us to that place of peace and the freedom to shine.

Everything has changed,

And yet, I am more me

Than I've ever been.

—Iain S. Thomas

CONTENTS

A Word To My Readers   *xv*
Author's Notes   *xvii*
Brandi Nue Learns Mormon Terminology   *xix*

1.	Traditional Fairy Tales	1
2.	The Blindside	3
3.	Plum and Cornflower Blue	7
4.	Self-Discovery	11
5.	My Perfect Mom and Her Perfect Osmond Cousins	17
6.	Cookie-Cutter Doctrine	21
7.	Crimson & Clover Girl	25
8.	The Devil Made Me Do It	29
9.	Unlocking My Magic Powers	33
10.	Eyes Like Dark Scotchmallow Candy	37
11.	Caged and Clipped	43
12.	When Music Speaks	47
13.	Be Mine, Johnny Valentine	49
14.	The Girl Who Helped Me Discover Me	55
15.	Visit From a Stranger	57
16.	BYU Bumbler	61
17.	Haight Ashbury Love	65
18.	A Pocket Full of Air	71

19.	It Had to Be Chad	73
20.	The Lost Window	77
21.	It Could Have Been Fireworks	83
22.	Red Flags and a Bright White Gown	87
23.	Honeymoon Funk	93
24.	My Biggest Mistake	99
25.	That Evil Magazine	105
26.	Don't Blame Me, Blame My Hormones	111
27.	Confessions to Bishop McDreamy	115
28.	Mormon Minion	121
29.	Reflections of a Desperate, Lonely Housewife	125
30.	Bad to the Bone	131
31.	The Unfulfilled Blessing	135
32.	Wannabe LDS Prophet	141
33.	Motherhood "Wonderland" (Part 1)	147
34.	Motherhood "Wonderland" (Part 2)	155
35.	The Day My Family "Died"	159
36.	Priesthood Conspiracy	165
37.	Grief, Loneliness, Peace, & Tranquility	169
38.	Quit Giving Men Podiums	175
39.	Ruthless Shepherd	179
40.	We All Wear Masks	185
41.	Thou Shalt Pay Tithing in Exchange for Bleached Breads	189
42.	Love Starved	193
43.	Eye-Candy Randy	199
44.	Beyond the Black & White	203
45.	Delulu Love in a Shaggin' Wagon	209
46.	Legs Crossed, Heart Open	215

47.	A Thousand Cha-Chings but No Wedding Ring	219
48.	Fever on the Dance Floor	227
49.	Night with a "Bad Boy"	233
50.	Confessions of a Non Strategist	239
51.	Vanilla John	243
52.	He Who Sins Against the Greater Light	247
53.	Hot Tears Upon the Hot Seat	253
54.	If Christ Were Here	261
55.	Bishop Roulette	265
56.	Happy at Kappy's	269
57.	Uncaged & Unclipped	273
58.	A Different Kind of Battle	281
59.	Right Guy, Wrong Time	287
60.	I Didn't Start the Fire	293
61.	Out of the Fire into the Frying Pan	299
62.	Making Love with My Heart	303
63.	Jet Plane Toward Redemption	307
64.	The Letter	311
65.	Dangerous Dave	319
66.	Old Habits Die Hard	325
67.	Jaw-Droppers, Shockers & Thunderclaps	329
68.	Dysfunction Comes in Many Forms	339
69.	Bedazzled by Beelzebub	343
70.	I'll Give You Real	349
71.	What's Your Emergency?	353
72.	A Much Better Hell	361
73.	Standing at the Crossroads	367
74.	Being Saved by Grace Takes Work	375

75. My Divine Matchmaker   379

76. Oh, Those Sweet, Sweet Lies   385

77. My Defining Moment   389

78. Life After Organized Religion   393

79. A Universal Religion   397

80. Free at Last   401

Thank You For Reading My Book! 405
Epilogue 407
A Glimpse Into The Author 409

A WORD TO MY READERS

People along my life's journey encouraged me to write my story. Although all these friends were not acquainted with each other, each one told me the same thing—my story is one crazy wild ride. In my memoir there are about a dozen chapters with light sexual content. As for the rest, to keep your compassionate tears from soaking the pages of your purchased book, I chose to lighten the moments of my harrowing life with my own brand of humor.

Only after making the courageous decision to leave the Mormon faith, did I exhume an essential part of me—a component long buried and forgotten due to puritanical shaming. As a Mormon, I loathed myself simply for having a healthy libido; and in turn, I decimated an integral part of my identity. How can we know and embrace ourselves fully if we are indoctrinated to disconnect with this most fundamental part of ourselves? As humans, we are hardwired for sex. We are sexual beings.

As you dive into my book, you will ride close beside me and learn about my private world's most intimate experiences along with Shame's relentless bullying. Why would I choose to expose myself in this way? Sex is often a taboo topic. It's the elephant in the room. I'm determined to develop a mature, emotionally intimate relationship with the elephant so that we might establish dialogue. Ethical sexual expression is a beautiful thing. Yet Guilt, Shame, and Sexual Pleasure cannot cohabitate in peace. Together they create a toxic trio and a lifetime of colossal suffering.

If you, my dear reader, are stagnating in a world of emotional or sexual repression, I humbly implore you to read my story with an open mind. In these pages, I share my experiences, from the most exhilarating to those painfully replete with hard lessons. By reading my memoir, I hope you find something that will help you avoid my pitfalls in your journey toward authentic peace.

I believe the newfound freedom that only your authentic self can offer will introduce you to a gloriously prismatic world filled with beautiful new colors—a world that will lead you straight to joy. Only then will you be able to identify the person who lives behind your eyes. And when you find out who you are and fall in love, the rest is easy.

PLEASE NOTE:

Chapter 2 and 3 include references to domestic violence. Chapter 8, 9, and 26 contain moments of sensuality and self-pleasure. Chapter 57 & 59 contain moments of sexual acts.

AUTHOR'S NOTES

This book is a memoir. It reflects my present recollections of experiences over time. Most of the names have been changed, some events have been compressed, and some dialog has been reconstructed.

BRANDI NUE LEARNS MORMON TERMINOLOGY

Bishop Gray: Hello, Brandi, welcome to The Sacramento 3rd Ward.

Brandi: But I'm not crazy.

Bishop Gray: No, no, no, it's not a psyche ward. A ward is another name for an LDS congregation. Our ward meets at 8:00 a.m.

Brandi: People must be crazy to get up at that time. Are you sure it's not a psyche ward?

Bishop Gray: Well, they say we're the craziest ward in the stake.

Brandi: Please don't talk about Sizzler on Fast Sunday. I'm starving.

Bishop Gray: No, no, no. I'm not talking about a restaurant. A stake is a bunch of wards under one jurisdiction that often meet at the stake house.

Brandi: So it's not like Sizzlers or Out Back? I'm truly starving.

Bishop Gray: Well, then you can bring cupcakes to the fireside tonight.

Brandi: How will we roast cupcakes? Can I bring S'mores?

Bishop Gray: No, no, no. A fireside is when a bunch of wards meet together at the stake house and listen to some really good speakers.

Brandi: Okay, I guess I'll see ya at 7:00 with a ribeye and bag of marshmallows.

CHAPTER 1

TRADITIONAL FAIRY TALES

What if you woke up one morning at midlife only to discover that everything you knew to be true was a big fat lie? That all you ever lived for and celebrated—your husband, children, friends, and religion were nothing more than a make-believe world?

All the years prior to my forty-sixth birthday, I thought I knew where I was going as I stumbled down the church's straight and narrow road to Absolutely Nowhere. Truth be told, my Mormon upbringing played a major role in my vapid wanderings, but it wouldn't be fair to give it all the credit for my continued weekly therapy sessions. Just like you, I am where I am today due to free will. And although my genealogical roots have tendencies to branch off in dangerously psychotic directions, ultimately, I owe it to myself to reach inside and find out how and why my choices led to my predicaments.

A product of my environment, I wasn't born lost. Like any impressionable child, I grew up believing in fairy tales. Especially the ones my parents told me. They said if I lived worthily, I would one day find a loving companion, marry in the Oakland temple, and live happily ever after.

It would be easy to scapegoat my parents for my rambling road to nowhere. But they just learned the same traditional fairy tale of princes, princesses, castles, Mormon temples, and "happily ever afters" from their parents. There was one catch, however. They failed to tell me the full story. My life story is the real version …

CHAPTER 2

THE BLINDSIDE

1977

I'm out cold and gradually coming to when I hear his reverberating cries—three faint words in the distance. "Talk to me." I have no idea where I am or how I got here. I'm sprawled out on a cold, hard surface, feeling drugged and exhausted. I try to move my neck to no avail. My eyes are imprisoned as if under a thousand-pound sandbag. Trying without success to open them, I finally give up.

Then I hear his cry again—the same three words. "Talk to me." Talk to me!" The voice approaches closer, echoing urgency, even desperation. Numb from the cold, I can't feel my limbs. All I want to do is move away from the harsh, demanding voice. *Is this real? Or is it just a bad dream?* A muscle involuntarily twitches at the corner of my eye as I hear his boots crunch louder. I think I must be in a cave or tunnel because his voice echoes in the hollow. I know there's no escaping. He's only a few feet away now.

In one last desperate attempt, I try to move my legs, but they're as heavy as melted tar. I can't even wiggle my toes. Then all at once, the creaking ceases. My skin tingles with the certainty of danger. I hold my breath and play dead, hoping he'll pass on by. But the phantom is too smart to be fooled. Suddenly he's on top of me, pinning my arms at my sides with his knees. I try to scream, but nothing comes out. *Is this it? Is this how my story is going to end? Murdered by the hands of a stranger in a dark cave where I'll never be found?*

Finally able to wriggle beneath his weight, I'm hoping to move his torso off my stomach so I can breathe, but he doesn't budge. Then one, two, three staccato blows to my head. I lay in shock as he wails to the rhythm of his slaps. "You never talk to me!" My brain finally registers that this man is no stranger. That all-too-familiar voice belongs to my husband. And now he's going to kill me. I try desperately to scream, but I have no voice.

YOU NEVER TALK TO ME!" The heat of his breath jostles me from my nightmare into the very core of a real one. On the bed, I try to wriggle free, but his strength overpowers me. I finally find my voice and screech in horror,

"What are you doing? ... You're a monster. ... Get off me!"

"We never talk anymore, damn it. Talk to me!" he demands. He's sitting on me. How can I talk when I can't breathe? I'm two months pregnant with our daughter, but within seconds I feel like a terrified little girl. I survey the room for a safe corner, at the same time, I scour my brain for a logical explanation to his madness. But there is none. If there's ever a moment I need my mommy and daddy, it's now. I long to fall into the safety of their arms and be whisked away from this madman who has taken over my husband's body.

Unlike the icy blue-eyed demon sitting on top of me, the man I married has always been respected in the LDS community. He honors his priesthood, magnifies his callings, and tolerates my occasional tendencies to be overly emotional. When we got engaged, I had the trusting heart of a child and believed he was going to make me the happiest bride in the world. Now, the only thing I want to do is to run far, far away from him.

Gary releases my wrists but clamps his knees tighter, pinning me down like a helpless animal. Searching for answers, I struggle to recall last night's events. Images appear in my mind—distorted images, yet as I close my eyes, the scene becomes more vivid ...

It was around 8:00 p.m. when I shuffled past the front room into the kitchen to fetch a light snack before retiring for the night. Gary was slouched in his La-Z-Boy and said he wanted to talk. I let him know I was brain-dead and asked if we could talk the following day. I don't remember much after that except for falling into a deep slumber before I had a chance to undress.

Like most young newlyweds, we struggled to stay on top of our bills. Every day after attending classes at the local college, Gary worked at his uncle's miniature golf course blowing leaves from walkways and dredging fishponds. I worked full-time at Redwood City Office Supply selling paper clips, staplers, and five-foot filing cabinets. Between both our schedules, there just wasn't a lot of day left over for conversation. I admit, I wished we had more time to enjoy each other, but for him to feel *angry* about not talking? Honestly, between the morning sickness and fatigue, I'd been far too tired to feel anything.

A sharp sting stabs my upper eyelid, knocking me from my reverie. He must have clobbered it pretty good. I wince in fear as I look up at him. I often hear of hell described as "fire and brimstone," but I never knew what it looked like until now. Everything I thought I knew about love has been shattered by this madman. I'm mentally trying to pick up the pieces of my broken heart as it falls in shards to the floor.

He finally peels himself away from my pregnant tummy and wanders listlessly into the front room. I breathe in a sigh of relief, but I'm still cautious. I have no idea why he left the room. Hearing rumbling sounds in the kitchen, I pray to God he's not looking for a knife ...

CHAPTER 3

PLUM AND CORNFLOWER BLUE

I utter a prayer under my breath, then ever-so-quietly roll to the edge of the mattress, pulling myself upright, making sure my feet are solidly on the floor. Wedging my toes between loose strands of dark green shag carpet, I slowly shuffle out of the room and down the hall. Then I hear it. The rising commotion His pathetic wailing and bellowing reverberate throughout the livingroom. Cautiously, I poke my head around the corner. Gary is kneeling in front of our old paisley-printed couch, praying. "Oh God, what have I done? Heavenly Father, please forgive me!" With his tear-stained cheeks buried in his hands, his lamenting howls echo through the walls.

I wait as he pounds the couch with his fists in the sudden transition from out-of-control lunatic to melodramatic repentant sinner. I fail to comprehend how the nightmare could get much worse, but it does. My husband's theatrical bemoaning continues for a full hour and now it's 5:00 a.m. At this point, I'm not sure who I feel most sorry for—him, me, or the next-door tenants who can hear everything through our paper-thin walls.

Amid this nightmare, I want to escape—run away forever. But six months earlier, Gary and I had been sealed for time and eternity in holy matrimony. We had made sacred temple covenants before the Lord. You can't just give up that easily when you make these kinds of promises. I remind myself that I need to do everything in my power to make this marriage work. Besides, I'm pregnant. I just can't pick up and leave. How would my child and I survive without a man to take care of us? I'm barely making minimum wage.

Before Gary left for work that morning, he made me promise not to tell my parents what had happened. He said he was sorry and wanted to talk when he got back home. *Sorry? That's it?* He must have used all his theatrics for God and had nothing left for me.

The apartment was empty now, and so was my heart. In hysterics, I threw myself on my bed and covered my head with my pillow wanting to smother myself. But it was Monday. I needed to show up for work despite my swollen eye, shattered heart, and hijacked night's sleep.

Hobbling toward the bathroom, I examined my face in the mirror. I was horrified. On most days my deep-set brown eyes and rosy complexion typically brought a warm glow to a frosty room. But not that day. I reached to touch my eyelid and winced. My eye was almost swollen shut a tiny, melted crescent, a murky mix of plum and cornflower blue. I despised the woman peering back at me. *This is not who I am. This day could not have happened.*

The form bearing some semblance of me gazed back and revoked my denial. "Welcome to hell!" it said. I blinked into the glass and could see the depth of pain below my discolored skin. My eyes welled up with tears that refused to fall. I was too broken to allow any other parts of me to do their jobs.

I had now joined the ranks of the millions of other abused women who were clueless about the battle that lay ahead of them. Through rattled breaths, my mind kept returning to Gary's last words when he pleaded with me to not tell my parents about his abuse. In return, he vowed to never lay a finger on me again. As tempted as I was to rat him out, I was a woman of my word. Although his tears of remorse weren't directed at me personally, I hoped they counted for something.

When I was a little girl, I had every reason to believe in a "happily ever after." But now I was just trying to get through the moment. My mind was a blur. It was as though my world had been tossed into a bone-chilling horror-story labyrinth with no way out. I was carrying this man's child. I had to do what was best for my baby. Yet at age twenty-two, I hardly knew what was best for me, or what "best" even looked like.

CHAPTER 4

SELF-DISCOVERY

Before I married a stranger, I grew up amid ryegrass and blue gum eucalyptus trees in the heart of California's Hayward Hills. Sandwiched between two older sisters and a younger brother, I got lost in the shuffle. To get them to notice me, I became theatrical.

As a preteen, I couldn't wait to grow boobs. But when they arrived, I felt conflicted. Flowing out of my Playtex DD at age thirteen, I ensconced myself in my happy place and admired my body behind closed doors. That is, until my church introduced me to Guilt and Shame.

In 1969, about forty years before women were purchasing their breasts by the pound, I was a rare specimen. When walking the streets, my outrageous bustline made me the focal point of all appreciating eyes. Guys of every age would go out of their way to meet me. Although their attention made me feel special, it also made me feel dirty.

Because the internet didn't exist in my day, you couldn't access information by the touch of a screen. Everything I learned about sex was from a little book my mom gave me. That book was it. Its rudimentary drawings forced me to use my imagination. A picture showed a sperm penetrating an egg floating down a woman's fallopian tube, but it failed to tell me the most important part. *How did that little polliwog get there?*

Porn in the '60s and '70s was Penthouse and Playboy. Stacks of magazines filled liquor store checkout stands and drew men in from the streets. As a naturally curious pubescent teen, I looked too. You can't help noticing a beautiful naked body, straight or gay. But I remained clueless about sex.

In my pubescent years, a church-adored leader, Spencer W. Kimball, began to preach about the evils of masturbation. My faithful adherence to his warnings kept me further in the dark about my body and its sexual responses. *Was I supposed to avoid touching myself altogether until I found a marriage partner who could touch it for me?*

Standing naked before the mirror one evening admiring my fully developed girls, I told myself they looked amazing. I leaned forward, examined my cleavage, then turned from side to side, pushing them up, fingers extending beneath them as if I were posing for Playboy. But the longer I stood admiring my nakedness, the more guilty I felt.

My predicament was paradoxical in that my heart was pure and good. I read my scriptures daily and loved my Heavenly Father. But I also loved my "bad girl boobs." Obedient to a fault, I believed that suppressing the overwhelming desire to admire and touch myself was what I needed to do to remain clean and pure so that one day I could be worthy to enter the temple. If I caved, I would blow my chances for a happily ever after.

At the same time, I couldn't help but wonder why God would choose to put me through such a test. Although I didn't understand the rules, I did my best to avoid even looking at my body, which is an insane challenge when your body is attached to you. Sometimes I'd get tempted to touch it lightly, then quickly stop. "The Lord is good," I'd say. "The Lord is great." And if I proved to be faithful, I knew that in His own due time, He would share the mystery to His madness.

FAKE IT TILL YOU MAKE IT

Sometimes, you just know when you're different from everyone else. Growing up was tough. For me, too much attention was never enough. When my belly growled, I alerted the national guard. I wasn't just hungry; I was starving to death. When cold, I was freezing to death. Obnoxiously loud and melodramatic, it comes as no surprise that I was often ignored.

At an early age, I noticed my mother's smile grow paradoxically wider when she worried, and an extra energetic bounce appeared in her step when she grew tired. If I complained about being sleepy or hungry or cold, her advice? —Fake it till you make it. No one likes a whiner." With all her many responsibilities, plus the effects of a severe sleep disorder, "faking it till she made it" was Mom's only coping strategy. It helped her get through the day.

By the time I was five, I could tell when she said things just to appease me, so she could move on to "more important things." Clearly, she was in survival mode, trying to keep her head above water. Still, I grew up feeling invisible. Don't get me wrong, I know she loved me deeply. But I was hard wired for connection, and I needed more than just love.

As introverts, my parents couldn't possibly fill my insatiable need for affection and connection. I often withdrew into my imaginary world, which to me was the real world. In my mind, I saw "him" clearly. Adorned in a gold dinner jacket and royal-red pants, my warm, genuine prince would be the one to rescue me from the "fake it till you make it" world. He would take me in his arms, and I would no longer be lost. I would be seen!

ME, MY MOM, & THAT BONY BROAD

In the '60s and '70s, you could never be too thin. As a high school freshman, there were several things that triggered my eating disorder. Having a mom who looked like a J.C. Penny's clothes department store manikin was one trigger. Why didn't she ever gain weight like I did?

The stress of being a teenager was my second trigger. My outbursts at home and my shyness and social awkwardness at school defined my daily defeat. I needed relief from the battle. If I had been raised to believe that my body was my best friend, a tool to use in moderation for both comfort and pleasure, I might not have developed an eating disorder. But when you grow up being told masturbation is a sin, you find another way to quiet the ruckus inside.

I'd often find myself creeping downstairs at midnight, stuffing myself with anything I could get my hands on—barbecued chicken, mashed potatoes, biscuits, leftover cake, anything to fill the emptiness. Hungry or not, I gorged myself until I could barely move—all while cursing Twiggy, that bony broad whose face was plastered on every Vogue magazine in America.

Thrusting my fingers to the back of my throat to trigger the gag reflex so my food could be expelled never appealed to me. Instead, I would starve for days at a time, eating the bare minimum until I reached my desired weight. When I did, I prided myself on having the silhouette of a trucker's mudflap girl. At least for a while. Yet, it didn't take long before Shame tore me down again. Shrieking loudly from the pulpit, it accused me of being walking pornography. On those days, I held my books high to shield my ever-expanding bustline as I slumped across campus like Quasimodo.

As a sophomore I was still shy and didn't talk much. But I didn't have to. I grew another cup size, and my uber ample breasts did all the talking for me. At five-foot-eight, if I turned sideways, my waist disappeared, but my DDD "church bells" could cause a serious collision if I got too close to ongoing traffic. When hearing, "nice rack" while walking down the hallways, was I supposed to yell back, "Thank you very much?" The exponential growth of my body's development ran circles around my social skills. At age fifteen, a good Mormon girl wasn't supposed to look like a porn-star. *How would I get good marks in heaven?*

CHAPTER 5

MY PERFECT MOM AND HER PERFECT OSMOND COUSINS

My mom made my Malt-O-Meal lumpy just the way I liked it. She showed her love for me by doing things. But we were two very different people. I was wired for connection. She was not. I saw her as a beautiful, untouchable rose that protected herself, not with prickly thorns, but with a wall. Or maybe I just imagined the wall because I was ultra-sensitive and needed a lot more personal interaction.

Second cousin to '70s TV stars, Donny and Marie Osmond, my mother was the picture of perfection all the way from PTA President to homemaker to adored choir director of our East Bay Latter-day Saint community. The problem? I wanted her all to myself. I wanted to sit at the table and eat biscuits with her and have a meaningful, unrushed conversation.

The Osmond genealogical family tree had a way of sprouting tall, long-waisted porcelain-skinned people with large white teeth and chocolate wavy hair. My mom was no exception. Still, she had her own insecurities, of which she kept tight reign.

As our ward choir director, she would flash her big, bright Osmond smile and wave her baton to the rhythm of joyful hallelujahs. Yet, I never had the ability to reach inside her and truly know if she served out of mere duty, or out of her love for the gospel. She once told me when I was around nine, that she didn't believe in Satan. I guess I needed to introduce her to her son, my extremely obnoxious younger brother.

In 1965, right before my tenth birthday, the Osmond Brothers came to San Francisco to perform. Mom invited them to our Bay Area home for a family day, which they accepted with enthusiasm. Our mother, elegant, efficient, and organized, was a perfect hostess. Nothing could be too clean or too shiny. How would I ever measure up? Especially when she told me I inherited my dad's "sloppy gene."

After playing in the backyard with my siblings and me, seven-year-old Donny decided to go inside. In doing so, he mistook my mom's spotlessly clean sliding-glass door for an open one and ran right into it. After a good smack to his braces, instead of whining, that little guy simply grinned from ear to ear.

That evening, the Osmonds joined us for a rewarding night of music. My cousins, siblings, and I huddled on the carpet and watched with rapt attention as Alan, Wayne, Merrill, and Jay took their places upfront in our spotless living room. It's like we had our very own front-row seat to the Andy Williams Show.

I glanced over at little Donny who was enjoying the music along with us. It seemed as though he kept smiling at our perfect mother who was the unintended cause of his injured mouth. Even when her uber-clean glass door caused bodily harm, she still came out a winner.

I don't think I ever saw Donny without a smile. He had been starting to make a few appearances with his brothers on the show. To think this little budding performer had no idea that his leap to stardom was right around the corner. We didn't get to meet six-year-old Marie who wasn't with them on the trip.

The four brothers sang a fun assortment of numbers, such as "Aura Lee," "Mr. Sandman, and "Sing a Rainbow." Then they sang a song which they dedicated to their mom. "I Wouldn't Trade the Silver in My Mother's Hair" was a gorgeous tribute. I glanced over at Olive Osmond who was beaming with pride.

After our cousins' wonderful performance, my dad boldly announced that his kids would be next. *Wait. What?* He decided we were going to sing for the Osmonds. From the time my three siblings and I were knee-high to a duck, we had been singing four-part-harmony a cappella for various cultural events and church meetings. We were used to performing in front of large crowds. *But for the Osmond Brothers?*

On "centerstage," we chose our favorite song, "Side by Side," our enthusiasm matching theirs as the famous brothers cheered us on. This was a moment in time that helped me appreciate my family tree—boughs filled with musically gifted ancestors going back many generations to the beginnings of Mormonism. As my eyes surveyed the room with its abundance of laughter and bright snowy smiles, my heart sang joyfully. I felt so blessed to have such a culturally rich Mormon heritage.

Not everyone has a perfect mom. But I had one. I eventually learned through the years that she wasn't so perfect. For in her beautiful, resplendent being was hidden a secret more shaming than shame itself—her fear of not being perfect.

CHAPTER 6

COOKIE-CUTTER DOCTRINE

When I entered LDS Primary, I learned through word and song that motherhood was a Disney World Wonderland—a place filled with rainbows and cookies and yellow balloons. I was three. Three-years-old. I was a baby singing songs about having babies. The road had already been paved for me whether I wanted that role or not: Someday I would become a Mother in Zion.

In 1967, when I was almost twelve, the women's rights movement emerged and feminist campaigns for radical reforms threatened the LDS family unit. Liberalized attitudes toward sex were slowly but surely weaving their way into the fabric of our society. My leaders worked to crush this "pernicious" movement by preaching all the harder about the evils of fornication along with emphasizing that a woman's place is in the home. Yet, as a preteen, I remained oblivious to what was happening in the world. In my own little Utopia, I wrote poems about safeguarding my virtue and fantasizing about my future husband. One of my poems went like this:

MY LIFE IS A ROSE GARDEN

My life is a package of rose seeds
Sent from the heavens above.
Its ribbon consists of gold stardust
That shimmers and glows with God's love.
This gift, my most precious possession
Should be planted with tender care,
Watered then sprinkled with sunshine
And nurtured each night with a prayer.
And if I attend to my garden,
After planting heaven's seeds
Each tiny bud that blooms and grows
Will represent good deeds.
My kindness will take on color
Of breathtaking yellows and reds
My grace will generate mind-blowing pinks
And whites in the garden beds.
Prickly thorns will show purpose.
My virtue they will protect
So I may bloom with purity
And develop self-respect.
I'll blossom through every rainstorm.
I'll thrive through each trial and tear.
I'll be a bouquet for the weary,
For those who need comfort and cheer.
And I will stand tall in the garden,
And never be afraid
To share my grace and beauty

Until my petals fade.
From heaven's seed to a rose bud,
Then opened, full bloom toward the sky,
I'll make this world more beautiful
Until the day I die.

As I grew older, while my high-school peers drank, partied, and got high, I took refuge in my bedroom chatting with the only person who tuned into my frequency—my Heavenly Father. Because I couldn't comfortably confide in my parents, I would kneel by my bed and pour out my heart to my Lord. Sometimes, I'd sit with Him for a good hour thanking Him for watching over me.

Was I a little fanatical in my prayer habits? Perhaps. But I didn't have many friends. Not close ones, anyway. The Lord was it. Perhaps I became borderline delusional due to my desperate need for a father figure. Not that I didn't have an earthly dad. He was just the absentminded professor-type. To get his attention, I would either have to hunt him down in the dust-filled haze of his workshop and shout above the roar of his table saw, or watch his eyes wander off to some distant land when the absence of noise distracted him. *But God?* A whispered plea, and He was with me.

As a teenager, every Tuesday night, I attended M.I.A (Mutual Improvement Association), an LDS youth program that teaches young women how to set spiritual goals. In her sweet, high-pitched voice, Sister Shoemaker stood in front of our class one evening and said, "Okay, ladies, it's time to work on our personal progress goals." *Ugh.* I hated goals. One important goal written in the handbook was "be worthy to attend the temple and have enduring joy on the covenant path." Sister Shoemaker was preparing us for marriage.

At age sixteen, I was a budding rose, pure and sweet. In my innocence, this so-called personal progress goal ironically set me on a panic-driven path to find my "one and only." And in obsessive pursuit of him, I ended up compromising my own social development. So much for personal progress. Furthermore, what first-rate guy would want to marry a one-dimensional woman with a one-track mind?

Most of my M.I.A classmates were high-school cheerleaders. I felt like a loser around them—the girl on the outside looking in. To make myself feel better, I judged them as supercilious and unladylike. I mean, how could they attract a righteous man by romping around in their fringe–layered skirts, flashing their panties for the whole world to see? In my dramatic assessment, it seemed that the world was becoming progressively more perverse. *Was this the sign of the times?* I wondered. *Maybe, the women's liberation movement would end us all.*

CHAPTER 7

CRIMSON & CLOVER GIRL

As a child, I was a spitfire who tried to get attention by hurling myself onto the kitchen floor—kicking, flailing, barking, braying, my long, thick dirty-blonde strands thrashing around my face. Then, I became a young woman.

At age fifteen, although I was still highly emotional, my explosive episodes were a little less dramatic although far from elegant. At least my outer shell looked more pleasing. My pristine smile replaced the braces on my teeth. Dark brown eyes with prominent cheekbones and a rosy complexion, I had outgrown my "not so comely" stage and looked more like my mom.

On the weekends, I would often shop downtown Hayward's Golden Strip. One afternoon on my walk home, something happened that helped me see myself differently. As I look back on this day, it was an afternoon driven by innocence, exploration, and exciting discovery. And although it lasted for less than a minute, I finally felt validated.

It happened like this …

I'm wearing my purple, white-polka-dotted, curve-hugging dress with a laced-corset bodice. My boobs look huge in it. With my ear to my little handheld radio, I'm getting into the groove of "Crimson and Clover," when to my left I see a column of connecting beams, a skeletal structure of a multi-story building.

I cup my fingers over my eyes to block out the sun and see them. Hardhats—an ocean full, pounding on the roof, sweaty, bulging, bronze biceps glistening in the hot summer sun. One of them spots me and is pointing me out to the others. The song's hypnotic vibrato along with all the male attention on the roof frees all my inhibitions and raises my heart rate. *Am I the Crimson and Clover girl in the song?* All those years feeling insignificant as a child, now as a budding adult, I'm finally getting a big payday.

I confidently sway my hips, clicking my white, round-toed go-go boots across the cement to the rhythm of the tremolo guitar. *Do I dare look up at them?* The warm breeze gives my hair a sexy tousle. The smell of fresh lumber permeates the air as my dress's soft fabric swishes to the "wah-wah" sound of the guitar. The mesmeric melody together with the muscly men on the roof make me feel like a flower-power Goddess.

I'm about three-quarters of the way past them when I cautiously look up to discover that some of them are no longer hammering. The men are staring down at me, their jaws dropping through the dust-covered beams. This is my moment to feel invincible, but what do I do? I look down at the ground, sharing my Mona Lisa smile with the sidewalk.

Still, just because I don't show it, doesn't mean I don't feel it. These are real men. Nothing like those acne-faced guys that pass me in the school hallways. Their attention gives me a confidence boost. I know I'm a head-turner because it happens a lot to me, but I'm still innocent and oblivious to the private male anatomy. I haven't seen what is hidden under their clothing, and I have no clue as to what it all can do. Deep down, I'm perplexed. *Why do I feel so invincible when strutting by a construction zone, yet so inferior, clumsy, and fat around my mother?*

I obsess about those yummy construction workers all the way home. *I wonder what they look like naked. Or even better, what if I married one of them and we had sex?*

Home, showered, and wearing only panties, I flop onto my bed and smile off into the distance as I think about that dreamy construction worker on the roof—the one that spotted me and pointed me out to the others. A deep burning fills my cheeks, and my throat feels constricted while picturing him without clothes. Still, a repentant voice within pleads with the Lord before I make my next move.

Lying on my pillow, I picture Fantasy Guy hovering over me, his spindrift curls, damp from sweat. I let out a slow breath as I ghost my fingers across my tummy, pretending to be him. I close my eyes and see his smile beaming brighter. Will he explore all my erogenous places?

As he ogles me with his expressive deep browns, I tell myself I should not engage in self-play.

Yet I take comfort in the thought that pretending to be married might make my sin less harsh. My sexy "husband" is huddling closer. I breathe in his smell. *What kind of cologne is he wearing? Or is that fragrance the soap he uses?*

As I reach to fondle my girls, this dreamy guy instantly transforms into a dark, shadowy figure. My studly hardhat has been replaced by Guilt. Guilt is on top, but it's not sexy. It's suffocating. Guilt is the predominant stink that overpowers the glorious smells of woody masculinity. I no longer feel exhilarated but unworthy. And for me, there is nothing worse than feeling unworthy. Even in my shame, I can't help but wonder why the Lord would allow me to experience a hormonal hurricane inside my body yet forbid me to act on it.

As the night draws near, there's a headwind inside my restless heart, propelling me forward, pushing me through the gates of private property, thrusting me toward territories that have not yet been discovered. I know I have a choice. The choice is mine. I can either mow down Guilt and hurl toward self-exploration or spread my wings toward heaven. It's all up to me ...

CHAPTER 8

THE DEVIL MADE ME DO IT

In the wee hours of the morning, I'm with a guy. I can feel his breath in my ear. His face gradually comes into focus. He looks at me adoringly, then moves in closer for a kiss. Then, I wake up. Damn! I close my eyes again, hoping to fall back into my dream, but this seriously hot looking stranger disappears into the shadows.

In my highly restless state, I kick off my covers, and while I'm at it, kick Guilt to the curb. At around 3:00 am, I find myself standing in front of my vanity, as the girl in the glass wearing a white silk slip and naughty expression, summons me. *"You and I are going to have a great moment,"* she growls.

I snatch a bottle of my English Lavender perfume from the drawer and puff the fresh-flowered mist along my clavicle. Pantomiming the temptress, I clutch my neck, nod my head in the mirror, and flash an indulgent smile.

The house is quiet. Everyone's asleep. I glance down at my slip's bodice and caresss my nipples through the lace. A pulse dances between my thighs as I trace a circle around my areolas.

My breathing is loud and laborious as I slowly remove my slip, one strap at a time, wiggling my garment down to the carpet, kicking it beneath the bed with my red-painted toes. Thoroughly naked, I feel elfish, unleashed, even a bit dirty.

My body reminds me of one of those girls on the cover of those naughty magazines I discovered in my brother's treehouse in the orchard behind our home. I remember getting aroused as I flipped through the pages. *Am I lesbian?* I don't think I am because I never think of kissing a girl.

Posing in front of the glass, my complexion is alabaster, my coppery eyes alight, my little pixie nose scrunched like an elf's. My dirty blonde strands are now a rich dark auburn thanks to Miss Clairol. I pile my hair onto my head, allowing looser strands to fall over my shoulders. Feeling ballsy and brash, I wink at an imaginary camera. "Click, click, click."

"You're hecka hot!" I say to my reflection. Aroused by my nakedness, I reach to glide my fingers across my soft ivory tummy and trace a circle around my naval. I lift the undersides of my breasts, then release them and watch them softly sway against my ribcage.

Turning toward the moonlit wall, I see my silhouette, a darker version of me. I reach behind and give my fanny a good swat. That's when I hear noises in the hallway, my heart palpitating frantically. *What if my mom heard me slapping my butt? Will she knock on my door?* I immediately dive onto my mattress and hide beneath my sheets. Rigid beneath the covers, I wait. Listen. Nothing.

As I lie in the shadows staring up at my glittered-stucco ceiling with its cottage-cheese-like texture, my mind is racing. I yearn to do more exploring. At the same time, I'm conflicted as sleep eludes me till early dawn. I conclude that my body's a drug. I'm hooked.

In its persistence, Guilt reminds me that if I continue down this road, I will end up in Hell. My body is so accessible. Unlike a Snickers bar, a snack that can only be obtained through driving to a corner market and purchasing before eating, my beautiful, sensitive breasts are a part of me, tempting me 24/7. *How am I supposed to dissociate from them?*

As I toss and turn on my sheet, that same headwind revisits my restless heart, propelling me to soar toward the unknown. In the stillness, my hormones are screaming far louder than my conscience. If there's any Shame to be had, I've managed to snuff out its haranguing.

CHAPTER 9

UNLOCKING MY MAGIC POWERS

After a night of exploring the regions below my waist, I conk out from exhaustion. No effort on my part has unleashed the genie of the perfect climax, no matter how much I rubbed my little magic lamp.

I wake up the next morning and notice some itching "down there." I don't know why. Perhaps from all those natural secretions they talk about in sex education. To soothe the irritation, I decide to take a bath while my family is out doing errands. Little do I know that this bath will be more like a baptism, a holy immersion, even a spiritual revival as I shout praises forevermore.

I abruptly slide out of bed, hotfoot toward the bathroom, and strip. Braless, my chilled nipples grow stiff, my ample breasts suspend as I reach to adjust the water temperature. That's when I get an idea. I lay on my back in the tub and straddle my legs in front of me, resting them on the ledge, my groin under the faucet. I need a stronger flow, so I turn the handle, rocking my pelvis beneath the spout until a powerful stream runs directly over my vagina.

With the water's warmth running over and in me, the itching gradually subsides. I feel much better, yet I'm not a bit prepared for what comes next. A contraction pulses between my legs, then another. I can't contain myself, whimpering louder with each hit, holding nothing back since I'm home alone. *Oh, my God!* Good little Mormon girls don't typically use the Lord's name in vain, but this feels too darn good! The Lord needs to hear his name!

Impressed with the water's ability to arouse me, I lift my legs from the tub's ledge and press both feet into the tile in front of me—the perfect position to allow the spout to run directly over my clitoris. After all, it needs a good cleansing too. As the water dances teasingly on me, I increase its flow and open my legs wider to welcome the first twinge. I close my eyes and tilt back my head as splashing waves rush through me, expanding my cavern, shaking my insides, sending pleasure pulses to every place unholy and impure. It gives me the urge to want to have sex, though I can't imagine what sex even looks like. But it's not over.

My heart is still pumping as I glance down at my drenched, fully blossomed rosebud of a clitoris. I reach to caress it. It feels swollen in my hand. Exhausted and spent, I lie limp in the water, my heart thumping inside my ears.

So that's the short and long of it. At age fifteen, I mastered taking my car out for a test drive and felt truly blessed that God gave me a bright pink Ferrari. I never knew my luxury model was designed for a twin-engine joyride. It was like having dinner and dessert all in one sitting. There was no more guessing after that. I had finally unlocked the magic powers of my body.

From that day forth, I never skipped my nightly baths. When I felt alone in the world, I'd spread my legs wide and welcome the rushing water, moaning beneath the sound of the flowing tap. My hollow, pathetic life seemed more bearable when I felt a tsunami fill my groin and shake up my insides.

Yet Shame had a way of tormenting me. The more I participated in this act, the more it clouded my mind with its damning lies. And I believed the lies. "You're nothing but a perverted sicko," it would say. "Getting turned on by your own body? How low can you stoop? No Mormon prince is going to want you!"

I knew that looking forward to nightly baths was kind of like premeditated masturbation, a far more grievous sin than a wet dream, because with wet dreams, guys ejaculate in their sleep. They can't control it. But climaxing in the tub? Shame made me feel like a first-degree murderer!

In no time, I was on my knees pleading for the Lord's mercy, promising to never masturbate again. Soon, I discovered I was trading one vice for another. To relieve my anxiety and depression, I'd stuff my face daily with a load of carbs. *Bring on the Hostess Twinkies, Snowballs, and Ding Dongs!*

One month and ten pounds later, I fretted about my bounteous behind bursting like a beach ball, straining the seams of my brand-new bell bottoms. *Why was masturbation so wrong if it helped me to keep my weight down?* I knew I'd be so much healthier and happier if the Lord would just put His stamp of approval on my tryst with the tub.

"Me time" behind closed doors was my therapy. It filled an emotional void that I otherwise tried to fill with food. Speaking of overeating, why didn't God require repentance for that? He told me my body is a temple. I couldn't see anything holy about defiling it with Hostess products and other unhealthy comfort foods. Still, as nonsensical as his rules were, I needed to fly straight so Heavenly

Father would guide me toward love no matter how monstrously huge I appeared at the altar.

Soon, I could no longer look in the mirror as my weight continued to climb. I also talked more frequently about suicide. My mom's suggestion of sending me to a shrink only drove me further to the edge. How could a bashful girl like me talk to a therapist about my raging love affair with the bathtub?

Then just like that, my life shifted. Little did I know that running into the one thing that would save me from Grief would end up being my biggest regret.

CHAPTER 10

EYES LIKE DARK SCOTCHMALLOW CANDY

I was doing my own thing, going about my business, drudging through the second half of my high-school junior year when I ran into Shame. Shame happened to be a tall, dark, breathtakingly handsome high-school senior named Jay. And his kiss, my very first kiss was … well, let me start from the beginning …

If it hadn't been for the LDS worldwide young adult dance festival, I would have never met Jay. So I can blame my mother. She was the one who wanted me to get involved. It was either that or charm school—anything to help improve my posture and social skills.

This spectacular "evening of dance" was a huge event, bringing together LDS youth from all corners of the globe. Scheduled for that coming June, I was lucky to meet the age requirement. In our Hayward community, members from all four wards were encouraged to attend. That meant I could meet new guys. But I had one problem. I was socially inept.

Although I had no trouble expressing myself at home, when I hit kindergarten, I clammed up. Unprepared for a socially stimulating environment, I became overly anxious. At school there were too many kids. They were all staring at me. Everything was overwhelmingly loud. I had a lot to say, but just couldn't say it. How could I connect with strangers when I didn't even know how to connect with my parents in a meaningful way, who in turn didn't know how to connect with me? They saw my shyness in public as cute. Without their encouragement, I remained a painfully silent observer.

Now I was in high school. Socially stifled for years, I desperately wanted to talk but didn't know how to emerge from my shell. Because I loved to dance, perhaps this worldwide festival would help me break free from my limitations and give me a chance to transform into someone more ... dazzling?

From February through May of 1971, I would be required to attend sixteen weekly rehearsals across town. I would also have to forgo my Saturday morning cartoons. My reward? The thrill of dancing in perfect synchronization with 7,000 other LDS teens at University of Utah's football stadium in Salt Lake City.

I met Jay at the very first rehearsal. On a Richter scale, he was a twelve. His earth-shattering looks and sex-appeal activated a launch sequence in my groin. When introduced, he cocked his head and offered an infectious smile, his eyes the color of dark Scotchmallow candy—rich brown with golden specks in the center. He had broad-shoulders, thick, wavy dark hair, and a waistline as lean as a cat. *Was he my happily-ever-after? Maybe dreams really do come true?* Jay Hawkins, a name I will never forget, was my first crush. He was outgoing and funny and everything I wasn't. At the rehearsals, he'd often hang on me, even when the music wasn't playing. On the inside, I wanted to curl up against his ribs and make little purring sounds. Even his body odor was intoxicating. But on the outside, I stiffened.

How was I supposed to react to his overly generous public displays of affection? I was so insecure, so rigid, I don't think he knew what to do with me either. No doubt he was used to girls falling all over him. I wouldn't know how to fall all over him if I tried. *But dancing? That was different.* I had no problem with it. Like most musicians, rhythm came easy. It was the only medium that allowed me to express myself without having to say a word. When rehearsing the waltz, every time he twirled me around to face him, my inner temptress dared me to kiss him. Like that was gonna happen. I could hardly look at him without blushing.

After four months of grueling practice, our dance team boarded the bus and headed to Salt Lake City. For early June, Utah's weather was hotter than Hades, but as I danced with my hand tucked into Jay's large palm, I felt an entirely different exciting warmth.

Before our big debut, we had one very long, last rehearsal out on the stadium lawn. Joined by young adults of every nationality, we practiced our heinies off in the warm afternoon sun. After our interminable rehearsal, drinks and sandwiches were served out on the field. That's when Jay took my hand. My jaw dropped as he led me through the labyrinth of dancers toward the refreshment table. I was completely caught off guard. I couldn't' believe he was holding my hand.

As we worked our way toward the beverage kiosk, my flash-in-the-pants "boyfriend" turned his head, his eyes fixed on me, a bemused grin twitching on his lips. With my hand still encased in his, I felt woozy and weak in the knees. Was it Utah's high altitude that brought on this sudden dizziness, or was it being head-over-heels infatuated with the young man whose hand was holding mine? Jay wasn't your average guy. He had good-natured charisma. And he looked like the kind of heartthrob you'd see on the cover of a Harlequin romance novel. I was dazed.

After lunch, we trudged up what seemed like an endless number of steps to get to the top of the stadium to view it from above. Shading our eyes with our hands, we looked down on the thousands of tiny people mottling the lawn with their mélange of costumes. It was an amazing sight. Then it happened. He grasped me by the shoulders, softly spun me around, and planted his lips on mine.

For my very first kiss, the timing, the venue, and especially the person beside me couldn't have been more perfect if I had tried to conjure it up myself in my incredibly imaginative mind. From shallow lips to deep tongue, I had no idea how to intimately kiss. I just went with it. I improvised. I tried to imagine myself in the movies as I breathed in his hot, musky, manly smell.

With our tongues intertwined, I could hear the faint sound of laughter from dancers who were practicing their moves on the stadium lawn below. A gentle, pleasant breeze grazed our faces and combed through our hair as Utah's fiery sun slowly floated toward the horizon. Jay glanced at his watch and saw it was time to join the others. The day couldn't have been more idyllic, yet the night was far from over.

The evening of our performance was magical. As the double bass punched its driving, energetic pulse beneath the stadium lights, my handsome partner and I gracefully fanned in and out and around thousands of other tango dancers, creating a spectacular kaleidoscopic aerial view. My stomach jumped into my throat each time he whirled me closer, his English Leather cologne stimulating a pulse between my inner thighs. What would it be like if he whisked me down on the field and had his way with me right there in front of tens of thousands of people that packed the stadium?

Clear up to our last number, I couldn't come down from my high. I didn't think I'd ever come down. And by his warm glow, I could tell Jay was far up there too. We were looking at each other differently after that. Electrically charged particles exploded in the air between us as we walked toward the bus to head back home to California.

Hoots and squeals echoed through the parking lot as a mass of teens waited to board their designated buses. I basked in the crowds' riant laughter which reflected the exuberance that was bursting within me. A gorgeous guy was holding my hand! After feeling so lonely and lost for so long, at last, I felt seen.

As we grazed arms, I timidly peered up at him, making sure this wasn't just some incredible dream. He was still up there, a half-foot taller, squeezing my hand, the tension crackling between us as he chewed on a stick of peppermint gum. There was no conversation. Just awkward teenage emotions of wondering and hoping. With my raging hormones, I was all over the map, my mind rushing in a thousand different directions ...

CHAPTER 11

CAGED AND CLIPPED

After the Greyhound doors finally swooshed open, and the exhaust pipe groaned, Jay and I climbed into the bus with the others. Although we got separated in the large crowd, my tall, dark friend reached and caught my hand, then escorted me to a row of seats near the back. As the bus rumbled down the highway toward our destination, he cupped my hand in his, drawing little circles on my palm, sending shivers up my arm.

This whole new adventure had my heart racing—especially when Jay glanced down at me and offered a raised, flirtatious brow while smacking on a stick of gum. Man, did he know how to light my fire.

After sundown, when all the noisy chatter from the day's excitement had turned to snores and the chaperones had conked out, I shyly gazed up at my … boyfriend? I guessed I could call him that. Peering up at him, he looked anxious in the shadows. That's when I sensed something wonderful was about to happen. I think he saw the longing in my eyes, because right then, he slowly lowered his lips to mine.

I hungered for more and got my wish. He cupped my neck and drew me in. Everything in my world narrowed to just the feeling of this guy—his stubble brushing against my cheek and the warmth of his peppermint breath in my mouth—my God, he consumed me!

As we continued to make out, Jay's large fingers floated purposefully, searching around my yellow pullover; and at first, I felt nervous. But it stirred something amazing inside me, something too good to turn down. I fought hard to hurl away the Guilt and allowed Jay to free-fall me through space. I'm not sure whose heart was pumping louder as we deep-throat kissed and petted through every bump along the road from Winnemucca to Sacramento to the Bay Area. I felt cheap, wonderful, dirty, transformed, shameful, reborn, all at the same time.

As the bus slowed to a stop at the Oakland Temple Hill parking lot, Jay and I exchanged phone numbers. After returning home, instead of basking in the exciting possibilities of this guy, Guilt would not let up, so I stupidly confessed all the gory details to my mother. Typically, I wouldn't have done this, but I grew up steeped in a religious purity culture. I had attended far too many young-adult conferences and heard far too many talks about moral cleanliness. I was conditioned to confess my sins—sins such as heavy petting, even though Jay's hands never wandered beneath my top. To me, it was more about how long we petted. There was no turning back after that.

Mom made it clear that high-school boys are nothing more than walking testosterone machines. She was most likely right, but the truth crushed me. I no longer felt reborn. Just cheap, dirty, and defiled, like I needed to wash him off me.

From that day forward, I walked around feeling worn down by Guilt, as Shame and Regret tagged along to give me an occasional good whipping. The moment I had a chance to be alone, I knelt and howled toward the heavens, "Please Heavenly Father," I cried. "Please forgive me for what I have done." I didn't ask just once or even twice. I can't count the number of times I begged for forgiveness as I waited for an answer while the carpet fibers duplicated themselves in red along my kneecaps.

Shame whipped me so hard that when Jay called me hoping to get a date, not only did I turn him down, but I read him the riot act. I raked both of us over the coals with my hellfire preaching, making sure to let him know the Lord was not happy with either of us. Then I pressed the phone into my ear waiting for his reply. Silence.

I was now in a dilemma. I wanted to date, but after what my mother said, how could I trust again? Choosing to date Jay might have been good for me. I needed to learn how to handle guys, not dispose of them. What better way to discover and create personal boundaries than through spending time with testosterone-driven horn dogs?

Instead, I went into hibernation and practiced my Chopin all summer. Sometimes I hid out in my room writing elegies about the Apocalypse and cannibalistic zombies. Well, I wasn't that dark, but I did pump out some pretty plutonian stuff. For sure I'd be the girl to grow old never tasting the sweetness of romantic love.

Near the end of my high-school junior year, a sweet guy from fourth-period English surprised me by asking me to the prom. We were both shy and he was as awkward as I was. The prom would be on a cruise ship. It would be a once-in-a-lifetime experience—an opportunity that might help me to practice sharpening my relationship skills. There would even be chaperones. But my parents told me I couldn't go because I turned down *Carl.* Carl was a member of our ward. Everything about him rubbed me wrong. But to my mom, he was a safe date.

You'd think Carl would have gotten the message when I turned him down the first time, but soon he began following me around campus, pestering me to give him another chance. Of all the guys in my chemistry class, I got stuck with him as my lab partner. Tall, sloppy, and unshaven, his definition of style was a '50s ducktail haircut and loud, tacky, oversized shirts. While I mixed and measured compounds, he'd sit across from me, his head propped up on one elbow, eyeballing me as if he wanted to eat me for breakfast. "But he's LDS," my parents would say. "How could you go wrong dating a Mormon?" I guess Mom already forgot about Jay the Groper?

When does being a Mormon, and a creepy one at that give Carl the edge over a classy guy? I think my folks felt sorrier for him than for me. They claimed him as lost—that he needed to feel accepted and appreciated. *And I didn't?* I eventually folded. As much as I didn't want to go out with Carl, my heart bled for anything slightly pathetic. At sixteen going on seventeen, I wasn't even the main character in my own life-story. I needed to change. Change had to come from within. And that would take time. Meanwhile, I allowed my parents to keep me "safe" in their little gilded bird cage. *It would be safe with Carl.* I consoled myself with this word: safe. Like feeling safe was better than finding love. Caged and clipped, emotionally whipped, would I ever fly free?

CHAPTER 12

WHEN MUSIC SPEAKS

From my birth, music filled my life. It was and still is as important as the air I breathe. In fact, it is such an integral part of me that I hear music almost every time the sun shines through my bedroom window. As a young deep feeling, sensitive girl, I couldn't imagine a world without a song.

It was music that caught my mother's attention. At age fourteen, after plucking out the last chord of my first original melody, I searched her face for approval. That's when it happened. The corners of her lips turned up, and the pride in her eye told me I had created something quite lovely. I had never felt that adequate in my mother's eyes, and in that moment, I was so overcome by her validation that I felt like crying. I smiled instead because that was the only thing I could do.

Music made me feel *worthy*. Music made me feel *whole*. But sometimes music can play on your emotions. It can give you a rush of endorphins. It can dominate your senses and enhance your delusions.

In the summer of 1970, right before my high-school sophomore year, I had the once-in-a-lifetime opportunity to sing in the balcony-chorus at the LDS Oakland temple pageant. Our 500-member close-knit group had been practicing for months. We were to perform for two straight weeks sharing our glorious music with nightly audiences of thousands of people.

One night, I got so caught up in the music, it was as though the heavens opened and we were joined by a heavenly choir. In my rapture, it was music that spoke to my heart and told me that the Church of Jesus Christ of Latter-day Saints was the only true church upon the earth. I couldn't imagine any other religion having what we possessed. We were it. We were the genuine article when it came to truth, revelation, and knowledge.

After that transforming experience, I became more motivated to read my scriptures, maintain my moral cleanliness, and prepare myself for temple marriage. But decades later, I became acutely aware that people of other religions or none at all — even people who use drugs to experience transcendence, describe similar spiritual awakenings. What about *their* truth?

CHAPTER 13

BE MINE, JOHNNY VALENTINE

At age 15, singing with the angels on Temple Hill was my defining moment. From that time forward, I didn't just believe the Church was true. I knew it. Or at least I thought I knew it. Yet my burning testimony didn't take away my hormonal drive. I knew my tryst with the tub had to stop if I expected the Lord to bless me with a good man.

As a teen, I was not a critical thinker. It never occurred to me to ask if the Church's infliction of Guilt and Shame was conducive to my spiritual growth. It was part of the package of being Mormon. I was raised in a purity culture and was programmed to simply believe. I saw "doctrine" and "truth" as one and the same.

By 1972 our bustling household had been reduced to my parents, my younger brother, and me. My two older sisters were married and gone. I was 17, and my sister who was only twenty months older than I, had married at that age. She wasn't even a legal adult. But her early marriage shook my hopeless single status into a woebegone doomsday. It just didn't seem fair. My sisters were getting all the sex they wanted without having to repent afterward. Instead of getting sex, I had to finish high school.

When I entered my senior year in the fall of '72, our Hayward bishop assigned a new home teacher for our family. We welcomed him wholeheartedly.

Johnny Valentine placed his hand on his crossed knee, shook his thick, strawberry-blonde bangs from his brows, then winked at me from across the room. *Was he flirting with me?* He was warm, relaxed, natural. Unlike Jay, he didn't look like a Harlequin hero, but did it matter? What a personality! He was on fire.

As he shared his love for the gospel, his eyes centered on each of us in turn, but mostly they would land on me, sparkling with an enthusiastic incandescence. I watched a playful smile grow wide as he talked about his missionary experiences. He had no idea what he was doing to me. Sparking up fantasies of marriage and its benefits, he made it impossible for me to concentrate on holy matters. He was the kind of man I had been longing for. I knew if I ever had the chance to go out with Johnny, he'd show me respect.

Every month on the third Sunday, my awesome home teacher showed up at our door to check on our family and present a spiritual lesson. Of course, I was always there soaking up his every word.

When spring arrived, our family took Johnny with us boating out on the lake. I'll never forget when he sang and played *Annie's song* on his guitar. His smile was most beautiful when he sang. It was like watching the sun come out from behind the clouds. I spontaneously joined him, singing the harmony. As our voices blended and our eyes met, my pulse started to quicken.

One Sunday afternoon, Johnny was casually talking to my folks when the topic of marriage came up. He unabashedly admitted that his mom was concerned that he was twenty-four and still single. The Brethren preached that if young men were not married within a year after returning home from their missions, they were a menace to society. I was okay with the pressure the church put on returned missionaries. I liked this pressure even more when my dad approached me one day and said he believed Johnny was interested in me. From then on, Hope was on my side.

Because my home teacher knew my family, I didn't have to put on any airs. I was just my bumbling, awkward self, and he seemed to be drawn to me anyway. At age 18, shortly after high-school graduation, I came to my senses. This highly charged, extremely confident man was six years older than I was and clearly out of my league. With his grounded sense of self and natural ability to relate to others, I had convinced myself that he wasn't interested; that he was more into the cute, flirtatious, cheerleader types.

Then, one day, from out of the blue, he called me and asked me out. I was dumbfounded. Once I moved past the shock, and the reality of a date with him set in, I began to hyperventilate. Even my highly circumspect parents would break out the Martinelli's and have a big Mormon bash if Johnny proposed to me.

But I didn't want to get too excited. I was the girl who often wore her meals on her shirt, heart on her sleeve, and kept her social skills hidden somewhere in a cluttered drawer. I was the fire-hazard toaster that someone pulled the plug on and chose not to repair. But if it did work out with Johnny, I would want to kiss God's feet with an apology for whining so much about my crappy life.

When the night of our date finally arrived, with all my nervous binging, I could barely squeeze into my size fourteen pants, the ones I reserved for my bloat days. Johnny arrived right on time and happened to be a perfect gentleman. As he held open the door of his green Chevelle, I plopped my ample tush on the seat so fast that I hoped he didn't have time to notice it. Yet I had far bigger problems to worry about than a chunky booty.

As his car softly purred its way across the bridge toward San Francisco, there was another sound—the high-pitched cry of panic in my head as I frantically thumbed my mental library for conversation starters, witticisms, anything. But I couldn't think of a single clever thing to say, yet I had to give him kudos for trying to fill the dead space between us with his kinetic charm. Still, charm can only get a guy so far when his date has no personality reservoir to draw from.

After that nerve-racking date, Johnny gave me another chance by inviting me as his "plus one" to his friend's wedding. It was a casual setting, a perfect venue for a do over. But I still didn't have a clever comeback for his repartee. I finally understood why people take up smoking. So they can do something with their hands. I ate wedding cake. Lots of it.

Two strikes and I was out. My delightful friend chose to occasionally sit next to me during sacrament meetings, but no more dates. Still hopeful, my fingers stayed crossed.

A month later, Johnny left for BYU. I just couldn't believe that this was the end of our journey together. Deep in my bones, I knew he was the one for me. Perhaps I could reach out to his mom and get his address? Maybe if I wrote him and let him know how I genuinely felt, he'd get in contact with me again?

The summer before I met my home teacher, I enrolled at Ricks College, an LDS institution located in Rexburg, Idaho. If I had only known the future, I probably would have enrolled at "the Y" so I'd be close to Johhny. But BYU had its drawbacks. It had a much larger, intimidating campus. And from what I had learned, Ricks was a tight-knit, friendlier, insular community. I was either very smart or very foolish to choose Ricks. To leave sunny California so I could trudge through blustering, snow-covered flatlands seemed insane. At the time, it seemed like the perfect platform to pursue a husband. But now, all I could think about was Johnny.

This would be his second year at "the Y," and I figured he'd be married in no time. But what was I supposed to do? Fly to Provo and scoop him up? I never got his phone number from his mom. And I was already heading to Rexburg.

CHAPTER 14

THE GIRL WHO HELPED
ME DISCOVER ME

Sprawled out in the backseat of our family's paneled wagon, I sprung upright as we rolled into the Ricks College parking lot late August of '73. Cranking down the window, I stared into the opened flatness of the campus. Unlike BYU, there was no breathtaking panoramic view of the Wasatch mountains nor any rolling hills. Just the city's rusty water tower. Yet the campus lawns were neatly manicured, and the surroundings had a pleasant, friendly appeal.

After meeting with my new dorm mother, I was handed the keys to a brand-new life. I had five roommates, but it was Mary Jo who helped me discover the real me that had been hiding out for eighteen years.

A plump, sharp-witted, wildly playful Southern gal, she became my best bud. Oddly, she didn't see me as shy. We just clicked from the get-go. When we weren't wrapped up in our studies, we'd be rolling on the floor, choking on our laughter, trying to catch our breath. Through her, I made an eye-opening discovery. I realized I connected beautifully with light-hearted people. My mom was proper and serious. Mary Jo was always a moment away from busting up.

Folks in my mother's "fake it till you make it" generation were taught that suffering in silence was more heroic. Mary Jo's heroism was her soul-saving sense of humor. She constantly had me in stitches and was as real as they come. I didn't know I was a goofball until I met her. We were great together. And for the first time in my life, I felt genuinely happy.

Yet I still struggled with men. Sheltered and dateless, I was a babe in the dating world. Because I didn't talk much through high school, I had a lot of catching up to do. The cuter a guy, the stupider I would become. But I wasn't too worried. I was waiting for my Johnny.

After only three weeks at Ricks, despite the fun I was having with Mary Jo, I suddenly got terribly homesick. Then something happened— something that I would have never thought possible …

CHAPTER 15

VISIT FROM A STRANGER

After trudging across campus one morning, I happened to enter the dorm lobby and guess who was sitting on the couch looking perfect in his casual BYU T-shirt and jeans? I stood there with my eyes and mouth wide open, gulping for air. Johnny Valentine had traveled 283 miles to see me. At least that's what I assumed until he told me that he couldn't wait to introduce me to his most favorite religion teacher, a professor named Dr. Keith Sellers. Johhny had met this warmhearted, brilliant man while attending Ricks prior to transferring to BYU. "Your Rick's experience won't be the same," he confidently claimed, "without a dose of Dr. Seller's weekly lectures."

Soon, the two of us were sitting across from this dynamic professor who gladly signed my add card. Afterward, Johhny and I had a disappointingly short visit and then he was gone. But I still hung on to hope. *Maybe Johhny's visit was an excuse to see me?* I thought. After all, he didn't hesitate to give me his address after I asked if we could write each other.

Not wanting to appear desperate, I waited an entire week before breaking out my notebook and ballpoint pen. I then constructed a five-page detailed account of all my adjustments to country living. After slipping my essay into a pastel envelope, I held my breath and carefully placed it into the mail. When I received his reply a month later advising me to date a lot, I was confused. I was too deep in denial to see his reply as a brush off. *He just doesn't know what he wants,* I told myself. *He'll come around.*

None of the guys on campus could hold a candle to my Johnny. After his visit, Johnny had my heart. He was always in my head. I saw no point in dating. On the weekends, while Mary Jo painted our college's little hick town with her dazzling charm, I sat home and studied with a bag of popcorn in hand that was larger than my romantic dating diary.

Six months later, on a cold February day, when the campus was covered in a thick blanket of snow, I received a letter from my mother. I ripped it open with eager anticipation. As my eyes scanned the first line, my whole world turned black. "Johnny Valentine is engaged to be married. He's found his wife at BYU and a June wedding is in the works." In disbelief, I stared at the stabbing words that marked my fate, written ironically in lovely blue ink in my mother's own perfect handwriting.

Tears streamed down my cheeks as I dropped the pages to the floor, threw on my Alaskan parka, and took a stroll in the crisp thirty-degree weather. I figured if I stayed outdoors long enough, I might freeze to death, which would be a welcome event.

As I look back on this time, I could blame no one but myself for my refusal to face the reality of unrequited love. The land of Denial is indeed a place of suffering.

At age 19, self-love and self-awareness were not on my vision-board. Just purity vows and eligible bachelors. Chasing a mirage—I was the mirage. Someone without substance or form. And the closer one got, the less one saw …

CHAPTER 16

BYU BUMBLER

At the tender age of nineteen, I was a horny, love-starved virgin who took the church's doctrine of marriage so literally, that my life became a revolving door fairy tale romance novel with a scattershot plot. I needed an M.R.S. degree like yesterday. And in my high-speed chase to get one, I chose not to return to Ricks. Instead, I enrolled at BYU, the Mormon marriage mecca of the world.

In the Fall of 1974, I lied to myself pretending that I loved college when deciding to major in music composition and minor in shame and low self-worth. My prerequisite courses focused on musical form and structure. Blah blah blah. I was a dreamer. I hated rules. I wanted to write music my way. But even more than that, I wanted to have "legal" sex.

My inability to focus on a course of study didn't really help my dating resume. And if I was lucky enough to get a date, I'd sometimes get so stressed, I'd fall into an abyss in the middle of a conversation. Not the best way to build a connection. In fact, I hadn't even found my voice until I met Mary Jo at Ricks. Socially, I had a lot of catching up to do.

In between course work and studies, I would often sprawl out on my bed and write funny skits for church talent shows. Sometimes I'd perform on stage—easy peasy when I could play the part of someone other than myself. I landed a few dates this way, but sooner or later they would meet the real girl behind the mask.

The guys I went out with in the pre-smart phone era had no way to text smiley emojis to soften the blow when they dumped me, which was usually after the first date. Don't get me wrong. I had marriageable qualities. At least I thought I did. I was genuinely sweet, fun-loving, open and honest. Perhaps a little too honest. When my dates asked me about my goals, I candidly told them I wanted to get married. Before I could blurt out, "I love you," they rambled down the road toward a more promising situation.

You see, most coeds wanted to get married as desperately as I did. They just knew how to play the game and didn't reveal their cards. I didn't know the first thing about holding and folding my cards.

Still there was hope. My puppy-dog eyes and killer figure always managed to pull guys from left to right. I just needed to learn how to reel them in. Maybe I wasn't ready for this grownup world. What guy would want a girl who stuffs herself with pink and white confetti animal cookies to relieve stress or dances in a store parking lot oblivious to the price tag still dangling from the collar of her blouse?

I've always been a walking contradiction. The guys I met on campus simply didn't seem to appreciate my endearing eccentricities. I felt (and still feel) comfortable in dirty, mismatched socks, even if one sock is halfway off my foot with the heel bulge in the center. Yet I insist on looking perfect in a dress. Even today, I have a strict eating and exercise regimen, holding myself accountable every minute of every hour. But I have no control over my runaway dental floss that decorates my bathroom drawers like a multi-sequenced game of Cat's Cradle. Perhaps it comes with a creative personality. Sounds good in theory, anyway.

As a first-year BYU student, with all my incongruences, how could I possibly change my one-date-wonder status? You'd think my ineffective efforts to find a man would have generated some self-reflection. But because I was so busy trying to catch him, I never paused to learn the game. Then I met Louie, and I was forced to self-reflect, because he broke my heart.

BYU BUMBLER

Tossed in the wind, a little off kilter.
A beautiful mess without a filter.
Creative and funny but can't parse the play,
They see me coming a mile away.
Without an agenda, I can't make the sell.
My childlike frankness doesn't serve me well.
This whirling tornado with no destination
Just wants to get married to end my frustration.
Not very patient as the gale blows through me.
I'm craving a man who desires to woo me.
Not far away is the eye of my storm,
He's funny and spiritual, tender and warm.
I squint through the cyclone and stingy debris
In hopes to detect him waiting for me.
Then there amid the fog and the rain,
I hear him calling, he's calling my name.
He reaches out, untangles the mess

And rescues this little lost girl in distress.
No longer tethered by the squall
With heartfelt devotion, he gives me his all.
My lighthouse and beacon hands me white roses,
Slips a ring on my finger and sweetly proposes.
My veil is bright, as white as my grin
As we seal our love,
In Jesus' name,
Amen.

CHAPTER 17

HAIGHT ASHBURY LOVE

With his wheat-blonde sweaty locks falling in knots around his face, Louie had become a permanent fixture on our living-room couch. Working out his guitar riffs till late evening, the guy had no place to go, yet oddly, he slapped me on a map and gave my desultory soul direction.

Louie was a BYU graduate. Go figure. Music degree. Go figure again. Someone's friend of a friend—we had no idea why he was in our house, but no one seemed to care. I was a music junkie, so it was easy for him to seduce me with his guitar. He simply swayed to the rhythm of his song, and I was his.

Slumped on the sofa across from him, my eyes widened with arousal as he strummed his fingers along the frets. I studied him. He studied me, his slow grin revealing a slightly crooked tooth.

I repositioned myself on the couch, my mouth curling up to one side, when all at once, this Haight Ashbury dude began strumming McCartney's "Yesterday." I was a decent guitar player and loved anything Beatles, so before he left, I begged him to teach it to me.

My intriguing friend surprised me by showing up on our doorstep the next day wearing cutoffs.

While I fetched my guitar from my room, he pulled out his Gibson and made himself comfortable on the couch. The second I sat down, Louie inched toward me, his lanky thighs flattening the lines along the dark-green corduroy cushion covers.

At close range, I studied his face. When he smiled, the corners of his eyes crinkled, and deep, crescent-shaped lines edged their way around the sides of his mouth. He was older, perhaps a decade or so, making him even more fascinating.

As Louie leaned in to reposition my fingers along the frets, all at once, I felt the air shift and change between us. Heat rose in my cheeks and my body tingled as he softly rotated my finger for that perfect placement. My throat felt constricted, and I grappled with the suddenly complex task of inhaling and exhaling. To muck up the awkward silence between us, I dug the pads of my fingers into the guitar strings and recklessly thumbed a glissando. My newly mastered bar chord, a thuddy twang, graced the room.

I searched my friend's eyes for approval. Shaking his bangs from his brows, he smiled indulgently. Then in a beat, his smile was gone, his eyes drifting away from me. He looked pensive as if he had escaped to a world of his own, enveloped in dreams that held him captive. Just like my dad. Just like me. No wonder I felt so drawn to him. I lived in that world too.

I didn't care if Louie wasn't a double-take looker. He was mellow. Confident. Sexy. And his laidback style was causing long forgotten lower-body twinges, reigniting a fire in my core. At last, I had finally found my muse. The kind of guy who preferred deep, sensitive reflection over trivial matters such as a dusty end-table or two-day-old apple core left on the bathroom counter.

After my lesson, while propping my guitar in its case, I suddenly felt Louie's hand on my shoulder. As I pivoted around to face him, he tipped my chin up and I had no choice but to look straight into his warm, walnut-colored eyes. I could feel my burning cheeks. I knew they had to be red.

"You're stunning," he whispered, his voice a sultry growl. I couldn't believe it was happening. He leaned in, his breath grazing my lips. As he kissed me, he was slow and thorough, our tongues dancing together so perfectly. The way he gently nibbled on my bottom lip brought my body to life, a tingling between my inner thighs that exhilarated me. Yet, I was scared. It had been years since my last kiss, which was in the backseat of a bus in the middle of Nevada. Now this man was bringing it all back almost too fast.

My head and heart wanted two different things. I missed this feeling. Yet I was overwhelmed. Louie was a practical stranger. Then just like that, he said he had to go. *Well, that solved that.* Now I just needed to know how to deal with my little pink Ferrari's revved-up engine.

Later that week, when my roommates were out, I invited Louie to our home. We danced barefooted to John Coltrane, on the rustic brown shag carpeting. I awkwardly followed his lead while taking in the scent of his strawberry shampoo. *And did I smell ragweed?*

My insides rose and collapsed as my friend gently unraveled his long mid-back ponytail and pulled me into his warmth. A heavy chain glinted from his opened collar exposing his chest hair. I wanted to trace my fingers around the chain, but I felt timid and inexperienced at those types of playful gestures.

As he held me to his chest, his heart thudded like a kickdrum in my ear. Although I was way out of my element, all my inadequacies melted away. I couldn't believe I was in the arms of an older man, a gifted musician in fact, who saw me as stunning. He was my sanctuary from the wind and the rain of a world so cold, so unaccepting. I was no longer the "one date wonder." At least for that moment. At last, I was beautiful. At last, I was loved. Oh, how I longed to remain beneath his Mary-Jane scented canopy, but Louie ruined it all.

Right then, he glanced at his watch, said he had to be somewhere, and poof, he was gone. *Again? Just when I was feeling so worked up. How could he leave me in this bothered state? Did he have another lover? Could he possibly be married?* I hankered for his touch, for his earthy smell. I didn't care if he smelled like weed. I hoped he wasn't married because I wanted him.

Unlike many college coeds, I held tight to my virtue. So when my hippie-love lit a fire in my groin and then left, I didn't know how to handle it. Then I remembered the flexible showerhead in the bathroom. *Guilt? What the hell was that?* I snatched the hose from its holder, leaned back in the tub, and spritzed away all the sexual tension. In my head, I was already making future plans. Marrying Louie would be my ticket out of here. That night as I settled into bed, I skipped my prayer routine and slept like a baby.

It was pouring rain when Louie called me a few days later and invited me to his place for lunch. When I arrived, he offered to heat up a peanut butter sandwich in his little toaster oven. Smoke filled the space between us as he retrieved my charred sandwich from his shitty second-hand broiler and set it on a plate in front of me. This was when I learned the literal meaning of the catchphrase, "starving musician."

That was the last time I saw him. To my utter grief and bewilderment, he simply vanished into thin air. After three encounters, I was madly in love. My dreams of a man to have and to hold forever, especially one as fascinating as Louie, were crushed.

A few weeks later, one of my roommates gave me a tip off; she said she spotted my hippie love in the supermarket kissing a guy in the bread aisle. The thought of Louie as bisexual was a horse-pill to swallow. And it hurt going down.

Allowing myself to become vulnerable with someone I barely knew was becoming a pattern. I was the desperate, needy "One-Date No-Wonder." I was certain I could never be happy alone. I had not yet to meet my inner woman who was strong, smart, and capable.

On my sunken mattress, alone and inconsolable, I coiled into myself. And just like when I lost Johnny Valentine, I entertained a death wish. But once I healed, I finally took control. I was never going to allow another Louie into my life again. I would be empowered.

CHAPTER 18

A POCKET FULL OF AIR

After being crushed by Louie, I wasn't just slightly guarded. A garrison surrounded my heart, ready and prepared for a lock and load moment at the first sign of trouble. I went from Lost and Needy to Militant. I was done wearing my heart on my sleeve. I finally decided to show up and become the main character in my own story. And I liked the new me. Even a few of my male friends looked at me differently.

In the winter of 1975, about six weeks after Louie vanished, I met Alan at a church potluck. His adorable baby face with a deep-dimpled ear-to-ear smile turned my knees to butter and felled the walls of my fortified heart.

When I accepted a date, I knew I was at risk. So, when he asked me out, I was one step ahead of him. I suggested a scripture-study session at my place. I figured that any guy who was truly interested in me would be game to unite in the edification of God's Holy Word.

The following Sunday after the church brunch, Alan showed up at my door in a sharp gray suit. He looked like a clean-cut Mormon missionary ready and eager to share "the good news." I was even more impressed when I spotted a set of leather-bound scriptures under his arm.

Because it was the Sabbath and the sky was blue, and his eyes were blue too, and I also felt really pretty, I let my guard down. A little. I allowed him to sit next to me on the couch. We opened the Book of Mormon, and because the print was small, we nestled a little closer. Everything was spiritual, and we were into Jesus and all things holy when I noticed Alan's arm creeping up around my shoulder. Warning lights immediately flashed in my head. I wasn't sure about his intentions, and I immediately started to put on the brakes just in case Alan was getting eager to run a few red lights.

I spotted his lips from the corner of my eye, approaching ever so slowly, ready to plant a big wet one on me. I had to think fast, so I swiftly turned my head in the opposite direction, forcing him to kiss a pocket-full of air. *Awkward!*

"You don't want to … um …" he fumbled, not knowing what to say. Not the most ego boosting moment for poor Alan nor the most pleasant one for me. After the "Louie experience," my trust in men had been firebombed. I needed time to rebuild. I couldn't afford another blindside by another shallow guy in search of a meaningless fling.

For good reason, I never saw him after that. That's why I was more than thrilled when Chad came along …

CHAPTER 19

IT HAD TO BE CHAD

In the mid-1970s, women throughout the US were starting to have a voice and slowly working toward becoming more equal with men. Instead of passively waiting by the phone for a date, girls were taking the initiative to actively pursue guys. Looking back, I wish I would have been one of them.

Instead, I had been programmed since the age of three, that girls should assume a submissive role. In her traditional role, my mother taught me by both word and example that hunting down a man is unbecoming, aggressive, and unladylike. There were no questions to be had. Men were the hunters while women stayed home and cooked the things they hunted. Looking back, my chances of experiencing marital bliss might have been far greater if I had been encouraged to assert myself and pursue men in the way I saw fit. Especially when it came to Chad.

At age twenty, I still had my blinders on, my heart guarded, and my vagina under lock and key. Clinging tight to my old-fashion values, I waited for my prince to show up with a glass slipper and hoped that he just happened to have a size eight-and-a-half wide.

When I moved to Provo, I lived off-campus with five roommates in a cute little peppermint-pink home. When you're a coed in off-campus housing, the church assigns a group of male students to look after you. We referred to these six guys as our family home evening brothers. When Chad McBride, a tall, sandy-haired, brown-eyed transfer student from the University of Michigan, joined our family home evening group, I found myself laughing all the time. Chad was playful and witty like Mary Jo at Ricks. And just like her, he "got" me from the get-go.

Typically, I shied away from witty banter. Especially with men. But Chad took me for the silly nut that I was, so sallying back and forth with him was easy. I didn't have to be someone I wasn't.

We're talking about a classy guy here. He always swallowed his food before talking, and his skin and hair always smelled clean and fresh. He even looked refined in casual wear. Whimsical and dry-humored, Chad constantly had his roommates and me in stiches with his pranks.

One time, he wrote a letter to his roommate, Paul, creating a professional letterhead and the whole bit. He gold-sealed the envelope and sent it to him pretending he was BYU president, Dallin Oaks, inviting him to an honorary banquet where he would be presented with an award for his outstanding academic achievements and service to his fellow classmates. Paul fell for it hook, line, and sinker until Chad revealed the ruse.

My smart, creative friend was a perfect balance of fun and thoughtfulness. Better still, he never made fun of my careless, off-beat mannerisms and occasional disheveled dress. As a political science major and history buff, with a goal to become a civil attorney, Chad would often enlighten me about past and current events. And because I was clueless about the world, he splashed my empty canvas with lots of color.

Chad and I became such good friends that I joined him at his apartment almost every afternoon. When our classes let out, we would stretch out on his top bunk and I'd rub his back (with his shirt on, of course) while he convinced me with a lighthearted chuckle that the Cold War did not get its name from brisk temperatures. When massaging him, I couldn't help but notice his muscles straining from the sleeve of his cotton-T. *Damn, he was in great shape.* With every back rub, his moans of appreciation made my crotch dance. I was becoming unhinged. He had no clue about the torture he was putting me through.

To have an excuse to see him every day, I volunteered to cook for him. His roommates found it hilarious when their kitchenware gradually became unrecognizable. It wasn't so much the food I burned, but the Tupperware that I thought was oven friendly. I learned that placing plastic utensils in the oven was not the best idea—even on low heat. Yet, Chad kept me around. He even hung the charred items on his kitchen wall and took a picture of me. *Maybe he had feelings for me?* If so, he never made a move.

Because I had a habit of falling in love too quickly, I convinced myself that the Lord put Chad in my life to help me slow down. He was a level-headed kind of guy that had the ability to keep whatever we had going in "the buddy zone." I would leave it to him to keep the flame low in hopes our friendship would one day transform into fiery romance.

Then it happened sooner than I had anticipated. A month into our friendship, Chad confided in me that he had a five-year-old daughter, Jade, a product of a high school romance. Shortly after her birth, he joined the church. To my delight, when little Jade came to visit Daddy, I had the chance to bond with her during the times Chad attended his classes.

After Jade had left for home, while working my fingers into Chad's neck, I mentioned to him how adorable she was. With raised brows and fixed eyes, my friend peered up at me from where he lay on the sheet. "Jennifer, Jade needs a mother." He jigged his brows two more times. "Jennifer?" My fingers wandered off his neck as I sat upright. All at once, that slow-burning flame grew brighter.

He was still looking up at me, but I couldn't tell if he was serious or joking. Was he testing the waters, seeing if I would take the bait and tell him how much I cared about him?

With his head propped in his hand, we locked eyes as he tendered one last flirty brow jig, his slow smile melting my heart. If non-verbal cues could relay a message, his were inviting me to close the gap between us. It appeared that he wanted to make it happen. Why was I so tongue-tied? He had me so confused. *Did he really want me to be Jade's mom? Was this a marriage proposal? If so, how was I to respond?* I was befuddled. To my chagrin, all I could offer was a nervous giggle. Pathetic.

When my friend extended his tease, his dazzling eyes fixed on me, I became immobilized. My window of opportunity to spill out any questions, or to tell him how I truly felt about him was slowly closing. Five … four … three … two … one …

CHAPTER 20

THE LOST WINDOW

I was a like a deer in the headlights—so nervous and so clueless about my friend's implication, that the window for me to speak up came and went without a word from either of us. Because I failed to communicate my true feelings, I might have missed out on the moment I'd been waiting for my entire life.

I never imagined that dating and marrying would be so complicated. Chad was the train I never saw coming, clamoring past me to see if I would jump aboard and say yes to mothering his child. If that was the best proposal he could offer, I needed to take a moment to redefine my girlish notions of romance. We hadn't even held hands let alone kissed. Nothing made sense.

While I chose to remain silent waiting for a traditional proposal, Chad's unconventional train chugged on. I was simple-minded and clueless when it came to matters of the heart. The more I grew to love the guy, the daffier I became. To stay hopeful, I continually tried to remind myself that it was my eccentric nature, my trusting candor, and little girl innocence that captured his attention in the first place.

On a whim one spring day, Chad and I decided to do something stupid like raft down the Provo River having had little experience. After climbing in the raft, the current became so strong, that it was hard to steer. A felled tree lay dangerously in our path and caught us by surprise. We were rushing straight toward it. Thank God my friend pulled me down before it lopped off my head.

After making it back to the safety of his truck, we began to giggle with mounting hysteria. I think that was what I loved about Chad the most. Although he was firmly grounded, he always had a yen to be playful, and whenever we were together, we laughed constantly.

Because he was into current events, at his kitchen table one morning, he discussed the topic of guerilla warfare. I turned to him and asked if jungle wars among guerillas was a thing. Chad didn't even smirk. He just pursed his lips to avoid doubling over with laughter.

Chad not only enjoyed his books, but we had a common love for music and we both played the piano. For an upcoming ward talent show, he volunteered to accompany me while I sang a silly song on stage dressed up as a man. Chad called me afterward busting out in laughter. He said he just couldn't stop laughing all night.

Even though Chad and I had a common love of the arts, my ignorance about the world may have been a deal breaker from the start. He was into academics and politics. I was not. Still, I couldn't help but see that he was enamored with my childlike charm. It was just a matter of how many points my charm was worth and if it balanced favorably with my not so redeeming qualities, such as ignorance about wars, my inability to choose a major, and my unhealthy relationship with food. In the end, would my charm be scintillating enough to outshine academic enlightenment?

That afternoon before school let out for the summer, Chad grunted and growled beneath me as I endured with heroism his torturous virile groans. We were fully clothed. I was on top, pressing my fingers firmly around his scapula, hanging tight to my virginity with no idea what the future might hold for us.

After bidding my friend goodbye that evening, I woke up the next morning to an empty house. My roommates had flown out early, heading back east for the summer. Chad was also on his way home to Bay City, Michigan. I'd be flying out that evening to California. As I plopped my last piece of luggage near the front door, I spotted a copy of Spencer W. Kimball's book, *The Miracle of Forgiveness,* on the coffee table. My parents purchased a copy of this book when I was an adolescent, and it was part of our library collection. That darn book haunted me wherever I went.

Since I had time to kill, I thumbed through the pages, allowing them to fall at will until they landed on a chapter devoid of white space. My eyes turned the size of Oreos as an army of sins swarmed across the page like little killer ants that bite and cause death.

Sins of commission, sins of regret,
Sins of omission, sins of neglect
Sins of adultery, sins of abuse
Bouncing to the rhythm of Dr. Seuss.
Red sins, green sins,
Fat sins, thin sins
Lock-'em-in-a-box sins
Fancy-colored-socks sins.
You hide 'em, you wear 'em.
Audaciously declare 'em.

Stupidly confessed sins.
Display-them-just-like-art sins.
The-list-goes-on-and-on sins
Like killer-ants-that-march sins.

I was already missing Chad. According to Kimball, every human soul is laden with sin. *With legions so copious within us, why even bother trying to be good?* Dealing with my strong feelings for the man I loved was challenging. Because Chad had never made a move on me, I felt like a reservoir behind a weakened levy. Solo play was the only safe way to release all that tension. Why did I open that book? Yet hadn't I held on long enough?

Alone in the house, I was finally free to do what I wanted. Through the years I occasionally practiced "giving myself a hand" behind closed doors. Now on my bed, this wasn't my first attempt, although a little rusty, like a piano novice.

Gracefully lowering my fingers onto the "keys," I began to tap. My fingers were the next best thing to the tub spout. A month prior, I attempted to play "Mary Had a Little Lamb." Although still a beginner, I confidently tapped out "Ode to Joy" and cheered myself on.

The more I practiced, the more proficient I became. A few beats later, I let out a slow wush, then played on through Beethoven's "Turkish March," accelerating full speed ahead to "Flight of the Bumblebee." I groaned low and wailed high through the scale of notes as waves of joy hurled through me. Then after a pause, I let out an ecstatic sigh, dramatically curling up my fingers as they drifted off "the keys." The music had stopped, and the recital was over. The only sound was that of my pounding heart as I lay in awe of my shining performance.

Yet my elation was but for a moment. Guilt and Shame were a rotten audience. Not one lousy applaud or encore for my ability to take myself to the moon and back. Instead, they had the audacity to shove me on my knees as I wept and pleaded for God's mercy.

As an artist, I grew up in a world where self-expression was boundless. I lived during the sexual revolution. The changing world could have helped me accept and appreciate myself as a healthy sexual being. But I was programmed to shut down my sexual self and feel Shame. Shame for my body. Shame for having carnal desires. Shame for wanting to go to bed with Chad. Nothing. But. Shame.

CHAPTER 21

IT COULD HAVE BEEN FIREWORKS

Back home for the summer again without a fiancé on my arm was a humiliation in my LDS community. The same question was asked. The same answer was given. "Are you engaged yet?"

"Hey, do you see a ring on my finger?" If I had been living in 2025, I wouldn't have had this pressure to marry. But I grew up in the 60s and '70s. And although in some ways my world was more simplistic, sociologically things were harder due to a more stringent set of expectations. In the US, the average age for women to marry was twenty-one. I was now twenty-one and a month. Above all else, my LDS community expected me to return from BYU with a fiancé. They celebrated temple marriage more than a college degree.

Around mid-summer, I received a letter from Chad. As cheesy as it sounds, his exact words were that he missed my sunny face that was now shining on the California coast. *How cute is that?* His sentiment tickled me. I sensed that he missed me as much as I missed him. But the question begged to be answered—did he see me as more than just a best bud?

With plenty of free time to think, instead of returning to BYU, I considered going on a Church mission. I guess deep down, I felt undeserving of Chad. He was far brighter and far more ambitious than I was. Serving the Lord as a missionary was an option for many women who couldn't catch a man by the time they finished college. But what if I wasted eighteen months out in the field and still couldn't find "the one?"

Near the end of August, after much prayer and consideration, I returned to my little pink house and met up with Chad. Even though I had gained a few pounds over the summer, he lied and told me I looked great. He must have really missed me. *Was there still a chance for romance?*

Because I had become increasingly doubtful about my academic potential, I decided to enroll as a part-time student to give myself time to figure out what I wanted to do when I grew up. In the meantime, I worked in the afternoons at the Provo mall dipping hotdogs on a stick for $2.10 an hour.

Chad happened to be strolling down the mall one afternoon and ordered a large fry in hopes we'd have time for a quick chat. It was the first time he had seen me in my brightly colored uniform and red, yellow, and blue-striped towering Fez hat. "You look like a walking, talking loaf of Wonder Bread," he quipped. I couldn't contain my laughter as he flirtatiously danced his brow at me while flicking his eyes up and down my "sexy" costume. After he left, that's when it hit me.

Although my friend never criticized me for deciding to be a part-time student, I knew he needed to be with an intellectual. He took college seriously. I was willing to take a break from it so I could sell deep-fried collagen-encased meat for minimum wage. The cold, hard truth about our deal-breaker differences punched me in the gut.

Near the end of the semester, Chad and I were in his room talking, when he shared the sad news that he would be flying back to Michigan so he could be closer to his daughter. He would continue his education there. All at once, I got a lump in my throat and tears welled my eyes at the thought of losing him. If only I had been more serious about college, perhaps Chad would have taken me with him. Even though I knew he had to go on with his life, I felt abandoned. I was like a leaf in the wind; tossed, scattered, and trampled beneath the shoes of the more driven as they mounted the stairwell toward academic achievement.

Was I far too feckless for my firmly grounded friend? Perhaps. But I knew one thing. I loved the man. I truly loved him. I couldn't say that about Jay or Louie. Rushing in with those two was like feeding a flame with paper, creating an instant explosion with no sustained heat. But with Chad, the flame burned low with a steady ember glow. Maybe it would have been fireworks if I had just impressed him with a few goals.

As a young coed, I was a truly remarkable woman with endless amounts of talent and capability. I just couldn't see it. If I hadn't been so set on marriage, I could have had the whole world in my hands. Who knows? I might have been able to spin it to my advantage.

But I was indoctrinated to believe that finding a husband was the goal. Perhaps Chad sensed this neediness in me, and it frightened him. My biological clock was ticking. All my roommates were engaged. Even more distressing, I couldn't connect with my family. My parents were introverts. My sisters were married and already had kids. Their lives were far removed from mine and abundantly full.

Because I was taught that I couldn't get to the highest tier of heaven without my Mormon prince, instead of getting more ambitious, I got down on my knees and asked God to help me find him. I hounded Him in the way a child would hound her daddy for candy. "Please Heavenly Father—if it isn't Chad; please, please, please help me find a husband!"

The next thing I knew, I was tossed upon the billows, swallowed up in the current of my delusions, fighting for each breath ...

CHAPTER 22

RED FLAGS AND A BRIGHT WHITE GOWN

Lost at sea, far in over my head, drowning in murky waters, sadly, no one was around to pull me to the surface and resuscitate me with a reality check.

My Mormon dream was to grow up, marry, have babies, nurture a family, and live on Planet Kolob in the eternities. Yet how would I even be capable of nurturing a family when I hadn't learned to love myself?

A week before the turn of the year 1977, I moved away from Chad, the only man I truly loved, into a mixed-gender apartment complex a mile down the street. Housed right across the terrace from a bevy of eligible bachelors, how could I not succeed in finding my special someone?

A day after I settled in, I was walking to the mailbox and silently pleading with God to find me a husband. Suddenly, I heard the Holy Ghost quote Proverbs 3:5-6. "Trust in the Lord with all thine heart; ... and he shall direct thy paths." Immediately, I felt at peace and knew something exciting would happen soon.

The next day, I discovered a promotional flyer peeking out from beneath our flimsy Astro Turf doormat announcing an upcoming campus dance. In my childlike faith, I was convinced this was a sign from on high. Yep. The upcoming event would present me with my Cinderella moment. The chance to meet my hubby was right around the corner.

I was thrown off guard when I ended up catching the flu on the day of the dance. Yet a queasy tummy wasn't going to get in the way of a chance for romance.

On that cold, January night in 1977, a week after Jimmy Carter was sworn in as the thirty-ninth President, I met Gary. Soon after we met, I learned we lived right across the terrace from each other. I saw it as no coincidence. This had to be divine intervention. Warning: Be careful what you pray for because you just might get it. Especially if you beg. I think God was tired of hearing me whine, so he threw me a bait and switch gracing me with my hardest lesson yet and said good luck.

At first Gary seemed to be everything I hoped for. Well, almost. He was a little on the controlling side, but what the heck. No one is perfect. Tall, reedy, and fair-skinned, his thick white-blonde waves rose and dipped. The whole look was effeminate; yet I was proud of my ability to look past it and see that he had a deep, abiding love for the gospel. *What more could I want?*

He and I saw each other almost every day after that. Nineteen days later, we were engaged. Gary told me the Holy Ghost told him I was "the one." *Who was I to argue with the Holy Ghost?* In fact, a few weeks prior, the Spirit had already assured me on my way to the mailbox that the Lord would take care of me. Because I trusted the Spirit, I felt certain that Gary's spiritual experience was real. I almost couldn't contain myself when he proposed. I jubilantly danced around my apartment shouting, "Hey, World! Jennifer is getting married!"

About a week after our engagement, up popped the red flags. One afternoon, my fiancé and I were sitting out on my backyard patio having a leisurely conversation when all at once he accused me of saying something I didn't say. Because it was so long ago, I don't remember the exact details of that conversation, but I recall feeling misjudged. When trying to defend myself, this new man in my life artfully twisted my words, using my own logic and reasoning to lead me to a place of self-doubt. He had me convinced that I said something that I had not said; a carefully created masterfully planned illusion to keep me enslaved and compliant. He was quite brilliant in his manipulations. But because I wanted a husband more than anything, I ignored that little voice in my head that whispered, "Break up with him, or you'll be sorry."

Maybe I'm making a big deal out of nothing. I reasoned. *What if I turn him down and never get an offer to marry again? After all, marriage is the most important goal for any young LDS woman. Besides, the Holy Ghost told Gary to marry me. Who am I to question a priesthood holder? He's also a biology major with a goal to become a dentist. Why would I want to flub that up?*

Gary was also a returned missionary. A missionary was considered a great catch. At age eighteen, young LDS men are expected to go out in the world and preach the gospel for two years, then find a wife shortly after they return home. We had a holy reason to want to rush into marriage. But we had to wait four grueling months to finish up the semester before meeting each other's families. Four months was an eternity for two obedient, over-eager virgins like us. And with my over-the-top libido, it felt as though that day would never come.

My fiancée had the physique of a bobby-pin and standing next to him made me feel like a house. But I convinced myself that a girl can't have everything. When there's love, there's sacrifices. That's just the way it was. Besides, I had a sparkling diamond on my finger.

On May 14, 1977, this practical stranger dressed in a white ruffled shirt and baby-blue tux accented with a pink boutonniere, took me by the hand as we entered the Oakland temple gates.

Anything but elaborate, our wedding day was a simple, sacred ceremony. In about a fourteen by twelve-foot sealing room, we knelt across from each other on a cushioned altar. Alabaster walls, gold-framed mirrors, and a four-tiered chandelier transformed this tiny room into an illusion of Heavenly Glory. But something was missing. *Was it joy?* Circled by family and close friends, everyone whispered. It reminded me of second-grade library hour.

I wore a pure white floor-length, long-sleeved, high-necked dress, with a pleated white nylon robe over one shoulder, a white veil on my head, and a small green apron tied around my waist. Gary was dressed all in white wearing what looked like a baker's hat and the same kind of apron. My prince and I ogled each other hungrily, ready and eager to participate in the physical act of creating a celestial family. After all, we had earned our place there.

Standing in front of the altar was a white-clad officiant whom we had never met until that day. He shared a barely audible, prosaic message, which my wandering mind neglected to take in. I just wanted to skip all the quiet and get on with the honeymoon.

After this stranger pronounced us husband and wife and we exchanged a chaste kiss, he led us to stand between two mirrors that faced each other. Smiling at each other in endless reflections, my new spouse and I vowed to live up to our temple covenants. In return, we were promised that death would not divide us. As a young bride filled with hopes and dreams, I was completely clueless about the rotten deal I had made.

As our guests pulled out their tissues and quietly dabbed their eyes, exuberant laughter was squelched. Family and friend's gestures of congrats were rigid and suppressed. A marriage event that would have otherwise been filled with so much rejoicing turned out to be a disappointing, sterile experience.

After the ceremony, we headed to the Hayward meeting house for our wedding reception. There was no lively dancing, no garter or bouquet toss, or loud, hearty guffaws. It was more like a family birthday party as loving ward members pitched in to decorate and provide music. Held in the church's multi-purpose room with basketball hoops and gym floor, the Carpenters and Bread hummed in the background on a '70s portable cassette player, lulling our guests with their mellow tunes. Tacky pink and white crepe paper zig-zagged around the basketball hoops and stands. But a basketball court will always be a basketball court no matter how hard you try to disguise it.

Refreshments consisted of a modest 3-tiered vanilla cake. But let's not forget the candy-coated almonds. Hungry kids popped them like hopheads since dinner was not offered. Guests paid their respects by shaking hands systematically down the reception line as their children ran loose, screeching their Sunday shoes across the freshly waxed gymnasium floor.

Would I find eternal bliss in this new chapter of life? If bliss was to be determined by the events that played out so far, I didn't have a chance. Time was drawing near. We would soon be heading toward the San Francisco Hyatt Regency to spend our first night together. *Would it be everything I imagined it to be?* A million scenarios flashed through my mind as we whisked our way through scattered rice.

Yet the sound of silence drummed even louder as our little Datsun B210 rumbled across the SF-Oakland Bay Bridge toward the City's hotel. Why was my new husband so quiet? Was he holding onto a secret? Was there something he wasn't telling me?

CHAPTER 23

HONEYMOON FUNK

Gary and I had finally arrived at The City's Hyatt Regency. This was the night it was going to happen. We now possessed a powerful sheet of paper; a marriage certificate, which entitled us to all the hot and heavy supersonic sex we could enjoy forevermore without a single shred of guilt.

Gary took his time when hanging his pressed tux in the closet, making sure the crease lines were perfectly lined up. *Who cared about neatness at a time like this*. My mind was on one thing only.

While my new husband unpacked his suitcase, I chose to bounce my heinie on the bed, my crotch quivering at the thought of what sex might feel like—the rhythm, the passion, the energy expenditure. I was never allowed to go to X-rated movies, but I did see a drawing of a penis that some sex-crazed girl passed around in seventh-grade art. Finally, the time had come, and I was dying to know what it felt like to have Gary's male hardness inside me.

After a hot bath, I waltzed over to my suitcase and pulled out my skimpy babydoll negligee, slipping it over my soft, ample curves. The sound of Gary's shower hummed in the background while I set my portable cassette player on the dresser and flipped on Roberta Flack's "Feel Like Makin' Love to You." In front of the room's cheval mirror, I swiveled my lace-covered hips in a slow, seductive manner. I couldn't wait to have my husband's large hands all over me.

Applying my favorite cherry lip gloss, I smooshed my lips together to even out the color, then applied my eyeshadow. Ocean blue turned my innocent eyes into deep-set, sinful bedroom eyes. I barely recognized myself all dolled up. I hoped my Gary would like my look.

The shower was still humming as I fumbled through my cosmetic bag, fetched the bottle of my sweet-scented perfume, and spritzed it in the air as I stepped into it. Right then I heard a big splash of water. *Was he swimming in there?* Settling into a seductive pose on the king-size mattress, my plummeting cleavage rose and fell with each anxious breath, as I waited. And waited. Still waiting.

Finally, Gary emerged in the doorway. Bonier than a graveyard and paler than a Halloween glow stick, I was taken aback at how different he looked without clothes. *And where were all his chest hairs?* My mother had often reminded me that a girl can't have everything. So I concentrated on his smile. And dimples. And full head of wavy hair. Smile. Dimples. Hair. That's what I needed to focus on.

Mom also told me to use Vaseline for "the sex act." Reserved and uptight, she couldn't even look me in the eye when saying it. My poor, rigid mother would rather die than talk about sex.

Back when we were dating, Gary mentioned that before he read the Book of Mormon and converted to the church, he had fooled around with some girls in high school. Nothing too serious. At least he retained his virginity. At age 22, my bona fide DDD boobies were screaming for experienced hands. I couldn't wait for him to rip off my lingerie and play rough. Not that I was into kinky sex. I just wanted him to work them over.

Now for the drumroll moment. The moment I'd been waiting for since I grew boobs ... Ready? Fifteen minutes later, it was over. *Almost a decade of anticipation, for what?* My hopes had been dashed, and sex hurt. It hurt a lot!

Here's how it happened ...

My new husband climbs into bed, slips off my blue babydolls, and plays sissy tetherball with my girls. Then he enters my Vaseline-filled vertical smile. It immediately turns into a frown, but I ignore the pain.

Admittedly, the sex could have been better. Because I had a boob fetish, I wished he would have focused his energy on my DDD's. Yet I still found the act of sex mind-bending despite the lousy foreplay. If I were to insist on having more, I may have had a hobbling gait for weeks. Yet the thought of going to town on Gary's man toy made my thighs quiver.

That night, as my husband snored away, I tossed and turned. How could he sleep so peacefully when we only did it once? Usually, it was the guy that couldn't get enough. *What was going on?* As he continued to grunt in his sleep, I obsessed about his penis. He didn't even feel pain with sex like I did. *Shouldn't he have been the one waking me?*

His penis and its magical growing powers fascinated me—the way it sprouted north toward his naval as opposed to sticking straight up toward the sky when he was lying on his back. I really thought that's what penises did. Stuck straight up. I wanted to watch the magic again. But I didn't have the heart to wake him.

For the next few nights, I obsessed about his unit. I was aching to be filled. I craved emotional and physical closeness and was not getting any. When we did make love, Gary's head bobbed back and forth like a bobblehead doll, and his barren eyes were nowhere near my face.

My trysts with the tub had been so much more magical than lovemaking. Warm running water had set the standard pretty high. *Why couldn't I feel that same growing intensity when having sex with my husband?* Although I heard Gary hollering out a few times when we were doing it, I don't think either of us knew how to get me to that magical place.

As our vacation came to an end, I was hugely disappointed. My new spouse was a healthy, red-blooded twenty-one-year-old male on a relaxing stress-free honeymoon. Yet he couldn't seem to rouse his sleepy Peter a third time in five days. I felt so rejected and unsexy. Gary noticed I was feeling down and came up with an excuse. He said men don't recover as quickly from an orgasm as women do. That didn't make sense. *Recover from what?*

Looking at my husband from across the sheet, for a moment it was like I've been sucked back into the temple. I breathed in far too much quiet. If only I had married Chad, we'd be laughing our guts out over nothing. And I bet the sex would have been over-the-top sublime. But I couldn't go there. I now had a husband that I vowed to be faithful to.

When the world charges full speed around you, silence can be healing. But not this silence. It spoke of disconnection, loneliness, and utter disappointment. Without much action on the mattress, I was so depressed, I wanted to cry. I couldn't shake the funk. I wondered if I was the one with the problem. *Am I oversexed? I'm a nymphomaniac? Can nymphos still go to heaven?*

After we returned home and settled into our new apartment, Gary told me he had a touch of the flu during our honeymoon. That would have been nice to know. I don't understand why he kept that from me. No wonder he couldn't get it up!

We eventually learned how to make each other happy in the bedroom. And despite Gary's quiet nature, I gradually become more fulfilled. I even saw him as a spiritual giant. Compared to the life I had before, he seems to be the answer to my many prayers.

Through time, I even conquered my weight problem. I was no longer obsessed with food. Now I was a purposeful wife. That hole in my heart was gradually closing, getting smaller. Until the unthinkable happened, and I could no longer look at him.

CHAPTER 24

MY BIGGEST MISTAKE

As life's train continues its momentum, I've gotten so much less young. Yet with age, I've attained a respectable kind of wisdom that can't be ascribed to the young and dumb. Wisdom comes through making mistakes, a landfill of them, some buried and forgotten, others surfacing decades later, revealing a past that can never be disposed of.

As I gradually got more familiar with my husband, I saw him as a trapdoor spider, cowering in his little hole. I was more like a social butterfly, the life of the party, making up for all the years I didn't talk.

For as long as I can remember, connection and affection have been as important to me as breathing in and out. Gary was my opposite. He stuffed his feelings in a box and carefully buried them beneath a shitload of trash. Communication that leads to emotional intimacy is my personal love language, and I desperately needed to understand what he was thinking—to the degree that I might have unintentionally pushed him further into his shell.

Like many men, my husband had an overpowering drive to work hard. As I look back on the life we shared, it's clear to me that this drive was more about proving himself to the world than doing the right thing.

In our first year of marriage, I put Gary on a pedestal and saw him as a deeply spiritual man. When he was asked to speak in church, his dynamic deliveries resonated as if God himself were handing him a script. And when talking with other church members. I sensed his peaceful, calm repose. I felt proud to be his wife and believed he was destined for greatness.

But then I started to notice his obsession about climbing the church's hierarchal ladder. As he grew more aggressive in his search for self-aggrandizement, his radical attitude frightened me. For example, he used the LDS motto, "A Woman's Place is in the Home," as a weapon and a whip to control me. He worked twice as hard so I could be a stay-at-home mom and belittled me fiercely if I tried to expand my horizons.

About a decade into our marriage, I enrolled in a college piano pedagogy class to perfect my piano teaching skills so that I could obtain students with the goal of bringing in a little extra income for our family. After dinner one evening, I wandered away from the table before clearing the plates so I could finish my homework assignment.

I was scribbling out my final notes in the den, when my spider-of-a-spouse suddenly appeared behind me. Before I had time to think, he reached around me and snatched my assignment from my hand, ripping it into shreds. "Wifely duties come first," he groused. I sat there with an incredulous expression. All my work was in a shredded pile. Why couldn't he have expressed his frustration in a kinder way? Instead, he chose to be cruel. Yet he was striving to be a saint. I couldn't make sense of it.

Trying to figure him out was like trying to put together a 5000-piece jigsaw with no clue what the picture was supposed to be. Over the years, I madly hunted for the missing pieces. But there were just far too many lost, broken, and distorted parts to have ever made sense of the picture.

With such little time to get to know him before we married, I never had a chance to experience his unhealthy behaviors. In his defense, he was trying too hard to be perfect, perhaps due to his lack of self-love. I saw him as a broken man. I was devoted to him because I didn't see a way out. We had been sealed in the temple. Our three kids were born under the covenant, which meant we were a forever family.

Gary's vicious assault on that fateful night when I was asleep and pregnant was the violent choice of a non-communicative man with a sudden pathological need to talk. It made no sense. Did he really believe that slapping me would make we want to talk to him? Was his need to control me so intense that he lost his mind? This was one of those distorted puzzle pieces that just didn't fit anywhere.

DR. JEKYLL & MR. HYDE

Neither my husband's shame nor his vows to never abuse me again had any power to stop Mr. Hyde. Dr. Jekyll would occasionally slip into the shadows and Mr. Hyde would emerge without warning.

One afternoon during a heated argument in the hallway, he plowed into my face so hard that he knocked the wind out of me. I lay on the floor, stunned and disoriented as the volatile Mr. Hyde stormed out the front door. Neither Dr. Jekyll nor Mr. Hyde returned for three long days. When Sunday arrived, I tried not to blink to avoid calling attention to my bruised eyelid. The last thing I wanted was for ward members to see my husband as a monster.

Although Gary was pretty messed up, I had plenty of flaws of my own. But I hated contention. I would often go out of my way to avoid it. Before we had children, I enjoyed working outside the home as a salesclerk at an office supply store. I was fun, outgoing, and gregarious. The lackluster little wifey had finally emerged from her cocoon as a radiant, colorful woman. Perhaps Gary was threatened by my newfound confidence, and the only way he knew how to cope was to strike out and belittle me. I, on the other hand, thrived on the energy of others. Being stuck with a man whose emotional barometer was broken threatened to suck the life out of me.

Seeing my troubled husband fly into a full-blown Mr. Hyde rage that seemingly sprang from nowhere was scary. Like the time he yanked our wall-mounted phone off the kitchen wall so I couldn't contact anyone when I felt threatened by his anger. But through the years, I made excuses for him. I mean, it wasn't like he hit me every day.

Eventually, I got brave enough to share his abuse with my parents. They had a good talk with him. It didn't help. He continued to put me down and call me names, destroying my sense of self-worth along with my ability to think rationally. I even convinced myself I deserved to be slapped. After all, I was highly emotional.

I was the kind of woman that when happy, I was over the moon; when I was really hurt, I'd sink onto my bed and cry into my pillow. When angry, my voice would speed up and get a little shrilly. But I was a lovebug and could forget about my anger in two seconds if I felt understood. It wasn't in my nature to retaliate with cruel digs or hit below the belt with ugly name-calling.

The thing that evoked anger in me the most was when Gary would attack my personal character and falsely accuse me of being someone I wasn't. Perhaps my quiet-natured, introverted husband just couldn't handle someone like me, a woman hardwired with strong emotional extremes. Yet, beyond all that he put me through, the worst abuse for me was his punishing silence. When he checked out, my world stopped. The isolation and lack of connection was the worst kind of hell I could suffer.

When I couldn't break the unbearable silence, it made me want to kill. His refusal to show any emotion only amplified mine. In time I learned that Gary's silence was his way of gaining leverage over me. "Look at you!" he'd sneer. "You're acting like a hysterical lunatic. You've got big problems!" He was right. At least I knew it. I went on a screaming rampage while he sat there like cold flint, gloating at the success of his torture.

As our marriage quickly deteriorated, my troubled spouse refused to go to counseling. By agreeing to get help alone, I hoped he would see me as a good example and eventually join me in this worthy self-improvement project. After I located a highly recommended psychiatrist and this man listened to my story, in his astuteness, he suggested that if I wanted my marriage to work, I would need to step up to the plate and own my goods. He had a point. Perhaps Gary would start to respect me if I learned how to become an empowered woman.

My first assignment toward empowerment was to purchase a copy of Cosmopolitan—a popular '80s women's magazine containing articles about fashion, relationships, self-improvement, and careers. It would never be approved or suggested reading by my church leaders, but I trusted the doctor's judgment.

When Gary walked through the door that evening and found me on the living-room couch casually flipping through the pages of my assigned magazine, his brain went into high alert. I glanced over at him with slanted brows. *Is he going to rip up the pages like he did my homework assignment?* His eyes looked glacial as he slowly edged his way toward me ...

CHAPTER 25

THAT EVIL MAGAZINE

Soon, Gary was standing in front of me, his feet flattening the blue fibers of the livingroom carpet. *What was that smell?* Oh, yea, foot powder. He always used it to keep his feet from sweating. From the corner of my eye, I could see his spanking new pair of dark gray socks.

"Ahem." He cleared his throat to get my attention, but I paid no heed as he proceeded to lecture me about Cosmopolitan and its worldly messages. He claimed it would fill my head with nonsense and teach me to be selfish. As he continued in his piety, I glanced up at his tumorous Adam's apple, the way it bobbed up and down his neck like an embryonic alien. "The next thing you know," he said, "you'll start getting ideas about working outside the home."

"That might not be a bad thing," I retorted, letting out a slow yawn. I then set my magazine on my lap, rested my head on the sofa arm, and flew up to my cloud. *Eyes closed, I see myself on stage, a world-famous singer/songwriter, eating up the mic, shaking my purple spiked hair to the rhythm of my chart-busting No. 1 hit, "Whiny Little Optimist." All my fans are screaming and cheering.*

If only I could've reveled in this moment a little longer, but in my happy state, a darkness appeared before my closed eyes. I opened them to discover Mr. Fly in the Ointment looming over me. He wasn't about to let this go. I didn't appreciate him invading my personal space. I had just come home from an intense counseling session and needed some downtime. Why did he insist on badgering me?

I immediately spoke up before he had a chance to reprimand me any further. I told him about the challenges I'd been facing as a wife and mother and stressed the importance of a badly needed hiatus to calm my nerves and frazzled spirit.

But rather than acknowledge my unhappy state, he lowered his head to meet mine and twisted his lips into a cocky smirk. I stared through him as he raised a condescending brow while preaching to me about the subtle craftiness of Satan and how he lay in wait to deceive weak LDS mothers like me. Typically, his tone went eerily flat when he was angry, and he took on a zombie-like semblance. That's the way he operated. I feared that at any moment, he would reach over and slap me silly.

"The devil speaks through all kinds of mediums," he said. "TV, magazines, newspapers, you name it." His sermon was as dry as weathered wood. He loved preaching, and I figured the less I talked, the sooner he'd be out of my hair.

But at that point, he decided to wedge himself into the small space between me and the arm of the sofa. He looked like the Devil's pale-faced brother. "Satan is real," he deadpanned, leaning in a little closer. His breath on my skin caused the hairs on the back of my neck to stand on edge. "And someday, if you're not watchful, he will lead you straight to hell."

Impossible! I thought. I was already there.

It wasn't long before Gary forgot about Cosmopolitan. I had a few magazines stashed under my bed and occasionally pulled them out when I got a little feverish for adventure. I'd read those spicy articles about moms who had run off into the sunset with their shiny typewriters and fax machines. But that was as far as it went. I was too indoctrinated to even consider joining the ranks of liberated housewives.

When the threat of divorce began to loom over our failing marriage, I stubbornly looked past Gary's fatal flaws and stayed on board, hoping to save the sinking ship.

In retrospect, the first and biggest mistake I made was marrying a stranger. And then, when the abuse started and continued, my thoughts turned to a popular quote by one of the church's prophets: "No other success can compensate for failure in the home." I didn't want to fail. I could not fail. I pressed forward, faithfully doing everything in my power to be the best wife and mother ever.

To think I could've been spared from so much trauma, if only I had been taught that sometimes success comes in the form of a healthy self-image, a good lawyer, and the courage to sign my name on the dotted line in bold, black ink.

JEKYLL & HYDE

I held my hands high to surrender,
Fully trusting the kind of love
That fell with ease thru the arm sleeves
And hugged my heart like a glove.
He cuffed me with careless aggression,
Robotically read me my rights—
A dog in the heat of the moment

With a bark as big as his bite.
My bucket was dry and depleted.
I hungered and thirsted for more.
I tasted his kiss at the altar
And believed I didn't deserve more.
I spilled out my heart as I trusted.
I talked about living the dream.
Of sharing a home and a family
And frolicking on the same team.
Pregnant and sick with our daughter,
I woke up and thought I was dreaming.
The weight of his torso was crushing.
His slaps stung so hard; I was screaming.
When life seemed so perfect and lovely,
He knew when to throw me off kilter.
This man that I knew, was a monster
Who had not a gauge nor a filter.
He offered me bread and Spumante
That turned to dry crumpets and water.
A lost little lamb needing someone
Was cunningly led to the slaughter.
Sang a song of angelic deception.
Played a saint in the light of the sun.
Satanically danced in the shadows
As he badgered and bullied and won.
Candles, chocolate, and roses
Shut me up if I dared to complain,
And soothed his joke of a conscience
Washed up in the tears of my pain.

Wore the mask of a blue-eyed cherub.
Had the dance of the devil inside.
A phantom behind the closed curtain
On stage was the Jekyll of Hyde.
He helped me to learn about karma.
It tends to bite hard when you're mean.
I lived to find love that is real.
He died chasing after his dream.

CHAPTER 26

DON'T BLAME ME, BLAME MY HORMONES

Through the years, as Gary struggled with his demons, I struggled with mine. My demon was my high libido. After I became pregnant with our first child, the surplus of hormones rushing through my blood had amped up my sex drive to the extreme. I felt like I was "Livin' El Libido Loco."

I also had a dark secret that lay hidden in my drawer beneath a pair of pink silk panties. I used my vibrator as advertised to reduce tension. When I purchased it, I told myself I had plenty of tension and needed this magic wand. Because it looked and sounded suspicious, I felt the need to hide it from Gary. But it kept calling me from the drawer. I wasn't sure which of us would win the battle: the toy that kept hollering my name, or me, by virtue of my stoic belief that "solo play" was a sin. But during weak moments, I would cave.

My leaders had often admonished me to cling to my spouse and nothing else. Certainly not a vibrating wand, egg, or silver bullet. *Were they worried I was going to run off into the sunset with my vibrator?* I had a lot of pent-up energy. Couldn't God make a few concessions and adjust his rules on a sliding scale in concurrence with my fluctuating hormones?

All I had to do was open the drawer and expose my wand to the light. *To use it or not to use it?* It had been untouched and locked away for about a week. It didn't deserve this kind of neglect. Unlike Gary, it never once yelled at me or called me stupid. It just hummed softly according to its packaged description.

In my nightstand drawer, my alabaster wand shined with confidence, as if it were goading me to let the good times roll. I often turned to the Book of Mormon to cope with such tempting moments, but my toy's warm glow beamed far brighter than any fair-skinned Nephite.

It was a Saturday, and Gary was working at the golf course when I got the sudden urge to undress and don myself in nothing but a handful of shiny, long, gold-chained necklaces. As I walked around the house, the mere touch of cool metals jostling around my breasts put me over the edge. My body, a multi-story warehouse of hormonal little she-devils, beckoned me to sunbathe in the backyard. I knew this was risky. Neighbors might spot me through their windows, but don't blame me, blame my hormones. They were completely unstoppable.

Butt-naked I lay on a skimpy towel, my protruding belly rising and falling as I breathed in the aroma of fresh grass, scented roses, and summer sweat. The thrill of the sun's erotic fingers tickling every curve and fold from head to toe almost had me in spasms. I would have loved to pleasure myself outdoors, but even with my temptress hormones, I would only risk so much.

Inside the house, I couldn't wait. I ran into my room to retrieve my magic wand. After snatching it from the drawer, I lay on my bed and within seconds, I was wailing loudly to its hum while that little vibrating critter took me places I had never gone. At last, all that pent up tension had finally melted away. But only an hour later I was ready for round two.

What was going on with me? Why were these biochemical changes commanding such power and authority over my thoughts and behavior? Why couldn't I stop thinking about sex? Who was I turning into? As far as I saw it, my hormones were the culprit, not me. I felt as if I were no longer in control. I even fantasized about running nude in the streets. I was already mapping out my route.

On Sundays, as I partook of the sacrament in my ankle-length dress, my conscience shamed my hypocritical soul for having the gall to eat of Christ's body and drink of his blood. Deep inside, I knew that no amount of bread and water could cleanse me from what I had done. *Why couldn't I release and relinquish this misguided Guilt?*

Guilt is what happens if you have a strong conscious like I did and you're highly impressionable like I was, and you have "the brethren" telling you at every corner that masturbation is evil. I wanted to be a good girl, but how could I feel good about myself when I had no control? Yet, was my strong hormonal drive really my fault?

My hormones had their name written all over my naughty impulses, still, I never gave myself a free pass. To maintain my worthy status as a temple-endowed Mormon, I was convinced that I needed to hold myself accountable for my actions. If my leaders required that sex crimes like masturbation be publicly confessed, then that's what needed to be done. Yet I shrunk at the thought of having to do this.

In his mid-thirties, my bishop had lovely sky-blue eyes that pierced me to the center. *How the heck am I supposed to waltz in there and share something so deeply personal, so incredibly embarrassing, so horrifically perverted to a man who has "do me" written all over him?*

CHAPTER 27

CONFESSIONS TO BISHOP MCDREAMY

My tummy gravid, ripe, and ready to deliver, I sat in the church foyer on a doll-sized folding chair, my buttocks flowing over the sides. The tiny, cold seat had to be for anorexic confessors. No normal heinie could mold to it.

Because I was a temple-going Mormon, I contacted Bishop McDreamy to set up my once-a-year temple-recommend interview. Just like a Costco card, my temple-recommend card had to be renewed annually. If it expired, I would not have the privilege of entering the temple to do the Lord's work.

Throughout the years, my church leaders continually reminded me that going to the temple and participating in the rituals would save the souls of those people who had passed on—those who hadn't been given the opportunity to accept the gospel on earth. They told me it was a blessing I should never pass up. After sacrificing my Friday popcorn and movie nights so I could rush off to the temple and sit through a three-hour ceremony to save a dead stranger, I had yet to feel blessed about anything except for my ability to crack the code to a backdoor escape route. If only I could. Too bad Gary didn't feel the same way. If he knew how I really felt about the temple, he'd see me as an ungrateful heathen.

A temple interview is a straightforward process. Bishops are required to ask a standard list of questions. If I answered yes to most all of them, I could pass go, allow my bishop to collect my tithes, get my recommend card renewed, and all would be well in Zion. But then there was the Chance card. How would Bishop McDreamy respond to my confession about solo play? I chewed off most of my nails thinking about it.

Finally, I heard some stirring behind the bishop's door. Maybe the interviewees before me were wrapping it up. I sure hoped so. I had a sudden urge to relieve my bladder. I could only hold on for so long.

A few seconds later, the door opened. Bishop McDreamy appeared in the hallway, spotted me waiting, and approached me with a smile. I reached to shake his hand, revealing my torn, scruffy nails. He asked me how I was. My bladder was about to explode, but I lied and said I was fine.

My bishop invited me into his office and extended a hand to show me where to sit. He smiled his usual warm smile as he lowered himself into a swivel seat behind his desk. Why did he have to be so damn hot? He had the most perfect head of dark hair. And sky-blue eyes rimmed with lashes so lush, I wished they were mine.

My kind, sweet leader wasted no time and dove right into the interview process. "Do you have a testimony of God, the Eternal Father, His Son, Jesus Christ, and the Holy Ghost?" When he smiled, he revealed his pristine white teeth.

"Yes," I said, almost too quickly, already in lockstep with this line of questioning. I was used to the drill. It was far easier than a traffic school quiz. My leader would pause, I would say yes each time, except when he asked if I affiliated with anti-Mormons. That was an easy "no."

But then he came to that one question I dreaded. I'd never been dishonest with my leaders. I knew a confession would cleanse me. It would wipe the slate clean. "Do you obey the law of chastity?" he asked. This time his words hung in the air like a black balloon. In my present hormonal state, his fetching looks caused me to blank out. I felt a hot flash coming on, so I brushed my sweaty bangs from my brows and played with a loose piece of yarn trailing from the cuff of my blouse.

Then somehow, I finally managed to spill it all. I confessed to my bishop about my obsessive need to pleasure myself while making sure he knew my raging hormones were the culprit. Because I tended to blurt things out, I made sure I was somewhat implicit in my confession. *But what if my lack of descriptive detail tempted him to fill in all the gory details?*

After getting everything off my chest, I looked down at my lap. What if he was picturing me naked? *Too late now.* I couldn't take back my words. My deepest, darkest secrets, my most personal and private doings were floating around in this man's head. I peered up in time to see Bishop McDreamy scratch his fingers along the stubble of his firm jawline. *What was he thinking? Why was he so quiet? His non-verbal gestures tortured me.*

Finally, he spoke. "I appreciate your confession," he said. I bet he did. I bet I made his day. I had naively believed since childhood that these high-ranking officials were immune to sin. Why had it not dawned on me earlier that bishops have carnal desires just like anyone else? I had no need for a mirror. Right then, I could feel my face light up like my bright pink flowering vagina. I didn't even have a fan to blow away the humiliation.

The following week in church, I spied him glancing down at me from the podium. *Is he picturing me on the bed with my vibrator? Does he do naughty things behind closed doors when thinking of me?*

I ran into him again in the foyer on my way to Sunday school. Because I was always drawn to his eyes, I never noticed how sensual his mouth was until that moment. His upper lip was shaped like Cupid's bow and it curled up on one side as he passed by. *Is he flirting with me?* I wasn't a naive college girl anymore. I knew I gave off a certain air that men liked, pregnant belly or not.

My confession was like lighting a match and igniting a lusty wildfire. As we brushed shoulders in passing, tingling sensations penetrated outward through my fingertips. I had to fight the urge to call out his name so I could lose myself in his smile. I longed to trace a circle along that firm jawline then press my lips against his. *What the hell's wrong with me? I should feel humiliated and ashamed after confessing. Instead, I was filled with lust.*

I knew I couldn't blame myself entirely for my horniness. Not only was I pregnant, but my husband, Gary, wasn't very attentive. He was all business, rarely smiled, and wasn't one for giving compliments. Because he rarely seemed passionate about life and showed very little emotion except for when he got angry, I wasn't that attracted to him.

✻✻✻

After the birth of our first child, I spent far too much time fantasizing about Adorable Bishop McDreamy even though my hormone levels had decreased.

I close my eyes and see him …

In the nursery, I'm rocking my newborn when, my sexy shepherd appears in the doorway. He walks toward me, slowly unbuttoning his shirt.

His chest hairs are dark and plentiful. He leans in to kiss me, then slips his fingers through my nightie without disturbing my suckling baby and caresses my breasts. I close my eyes, almost tasting the sweetness of his lips on mine, when a sawing snore rattles me into a hellish reality.

I open my eyes. My sexy apparition is no longer there. In his striped pj's, Gary is drooling on my shoulder. I need to face it whether I like it or not. I'm joined at the hip to a self-righteous, all-work-and-no-play bully for time and all eternity.

Yet, I know all will be well in Zion. It simply comes down to a choice: *To use it or not to use it?* My Hitachi vibrator knows how to keep a secret. If I don't tell, it won't.

CHAPTER 28

MORMON MINION

I was called to be in the Primary Presidency when I had a six-year-old, an unmanageable three-year-old, and a three-month-old newborn who required around the clock feedings. I felt physically depleted. But because I had been taught to never turn down a church calling, I looked into my bishop's hopeful eyes and mustered a weak smile and a yes.

Being in the Primary Presidency would require time-consuming preparations of weekly presentations for more than 100 children every Sunday ages three to eleven. My list of responsibilities was endless. And my dynamic deliveries needed to outplay all attention deficit disorders, hungry tummies, and saucy preteens.

After finishing my Sunday presentations, I'd find myself locked in my room already preparing for the next one. But I never complained. I was a good soldier marching as to war, forward into battle, doing my duty with a helluva heart full of song.

What I really needed far more than any calling was a seriously overdue afternoon nap. With all the chaos and responsibility around our home, I was gradually losing it. I began to yell at my children all the time; and even though I felt like a terrible mother, I just couldn't seem to stop. Trying to get an uncooperative toddler and newborn out the door along with a duffle bag filled with snacks, crayons, coloring books, and fidget toys to keep them fed and entertained was like trying to prepare a trip to Patagonia.

As my children argued and punched each other on the pew, I fought the urge to laugh since I couldn't cry. The opening song mocked me with its words:

> Welcome, welcome, Sabbath morning
> Now we rest from every care
> Welcome, welcome, is thy dawning,
> Holy Sabbath, day of prayer.

Ebenezer Beesley, polygamist father of sixteen, and co-author of this hymn, undoubtedly felt inspired to write it after escaping the family madness and hiding in the confines of a nearby chapel.

Throughout the years, the list of my callings was as follows: Church Organist, Chorister, Cultural-Art Specialist, Talent Scout, Stake Roadshow Director, Church Organist, Primary 2nd Counselor, Primary Pianist, Primary Teacher, Spiritual Living Teacher. I attended sacrament meetings, Sunday night devotionals, Relief Society homemaking meetings, stake meetings, ward activities, yearly tithing settlements, and temple-recommend interviews. Every month I visited my assigned ward sisters and taught them a lesson, attending to their needs. I made quarterly trips to the temple to do work for the dead. And finally, I made special trips to the Beehive Clothing store to purchase my sacred underwear. Ironically, while my leaders kept me hopping with all these time-demanding duties, they constantly reminded me that families come first.

Back in the '80s church was an all-day affair, especially for musicians like me. There was never enough of us to go around. I often had to skip meals to keep the music going while my husband hid out in the church house like Ebenezer Beesly. How could I possibly feel empowered when my world was a never-ending cycle of madness?

Today, I look back on my "put your shoulder to the wheel" determination and realize I was far too busy pleasing others to notice my family falling by the wayside. Along with church peer pressure, that overused, omnipresent cliché, "What would Jesus do?" guilted me into submission every time. The Lord gave His life for me. *Couldn't I do just one more little thing for Him, then another, and another after that?*

Welcome, welcome, Sabbath morning
Now we rest from every care.
Welcome, welcome, is thy dawning,
Holy Sabbath, day of prayer.
Rest, my ass!

CHAPTER 29

REFLECTIONS OF A DESPERATE, LONELY HOUSEWIFE

It's summertime as I lay on my towel in my backyard wearing my tiny yellow bikini and a pair of UV protected shades. Finally, I'm taking a break from my endless list of responsibilities. I look up at the sky and watch a flock of fluffy phalluses float by. *Wait What? Phalluses as in penises? Male anatomy?* I'm the second counselor in the Primary Presidency. My thoughts should be pure. Instead, I see penis clouds.

Near my feet, a family of freckled ladybugs sway on cool green blades of grass that tickle my toes in the warm summer breeze. Across the sky, a jet streaks a thin vapor trail, its hypnotic rumble lulling me into a trance.

It's eighty degrees in my East Bay neighborhood, and because my kids are in school, I'm taking a break from the insanity. As the sun sprays a tan along my girly curves, I can't stop thinking about young Roddy, my next-door neighbor.

I picture him ogling me through the fence holes as I lay here practically in the buff and shiver as I dream about him. A sturdy redwood paneled fence dividing our property is the only thing standing in the way of a great love affair.

I'm done having kids and although I no longer have that crazy libido, it's still high. Just not crazy high. Maybe it's all those green M&M's I'd been snacking on, or my new body, or both?

Baby Drew, my last born, is now in preschool, and my once-deflated boobs due to nursing have been pumped back up to my original perky DDD's thanks to my recent breast lift. I've also been religiously working my tail off at the local gym and look even better than I did in high school. To show gratitude to Hubby for throwing his hard-earned money into my boob job, we have a lot more sex. But it doesn't change the fact that I'm unhappy in the relationship.

As I roll onto my tummy, pondering my troubled marriage, a soft, warm breeze blows through my reddish-brown locks. There's a frisson of excitement when I'm one with nature. I feel so alive outdoors. *Am I bad if I can't control my thoughts about my hot neighbor?*

It's not like I haven't tried to block Roddy from my mind. In fact, I've work hard to feel attracted to my husband. I've even gone to counseling and poured my heart out to my therapist. So far, no amount of counseling has helped. I've even tried hypnotizing myself so I could see Gary in a different light. I repeat in my mind, "I'm attracted, I'm attracted, I'm attracted," hoping one day I'll wake up and find him dashing. So far nothing has worked. I believe my lack of attraction goes beyond the skin. I think it has everything to do with how he treats me. *What is a desperate, lonely housewife to do? Especially when I'm holding onto a big secret.* I want to kiss Roddy, make out with him, have sex with him. There. I said it out loud. Dear God, have mercy on my soul!

In church I'm told that lusting after someone is the same as committing adultery in your heart. That's pretty damning. Why not beat down Roddy's door and "do the deed" right now since my thoughts have already condemned me? If I'm going to hell in a handcart, shouldn't I at least be enjoying the ride?

Back in the real world, my kids and I finish off most of the stove-top macaroni when Gary walks through the door late from work. He's a real workhorse. Through the years, I've tried to ease his load by doing daycare and teaching piano lessons. Yet he continues to overextend himself. He's a one-man battalion fighting his demons alone.

I embrace my demons by fantasizing about the stud next door. Although the church keeps me plenty busy, with all three children enrolled in school, I feel less purposeful. That's why my head is often in the clouds, forever dreaming about naked Roddy.

As I lie in bed at night, I imagine my hunky neighbor leaning against his car, smoking a Marlboro while gazing up at the stars. I'm on a midnight stroll when I approach him. I catch him off guard and suddenly lean in and kiss him. The next thing I know, our passion has gotten way out of hand as we kiss and grope and … In no time, he's having his way with me on the hood of his unpolished junker, each thrust robbing me of breath as our bodies grind to the beat of the R&B song, "Do Me." In my fantasy, Roddy and I are sizzling hot lovers. Why can't my husband take my breath away? Why can't we have that same carnal rhythm?

I don't know how I have managed to stay married a full decade to a man who fears emotional closeness. I believe Gary also needs connection, yet at the same time, he protects himself. In fact, today, as I look back on us, I see a clear pattern. Almost every time we went out on a Friday-night date, if we started to get too close, he'd suddenly push me away by picking me apart 'til I was in tears. From experience, I came to know that sabotaging our intimacy made my husband feel safe. Vulnerability was terrifying for him. It would have meant having to show me who he really was underneath his façade. No way was that going to happen. My husband's behavior was typically punishing and cruel. Daydreaming about my next-door neighbor made me feel warm and happy.

In his early twenties, my Latino neighbor is brawny and bright-eyed. He's always in his driveway tinkering with his '56 broken-down Chevy. His eyesore-of-a-car downgrades the value of our nice, tidy cul-de-sac, but Roddy is a sight for sore eyes.

Whenever I leave the house to do errands, we often make eye contact. His eyes are not sterile like my husband's. They're big and black and warm and filled with desire. Whenever he sees me, he nods his head and grins, bringing me back to life.

On Sundays, when the primary children give talks about Jesus and how they strive to follow him, I dream about this swarthy, six-foot grease monkey with a five o'clock shadow soaping up his Chevy. He's always in my head taunting me with those suds.

On the Sabbath, I'm both a saint and a sinner. The saint reminds me that my body's a temple. The sinner in me wants to arouse Roddy when he's out washing his car on the mornings our family heads for church. On those days I'd choose to wear my dipped-collared blouse with a skirt that shows a little leg. Strutting down my front walkway, I'd feel the heat of his gaze, and if eyes could talk, they'd be saying, "Let's roll in the sheets, girl!" Sundays like this make me want to run away with him. *Why does being a sinner make me feel so happy?*

One day after work, my husband pulls into the driveway in a Triumph TR6. This British sports car with its four-wheel independent suspension is cool. Gary doesn't fit this car. He wears pressed slacks daily. He's as one-dimensional as a postcard. His mouth looks as expressionless as a Muppet's. The good news is that his boss loaned him this fun little car for the weekend. Gary tells me that he wants me to try it out. *Maybe he is thinking of purchasing it?* I can't wait to drive it.

The next morning, he's installing an alarm across town. He calls to ask me to do an errand. We end up getting into a dumb argument and he hangs up on me, leaving me in tears. I'm so upset that I don't know what to do. I look out the window and see Fantasy Guy working on his car. The Triumph is still sitting in our driveway. *Would I be forgiven if I stole Gary's boss's car and drove off in the sunset with this stud muffin?*

CHAPTER 30

BAD TO THE BONE

I hate it when my husband gets angry and hangs up the phone in the middle of a call. From the kitchen window Roddy is still in the driveway, but now he's got the hood down on his car and is waxing it. My heart races wildly as I grab my purse and keys to the TR6.

When I see him, I choke back my tears and flash my pearly whites as I head toward the sports car. Roddy's in his usual spot, his biceps flexing as he rubs a blue cloth along the hood of his dull gray wanna-be hotrod. I'm donned in a bright amber V-necked sundress and my jumbo cat-eye sunglasses. Not too overstated yet alluring enough to catch his attention.

I stroll toward him, swiveling my hips, my heart pounding. I'm so nervous my throat is dry, and my hands are shaking. He glances up, tips the edge of his baseball cap, and politely nods. At only two yards away, I think I'm going to stop breathing. Then without warning, words spill out without my permission. "I'm gonna test out my new wheels. Wanna tag along?" *Did I really just say that?*

Hotrod Roddy pauses and reaches to scratch his nose as if he's laboring over a math problem. Most likely he's weighing his options: *Should I go for a spin with this hot, older broad or finish polishing my rattletrap?* He lifts his shirt to wipe the sweat off his face, flicks his eyes down my dress, then strolls over to the car and jumps over the passenger door without bothering to open it.

I tear out of the driveway like Cruella de Vil minus the Virginia Slim. We circle the block as I vent about my husband. From across the seat, Shotgun Roddy's breath smells like a mixture of Budweiser and cherry juice as he chomps his Bubble Yum bubble gum. I'm whining about this and complaining about that when all at once, my delightful neighbor does the unexpected ...

He suddenly breaks out singing, "Bad to the Bone." I'm laughing so hard that I'm in hysterics. Shotgun Roddy has those bumblin' B's down without missing a beat. Sitting across from him is like having a front-row seat to a younger, better-looking version of George Thorogood.

The mood is light until suddenly the ominous cloud of Guilt rolls in and darkens it. Yet I have more than Guilt to worry about. I'm not young and single and bubble-yummy like my friend. I feel miserably stuck. How I long for a chance to be in my twenties again. A chance to be in Roddy's arms. A chance for him to do unimaginable things to me.

Time is short as I blubber to him about how jerky Gary can be. I know I'm betraying my husband because all I can think about is running away with Roddy. He's so alive. He even sings on key. And what a great listener. At least he's making the effort.

After circling the block a few times, I spin my wheels back toward the cul-de-sac and slam on the breaks, hoping to impress him with my hotrod skills. I don't want to boot him from the car, but a booty call would be nice. I might not have made the best choice going for a joyride with a guy who turns my loins to putty, but I know I won't allow myself to get too close. *Or will I?*

My sexy friend jumps over the door, then leans up against the car, his eyes glowing like candles on a birthday cake. "Adios, mi amiga." His whisper is low and guttural. I suck in a slow breath as he strolls away. My eyes target the mangled curls that spill from his old worn cap. His tight, round tush looks like an edible peach as he rambles toward his driveway. *Holy Mother of … Gosh?* I never felt comfortable using the Lord's name no matter how hot a guy looked.

Only a small moment with him and he's tucked away in my heart. Even more in my groin. Instantly, my vagina twitches, then pulses. I mean, there's a whole lotta below-the-waist activity going on. It's dancing, it's jigging. *Is this how I'm supposed to feel when turned on? No wonder sex hurts with Gary.*

Since having kids, I've been to the shop, tuned up, and remodeled. At age thirty, I'm finally becoming the woman I have always wanted to be. Paradoxically, I find it easier to strike up conversations with complete strangers, but I'm stuck with Mr. Burnt Toast. I want to cry an ocean. I want to test the boundaries, live on the edge eight years too little too late. It's not like I can jump into a time capsule and start over.

When my kids are in school, I exchange smiles at the supermarket and grin at guys who wink at me at the 7/11 checkout. As I stroll down the street, I pull back my shoulders and eat up the whistles and the honks. That's about as racy as this good little Mormon girl gets.

I know myself all too well. If I did end up having an affair, we're looking at a woman without a filter. After committing the crime, I'd end up spilling the beans to Gary before I even had a chance to shower away the DNA. What I needed was to fix my marriage. *But how?*

CHAPTER 31

THE UNFULFILLED BLESSING

"The blessing" softly killed him. And if I had been paying closer attention, I might have noticed the signs sooner than I did.

In September of 1972, when Gary was seventeen years old, he visited his bishop and inquired about a Patriarchal blessing. Like all youth in the LDS Faith, he was encouraged to prepare himself for this special blessing, which would not only serve as a guide throughout his life but supposedly open the door to an understanding of his spiritual potential.

LDS members believe that the Lord speaks through divinely appointed patriarchs when called upon to give a blessing. When Patriarch Stephens laid his hands upon Gary's head, he revealed that one day he'd be called to sit among the Church's elite. Mind you, Gary was only in high school. Near the end of the blessing, his patriarch stated, "Study the words of the prophets, for you may become like unto them."

Like most members' blessings, Gary's was tape-recorded and later transferred to paper. He tucked it in a safe drawer and during times of self-doubt, pulled it out to remind himself of his noble calling. His dear patriarch cautioned him that the fulfillment of these blessings was conditional upon his righteousness.

Gary and I were engaged four years later. One evening, we sat down together as he solemnly shared his blessing with me. One part in the blessing still rings clear in my head today: "As you teach of my doctrine, many of the words you speak shall be written and published to many whom you will never meet."

After reading his blessing, I felt nothing but awe for my fiancé and saw his piety as genuine. But through time, it became more apparent that his deeds were efforts to be noticed. The gnawing, hollow parts of him were starving for recognition and validation.

This blessing seemed to be fodder for his obsession in wanting to be great in the eyes of the church. It filled his empty soul with purpose and made him feel important. If the blessing was administered to a psychologically healthy man, it might have been nothing more than an admonishment to prepare for spiritual growth, but Gary couldn't see it that way. He would be a prophet one day. That's all there was to it.

In his quest to see this promise fulfilled, the rest of his family became his props. I was a lousy prop despite my efforts to be everything he wanted me to be. I didn't give up easily, and as I tried and failed to get his approval, my sense of self crumbled until there was nothing left of me.

I couldn't help but wonder if he cowered in the shadow of his more athletic, better-looking, older brother, Blake. Gary always seemed uncomfortable around Blake at family gatherings. And because his older brother was a free spirit who easily attracted beautiful women, Gary told me he saw him as a lost soul. My husband's "holier than thou" attitude was no doubt fueled by his own insecurities. It was his lack of self-love that eventually destroyed any peace in our home.

Gary's blessing offered him a ticket to a world where someday he would be recognized, maybe even revered. Convincing himself of his destined greatness was the easy part. He then had to earn his destiny by doing the impossible—becoming perfect.

What made him different from other men is that his life was consumed by a need to present a gleaming image to the LDS community. His decision to be the sole provider had little to do with my welfare or the welfare of our children. "The Lord is pleased with me," he'd tell me. "You don't have to work. We have a three-bedroom home and live in a nice area." He might as well have added, "Others will see me as a great provider and a spiritual giant as I climb the Church's hierarchal ladder."

His self-talk didn't come from a place of spiritual peace, but rather from a place of turmoil. Yet as a young bride, my inability to figure out the driving force behind that turmoil was unsettling.

Later in our marriage, Gary revealed to me that as a child, he struggled to be seen and heard as he floundered through each day feeling unnoticed while his parents attended to "more important things." Sounded like we had the same childhood. Yet at age seventeen, everything changed for Gary when he chose to embrace the Book of Mormon. Shortly after becoming fully converted to the gospel, he received his Patriarchal blessing. What a relief to learn that he would no longer remain a nobody. According to Patriarch Stevens, his potential was limitless.

In the years following the pronouncement of the special blessing, Gary's parents gloated on the idea of their son becoming a renowned LDS leader. I witnessed their gloating firsthand, and it made me sick. Gary's two siblings fell away from the church in their teens and never returned to embrace it as he had. His folks often referred to their other two children as heathens. But their middle child had a shiny-star collection on the family sticker board. He was "the righteous, obedient one."

Aggrandizing him was most likely a feeble attempt to melt away their own inadequacies. In doing so, they missed the mark and failed to notice his mental deterioration. All the bragging about his great destiny caused him to teeter on the pedestal that he knew would topple if his lies and abusive behavior were exposed.

Heck, he was only a teenager when he received the blessing. The stress of living up to it would make any kid bubble over to build a scalding head of steam like a slow pressure cooker. Trying to keep the lid on tight was his life's challenge. He couldn't always do that though.

I know his fear of failure was real because I often became the victim of it. As much as he'd try to bury it, without warning, his feeling of inadequacy would raise its ugly head in the form of shame and unworthiness and strike out at me. How could he possibly live up to all those gold stars and ballyhoo?

Gary often expressed frustration about being forever stuck in his church callings as an ordinary worker bee. His deep need for Mom and Pop's validation made for austere family visits. I could only imagine how brightly he'd beam if he could walk through their door saying, "Guess what Dad, Mom, I was just ordained a bishop." He had to start somewhere. If he was lucky enough to be called as one, it would surely get the ball rolling and place him on that path toward greatness.

So here we are visiting his parents. I'm curled up in the guest room with a novel. Gary plunks down beside me on the mattress, displaying his unique find from his parent's library: Brigham Young's biography. He has always admired this LDS prophet who bravely led the Mormon pioneers across the plains. We sit in silence for a while, both of our heads engrossed in our own stories.

Then out of the blue, he snaps his book shut, adjusts himself on the bed, and clears his throat. Being married to him for a decade, I'm quite the expert at picking up his nonverbal clues. Using my hand as a placeholder, I flip my book shut and wait for him to speak. But before he even says a word, I feel his arctic blues dissecting me with their sharp edges. *Uh-oh. This is not going to be good ...*

CHAPTER 32

WANNABE LDS PROPHET

Gary is on the bed next to me, clearing his throat one more time. I tend to flinch when he glares at me with such disgust, in fear that he might strike me. This time, I blink nervously, waiting for him to speak.

With his prized book in hand, he proceeds to tell me that after reading a few chapters about Brigham Young, he can't exactly envision me as "wife-material" for an LDS prophet. His tone is flat and condescending. *What?* I instantly slip my hand from my book and shift to an upright position. "What are you talking about?" I ask indignantly.

"You're not as spiritual as Sister Jones," he says with a snark in his voice, "and you're not as organized as Sister Cunningham." (These two ladies were members of our Newark ward). If I were wittier back then, I would've told him that when he was ready to act like a prophet, I'd be there by his side. Instead, I bottled my hurt.

The thought of how easy it would be for my husband to toss me aside for someone like Sister Jones or Sister Cunningham made my blood run colder than his. *What a jerk.* For the first time since we'd met, it became evidently clear that I was the blockade on his pathway toward snobbish ambitions, while his own inadequacies remained locked away in the shadow of his denial.

My first reaction was to grab my bags and leave him with Mommy and Daddy. I was in no mood to pretend that I was in love with their son. But our children were asleep in the other room.

The next day was Sunday, which meant I had to slap on my happy Mormon mask. Gary's mom wore one naturally. She never seemed authentic to me. She had a knack for turning the meetinghouse into a humdrum game of show-and-tell. I'd lost count of the times I'd yawn in the foyer while she dragged Gary down the hallway with overzealous pride. What was the point of going to church if she couldn't introduce her future-prophet son to her niche of friends?

When Gary's parents arrived at our house for his thirtieth birthday, we happened to be fighting. They made themselves at home while I tried to escape out the front door. I was in no mood for company and needed my own space.

With keys in hand, I headed down the hallway, but Gary barricaded my way, his arms folded over his chest like a nightclub bouncer. I wanted to rip that smirk right off his face. When I tried to pass by him, he grabbed hold of me and pushed me into his mother who was standing inches away. She didn't seem at all phased by his physical assault or concerned that he could have injured her and/or me. Instead, she reprimanded us both, as if we were kids fighting in a schoolyard.

A few weeks later, the two of us were sitting before our new bishop, spilling out our latest feud, when I spoke up about Gary's abuse. I couldn't hold it in any longer. I'd always been too afraid to call the police during those times when he left me bruised or bleeding. I felt safer spilling the beans before "the father of our ward."

When our bishop told him that he was required to document his misconduct on church records, Gary became outraged. How would he ever be able to become a great leader in the church if "Guilty of Wife Abuse" were stamped beside his name on church files? It sent him into panic mode. He would have to run faster to earn his destiny while seeking laud, honor, and recognition.

My husband also had a rapacious need to prove God's favoritism toward him. As we were sitting on the bed engrossed in the Book of Mormon one evening, he turned to Alma 3:6-19. Here, he read out loud about how God cursed the Lamanites, a wicked and disobedient people in the Book, with dark skin due to their transgressions. "But there's hope for them," he said with a little more zeal. I had never seen my husband more alive than at that moment as he thumbed madly through the pages, hunting down his favorite scripture. When he found it, his eyes were brighter than the Christmas star.

"Get this," he said. I was on the edge of my seat. "If these dark-skinned Lamanites decide to convert unto the Lord and unite with the Nephites, the Lord promises that He will remove the curse, and their skin will become white." (3 Nephi 12-15).

"And your point is … ?" I said, with an eye roll and a yawn. That's when he removed his glasses, set the book down, and expressed how blessed he felt to have fair skin. *What?* I never considered my husband a racist. At that point, I just knew that he was off his bloody rocker.

Drenched in indoctrination for thirty years, I was programmed to believe that no matter how nonsensical and bigoted the Lord sounded, the Book of Mormon was His Holy Word. The only thing I questioned at the time, was Gary's mental wellness.

Through the years, my husband held many respectable church callings, including Ward Clerk—a position that could have been extremely fulfilling. He had an opportunity to work by the bishop's side and personally get to know him. I'd say that was an honor on its own. But I watched him grow restless through the years as he worked behind the scenes. He had a strong need to be in the limelight. He wanted to shine from the pulpit.

In the thirteenth year of our marriage, we moved from the Bay Area to the San Joaquin Valley. The Atwater Ward was new to us. One day after church, I studied my reserved husband loitering in the foyer after church, mapping out his moves. He'd often shuffle his way toward the bishop's family and hang near those with clout. His effort to make friends and rub shoulders with important people was like me trying to organize my sock drawer. He wasn't very good at it.

Of the two of us, I was the fun-loving mingler. Over the years, each time we moved, I became close friends with the bishops' wives. Gary and I were different in that my agenda wasn't to impress. I was simply drawn to good, kind people.

Hannah, a lovely friend who served as Primary President, was a genuine sweetheart. When her husband, Joel, was set apart to serve as our bishop's first counselor, Gary was appalled. I watched him approach Joel in the foyer and overheard him quizzing him on how he got picked. But I knew my husband. His curiosity wasn't motivated by an opportunity to learn something from this guy. It was straight out passive-aggressive interrogation.

My poor, out-of-touch spouse was baffled, angry, and jealous. He had expressed to me on numerous occasions that he considered Joel to be rough around the edges, irreverent, and unrefined. How could this man possibly be more Christ-like than he was?

That's when the picture became clear to me. Gary viewed church callings as an entitlement, like reserved seats for those who obsessed about them the most. His stairway to heaven was built on a people-pleasing point system—how he appeared in his dark suit and tie, how his happy, shiny brood dazzled on the pew, and let's not forget his hoped-for "prophet-material" wife.

In the last year of our marriage, I saw a broken man. I envisioned wistful tears in the pools of his eyes that could not fall, and a heart that could not break because he had to be stoic— lips that dare not speak of the "unfulfilled blessing." He sat in the dark with his head in his hands while those nimbler and quicker jumped over the burning wick to the top of the "Chutes and Ladders" game-board.

Today, I look back and try to imagine how he felt as a young teen when his Patriarch admonished him to "be like unto the prophets." This blessing was pretty much left to his own interpretation. It would have never hurt him to emulate the lives of these good men.

But for Gary, his blessing was the key that would open the door to a world of becoming something—becoming *anything*. For him, making it to the top would convince everyone around him (including himself), that he was, indeed, that which he was so afraid he was not—a most honorable and worthy man.

Tragically, for him, his elusive destiny was never realized. He remained a bottom-of-the-totem-pole ordinary Mormon worker bee. Perhaps all the stress and negative energy in his life played a part in incubating the cancer that covertly wormed its way through his colon. Of that, I can only speculate.

When Gary died of colon cancer at age 53, I believe he also died of a broken heart. He had been estranged from all three of our children; but oddly, that wasn't the reason for his sorrow. While on his deathbed, my daughter, despite having been estranged from him for years, reached out in compassion and hope that he would express some regret for their broken relationship. His controlling, manipulative and obsessive self-righteousness had forced him to reject his "unfaithful" children, who had stepped away from the church, and even deny them funds for college unless they chose BYU.

But instead of an apology, he described his haunting regret with the same harmful rhetoric that had exiled his children in the first place. He mourned a life cut short before the fulfillment of the prophetic blessing entitling him to grandeur and influence in the quorums of the LDS elite. Because of those unfulfilled promises, he went to his grave believing he was a failure.

In the process of relentlessly seeking laud and honor, he lost the faith and admiration of his family. It was the blessing that softly killed him—a blessing given to him at age seventeen by a stranger sitting in a dark corner—a man who neither knew him nor the extent of his emotional illness.

Today, I question the wisdom in giving anyone the responsibility of receiving "revelation" from God to pronounce blessings and promises on any young person. Inspiration is not measured or guaranteed, and such blessings are universally subject to misinterpretation.

It's unfortunate that my husband never had a clue about what love was. Nor did he understand the infinite grace of God who dwelled within him—the God who dwells within all of us. He was too busy trying to earn his salvation; instead of simply letting go.

CHAPTER 33

MOTHERHOOD "WONDERLAND" (PART 1)

In LDS primary I was made to believe that motherhood was a Disney World wonderland—that bearing and rearing children was a picnic party. For some reason, my leaders left out a few important details, such as the near-death experience of childbirth, zombie-producing sleep deprivation, and warfare on the child-rearing battlefield.

Because I was married to a man who was emotionally unavailable, I prayed for lots of babies in hope that they would fill the void inside. Only the Lord knew how truly remarkably independent all three children would become, so he laughed, and said, "Ok, you asked for them."

CLAIRE

In 1978, my extremely gifted daughter, Claire, sprang into the world giving Ted Talks and writing New York Times best sellers. From the moment she arrived, she had me second- guessing myself. How could I possibly nurture a prodigy?

When she was three years old, I exposed her to music—the subject I excelled in. At age four, she quickly mastered a long repertoire of songs and performed them for our church and the community. As her most enthusiastic supporter, I hoped our common love for music would bond us.

As a young mom, I did some incredibly stupid things. I had high expectations for my brilliant daughter and ran her song-practice sessions like a Gestapo, giving her no room for error. My impatience was mostly due to my immaturity, and the fact that I was a very hangry dieter. Young, vain, and ignorantly selfish, as a young mother, my constant need to look trim and svelte took precedence over everyone's emotional well-being, and my poor daughter paid the price.

I occasionally took advantage of Claire's confident nature and adult-like maturity by burdening her with grownup tasks. One of her responsibilities at the tender age of six, was to call the family babysitter when her father and I planned a night out.

One day, she challenged me on the matter. I was in the kitchen when she approached me. "Mom, why are you having me call the sitter? Do you know how humiliating it feels to say, 'Hey Amber, can you come over and take care of me?'"

Truthfully, I hadn't considered how it made her feel until she brought it up. In many ways, she was more grownup than I was. Maybe I was the one who needed a babysitter. I tended to be overly theatrical and childlike, whereas she was rational and level-headed.

Because Gary would often decimate me at the dinner table, insisting that I was dumber than a lug nut, Claire grew up believing I wasn't very smart. Due to her limited knowledge about my intelligence, she believed she had to rely solely on her father to help her with her homework. When I look back on this, it saddens me that I didn't have the required self-love to help her balance her life and give her what she needed, which was a capable, strong, confident, self-assured, attentive mother.

LANCE

In 1980, I gave birth to a beautiful, content little boy—the angel who I believed would fill my emotional voids. I had my girl. Now, I had my boy. I couldn't wait to live that Motherhood Wonderland dream filled with cookie and ponies, and yellow balloons.

Three-month-old Lance adored his colorful butterfly mobile. As he watched it slowly gyrate above his head, he'd kick his little booties and squeal excitedly. He was so easily entertained. I often took advantage of his good nature to get the housework done.

As the holidays approached, a still, small voice within prompted me to give him more attention. I took him from his crib and set him safely in his infant seat on our kitchen countertop. Claire and I would tap him on the nose and say boo as we rolled out the gingerbread dough. He would giggle so hard, he'd have to catch his breath. We felt so blessed to have such a happy little tiger in our home.

This was our last memory of our beautiful baby boy. Lance passed away sometime during the night from SIDS, December 20, 1980, twelve days after John Lennon was murdered. I discovered my baby's lifeless body that morning. The anguish and devastation that followed could never be described. At the time, I couldn't imagine ever feeling whole again. The sound of popping yellow balloons was deafening. THEY EXPLODED LIKE GUNFIRE!

But then,

I saw him.

There were no pearly gates.

No judgment or St. Peter.

Imagine.

Only John Lennon.

He was holding little Lance

And singing him lullabies.

Also ...

You guessed it!

A whole sky filled with

YELLOW BALLOONS!

Picturing Lennon singing to my angel son tickled my heart and consoled me for a time, carrying me through the grief. But the emotional boost was short-lived. Soon came the gnawing hollowness that ate me from the inside out. If I had to keep looking at that barren crib—the one I couldn't bear to take down, I'd lose it for sure.

A few months later, after sharing my grief with Heavenly Father, the emptiness no longer haunted me. I felt as though my heart had been wrapped in a warm blanket of love. Whether Lance was with Lennon or not, I knew he was happy. And for the first time, Christ's Sermon on the Mount spoke to my heart and rendered total peace. "Blessed are those who mourn," He said, "for they shall be comforted."

ZACHARY

I didn't waste time getting pregnant after losing Lance. Eleven months later, on a cold, wintry night, Zachary sprang from my womb squealing like a crazed banshee from the underworld. Here's where Motherhood

Wonderland begins to morph into something else entirely. My first-born son was perfect and rarely made a fuss. In contrast, Zachary was a shrieking, flailing, noggin-banger.

As I battled Zach's around-the-clock tantrums, my husband insisted on taking twenty college units while holding down a full-time job. We became two ships passing in the night, but he refused to slow his sail, even if it meant risking going down like the Titanic.

Zach's pediatrician tested him for every physical and mental ailment out there. But everything came up negative. Rocking my troubled infant to sleep and getting him to stay asleep was a major challenge. Yet once he'd finally drift off, in my mind's eye, I would see my first son's lifeless body on the sheets and would frantically rouse little Zach from a peaceful dream. PTSD is hard to shake, and losing a baby to crib death is something from which a mother never recovers.

Sadly, my second son and I were both broken from the start and unable to fix each other. At age three, he was still a bundle of undiagnosed behavior problems, and I was a bundle of nerves. *Where were the answers? Didn't we both deserve just one moment of peace?* As his persistent howls continued to haunt me, I gradually became as functional as a worn-out hex nut, stripped of threads, soon to be spinning in circles.

Just as dogs raise their legs to mark their territory, Zachary raised his lungs to mark his domain. His capricious wailing echoed through bank lobbies, supermarkets, the post office, the mall. Everywhere we went, panicked shoppers tightly covered their ears and exited in droves.

What was a mother to do? I just had to keep reminding myself that those squinty-eyed folks who watched in judgment probably had zombies for children. Meanwhile, we put our unhappy son through more tests. Still, everything came up negative.

Where was that proclaimed Motherhood Wonderland my Primary and Young Women teachers had described? I felt I was losing my sanity when I actually imagined him running out in the street and getting mowed down. *Who was I turning into?* All I knew was that I was physically and emotionally depleted and had nothing left in the tank.

As my son grew older, occasionally the sun would come out. He had rare golden moments—moments when he connected with me on a deeper level than my other two. At age nine, he was profoundly sensitive. And when he saw snowfall for the first time, he wept.

Like Claire, Zach excelled in all subjects. A master musician, there wasn't anything he couldn't sing, play, or compose. But as my son grew to adulthood, something wasn't quite right. He was all love when he loved. But when he wasn't love, look out. It was all about the play. Foul. Deliberate. Unpredictable.

One minute I'd be laughing with him, the next; *bam*—he was enraged for no apparent reason. It would often start with a cock of his head and an emerging condescending smile. And that icy-cold stare. Then the badgering, bullying, and belittling would begin in crushing verbal blows.

"The whole family thinks you're retarded and delusional, and that you must have been dropped on your head at birth!" This was one of his favorite's along with "I don't have to honor you as my mother just because you gave me birth. If you want respect, you'll have to earn it!"

He would twist my words to his advantage, set a trap to make me look like a fool, set out to prove his theories, then articulate his "holier than thou" conclusions in manipulatively clever ways.

In recent years, as I became more familiar with narcissistic personality disorder (NPD), I look back and solely regret not putting Zach into therapy when my intuition prompted me to do so. But my

Priesthood-leader husband, who most likely had NPD himself, was dead set against it. The tragedy is that Zachary continued these destructive behavior patterns until he cut off all communication with the family and vanished at age thirty-five.

But my husband was not the only one to blame. My emotional state limited my ability to understand my son's needs or the turmoil he was going through. I was preoccupied with my overflowing plate of church and home responsibilities. In retrospect, I ask myself: Was I blind to his needs because I was so focused on the many demands placed on me, or were those demands a welcome distraction from the pain of raising my difficult son?

CHAPTER 34

MOTHERHOOD "WONDERLAND" (PART 2)

DREW

When I became pregnant with our fourth and last child, Drew, as with all my pregnancies, my breasts were so engorged, I could pump my milk into enough containers to fill a world warehouse of Neonatal Intensive Care Units.

Yet when baby Drew was only three weeks old, he couldn't digest my milk. Breastfeeding soon became an all-night affair. For an entire week, the two of us camped out on a blanket on the kitchen floor due to his excessive vomiting. I was worried sick that I might lose him.

When I voiced my concerns to Gary, he told me I was being overreactive. "All babies spit up," he said. Thankfully, I didn't listen to him. Instead, I drove our sick newborn to the nearest emergency room.

The doctor informed me that Drew had an intestinal blockage, a condition called pyloric stenosis, and that he was literally starving and in critical condition, I had no idea. I felt guilty for not acting sooner, but I assumed that my little tyke had indigestion. While the doctors prepped him for emergency surgery, I fell asleep on a hard, plastic chair in the waiting room.

A week later, my sallow-skinned, wiry infant was released from the hospital. Dangerously underweight, he had to learn to breastfeed all over again. It was a scary time for us. I was so relieved when he gradually started gaining weight and returned to full health.

At age two, Drew's summer-sky blue eyes, little button nose, cherubic red lips, and thick mop of white-blonde curls drew the attention of shoppers everywhere whenever I took him with me to do errands. "He's so beautiful, what's his name?" they'd say. Maybe I should have had him sign autographs. He was not only a beautiful baby, but his sweet disposition shined away the rain during life's storms.

One afternoon, when Drew turned three, I took him with me to J.C. Penny's Department Store. As he sat on the floor beside me, I sifted through the clothes catalog looking for dress patterns. Like many women of that era, I enjoyed making my own clothes. After two-hours had passed, my princely son was still sitting on the floor like a happy little buddha, barely making a fuss. Suddenly, it occurred to me that something must be terribly wrong with him. He wasn't challenging me with ear-popping shrieks or head-bashing explosions like his brother. *Was he mentally retarded?*

You can imagine my relief when time revealed that he was just as brilliant as my other two. He just loved soaking up everything around him. Spellbound by his environment from where he sat on the floor beside me, he appeared to be examining the dust particles floating down from a sunlit window as they settled on the table legs in front of him.

After that day in the catalog department, I observed him observing everything. I found it impossible to hold back over-exuberant hugs and terms of endearment for my good-natured son. I tried my damnedest to balance out my affection by giving Zachary more attention, but he knew I had a favorite. So did Claire. The score was never even.

One morning, I was helping nine-year-old Zach with his homework, when all at once, he flew into a full-fledged rage, unable to articulate what was bothering him. He just continued to scream and call me names. After I miraculously got him out the door, I threw myself down on the living-room sofa, too distraught to cry. I will never forget how six-year-old Drew snuck up from behind, threw his tiny arms around me, and held them there, making sure the world stood still for me. He was my guardian angel.

At bedtime, little Drew and I loved to play "The Hugging Robot" —one of his many clever inventions. He would first share his list of the types of hugs he could give. Then he'd have me tap a pretend button on his chest, and all at once, his little eyes would light up and he'd teeter his arms in a stilted fashion. "What kind of hug do you want tonight?" he'd say in his best android voice. If I chose Wimpy, I'd get ready for his hug, but then his hands would flop like a fish onto my shoulders, and he'd showcase his best snarl-toothed derelict smile. When I chose Bear Hug, he'd wrap his arms around me so tight I could barely breathe.

Motherhood Wonderland was turning out to be freakin' awesome. Then one day, before he turned seven, his dad took him away. Drew was my world. I fell apart.

CHAPTER 35

THE DAY MY FAMILY "DIED"

October 3, 1990, was my 9/11. It was the day my life went up in smoke. It was the day I signed my name on the dotted line and unknowingly gave my kids away. Two months prior to my 9/11, the Iraqi Army invaded Kuwait, triggering an international conflict. The world was a mess, but I was too numb to care.

I woke up at 7:00 a.m. as the San Joaquin Valley's October sun thrust its glazed fingers through my battered blinds. The whole room was amber light, yet I couldn't chase away the darkness. On a rust-stained mattress in the center of my room's puke-green shag-carpet, I rocked back and forth, nearly catatonic. As I folded into myself, the smell of cat urine seeped through the carpet fibers and burned my nostrils. I guess this was my landlord's standard of "deep cleaned and sanitized." Across the hall, the kitchen refrigerator mocked me with its loud hum, my walls too quiet to be good company.

I tried my damndest to be a loving wife and mother. Now, I was alone. Still, somehow, I was supposed to put it all behind me and soldier on. I just couldn't do that. Only those who have had their families snatched away would understand this type of pain.

My family was my world. What could I hold on to now? All that was left of my memories were shuffled inside a box in my storage shed—photographs sketched with smiles of the past that were just too hard to look at.

As divorce proceedings began, I knew nothing about family law. Gary made the dividing of property sound like I was getting a real bargain. I packed light after he agreed to hand over our old, dented ironing board, a kitchen mop, and our family's Nissan pickup truck, which happened to be a jumper-cable insured, fender-bent oxidized piece of junk that dripped oil in the outside parking stall. I may not have been able to afford rent or food, but at least I could mop my floor, iron my clothes, and get as far as the corner market before my old beater broke down.

At the start of the year, about ten months before my 9/11, Gary had suddenly decided to quit his job during the crossfire of the 1990 recession. In consequence, we ended up losing our bay-area home. To avoid a dire situation, we ended up moving to Atwater, CA, into his parents' family rental—a dilapidated stucco dwelling.

Living in a low-income neighborhood where the school picked up the bill for latchkey children's lunches was a culture shock, but I honestly didn't mind. I grew to love the simplicity of country living, even so much that I wrote a poem about it.

Tire swings,
Willow vines,
Rooster weathervanes,
Clothes flapping

On the clothes lines.
Garden bridges,
Waterlily ponds
Stone-wall wells,
Lush, green lawns.
Moving to the country
Out of the rush
Has taught me to revel
In the essence
Of hush.

Sadly, my husband didn't share my same love for simplicity. His obsession with earning back the money we'd lost shut out all beauty and hush around him. I knew exactly why he was depressed. Since I had known him, his goal was to become financially successful. He never knew an LDS general authority who wasn't wealthy. Yet he invested in a home we couldn't afford, then quit his job when the housing market stunk.

I really tried to raise Gary's spirit after our move. I assured him that I adored country living and was happy in our tiny home. But he was so blinded by his delusions of grandeur that he couldn't see his own priceless treasure right in front of him—his family.

While doing errands one day, to break the silence between us, I tried to get him to open up. I should have known better. He immediately got defensive, and we both got into a yelling match. I just couldn't take it anymore. I jumped out of our slow-moving van a few blocks from home, slammed the door and told him I wanted a divorce. I had finally reached my breaking point.

Shortly after that, we separated. And that's how I ended up in a rinky-dink, grunge-yellow apartment complete with complimentary spider-webbed curtains. This awful dwelling was located only two blocks from the kids, but in my broken-down state, I might as well have been on Blackwell's Island—a New York City asylum for patients in the 1900s.

Lying on a flimsy mattress, aching to be with my kids, I was clueless about knowing how to support myself. I didn't even have a college degree. The church demonized working mothers in the era in which I grew up, labelling them as one of the causes of society's moral decline.

In my desire to be a stay-at-home mom, I couldn't conceive of any reason why an LDS woman would not want to follow the prophet. But as I lay there in my Hello Kitty pjs on a sagging, stained mattress in the middle of my bedroom floor, I finally understood why wiser Mormon mothers prepared to take on jobs. They were far less likely to face a situation like mine—broke, aimless, and alone in the dark playing footies with mattress buttons.

Funny thing, my entire reason for marrying was so I could have that happily-ever-after fairy tale. Instead, my husband was closed off and cruel, Claire and I struggled with our differences, and Zach's round-the-clock fits of rage had depleted my energy reserves. At least I connected with Drew.

At age six, little Drew always gave me love pats, shared his stories, and sang me songs. He lit up my world like a big bright yellow umbrella. Yet I couldn't expect a six-year-old, no matter how bright his umbrella, to rescue me from the winds and rains of life. I needed to seek refuge on my own. I needed to rest and renew myself before I had nothing left to give. I also knew deep down it would be traumatizing for him if I snatched him away from his siblings and familiar surroundings. So I made the painful choice to leave him behind—a temporary arrangement while I prepared for our reunion.

Divorce was inevitable, but the very thought of it terrifed me. I knew nothing about family court or my rights as a wife. I could no more air my family's dirty laundry before a judge than I could bungee jump over a river gorge. And get this—I had no idea I could hire my own lawyer at my husband's expense. Not that I was the kind of woman that would take advantage of my situation. But I had chosen to be a stay-at-home mom over a career. All our money was in one account … *his*.

Since the day we married, Gary was always one step ahead of me. As he went out into the world and mastered the art of becoming manipulative, cunning, and cruel, I stayed home and learned to be compliant, gullible, and stupid. Guileless in my faith, I willingly complied with the church's patriarchal order, with the husband as the leader in the home. I was told to obey him in righteousness. I never once stopped to consider my own insight into what "righteousness" looked like *to me*.

My "worthy" priesthood bearer made all the major decisions for our family—from how to spend money, to purchasing our home, to moving to the area where we now lived. The second I told him I wanted a divorce, the game was on. He told me I looked exhausted and said I could really use a permanent break from Zach. *Where was he all those years when I battled our incorrigible son alone?* And what made this abusive man think he could handle Zachary better than I could?

Luck was definitely on Gary's side. His supportive mom, the grandmother of our children lived right down the street. My folks lived two states away.

In fear of losing her grandkids, Gary's mom told me I'd be much happier if I handed the children over to him. With my husband's voice in one ear, and his mom's in the other, they both wore me down and convinced me to doubt my competence as a mother.

"You'll find a new husband in no time," Gary assured me. Anything to get me to think that I didn't need his monthly alimony check. He knew how to play on my vulnerabilities. How cunning he was to change his tune from those repeated verses about how inept and stupid I was to a new grand hook describing me as an invincible woman who would make gobs of money with my music skills.

CHAPTER 36

PRIESTHOOD CONSPIRACY

When Gary and I agreed to divorce, he promised to pick a fair lawyer, and in my naïveté, I thought that meant a lawyer who would represent us both equally. Little did I know this is not how attorneys operate. I anticipated a simple, drama-free arbitration. Especially when I learned that his attorney was a Mormon bishop.

For Gary, sporting a good game in court was critical. To save face in our church community, he'd parse the play that would make him appear as the "winner dad." He couldn't afford to lose. After all, he was climbing the church's hierarchical ladder toward superbness.

First on his agenda, my sneaky spouse and his lawyer made sure Gary got all the power. As a submissive wife, I didn't see the train wreck ahead. *Why should I not trust my own husband? And why not trust a bishop?* I had been taught to put my trust in ordained priesthood holders all my life.

Unlike my spouse, I never learned how to play dirty. My desires were simple. All I wanted was a cordial parting of the ways. "Trust me," he said. Blissfully ignorant, I did just that.

So, there you have it. My trusting nature, my overwhelming feelings of inadequacy, along with my duty to submit to my so-called righteous husband—all came together to create the perfect storm. At my most vulnerable moment, when emotionally raw and depleted, I was tricked into signing an order that awarded my husband full custodial rights.

His attorney informed me that the "transitory" waiving of my parental rights would buy me time to get counseling, find employment, and relieve my stress. He affirmed that when I was ready, I could have the kids. But after I signed on the dotted line, I learned that I forfeited all custodial rights.

After fourteen years of being a dutiful wife and mother, I was tossed out like a dirty old dishrag. Gary's attorney insisted I got a great deal. He affirmed that my husband was more than generous to hand over the kitchen mop, ironing board, and our prized twenty-year-old Nissan pickup truck.

A gnarled old mop, instead of Claire
An ironing board, instead of Zach
A junky old truck, instead of Drew
What's a mother to do?
Tie up the Ex with yarns from the mop.
Knock him out good with the board.
Pile the cheap rat in my old rattletrap
With a sign that says, "Steal for Reward."

I get it. I should add myself to the "Top 10 List of America's most foolish women." I can't tell you how many times I've looked back on this most tragic year with tears and regret. To think my children and I could have been spared from all this grief if I had only listened to my older, wiser sister. She begged me not to trust Gary. But she lived two states away. My husband, a master manipulator, lived right across the street. It's hard to describe this kind of remorse. It changed me forever.

I condemned myself for years for having innocently trusted my priesthood leaders, as I had always been taught to do, never thinking they would betray me and lead me carefully down to a waiting hell and close the gates.

In the end, Gary got everything he wanted. And although his win didn't come in gold or greens, he ended up with something far more valuable than any earthly treasure—my three precious gems. He even worked my compassion to his advantage, talking me out of spousal support. "The children won't be able to attend college if I pay you alimony," he whined. With his high-paying salary as a computer software analyst? I highly doubted it. Still, I made sure the kids' needs came first. Finished with the fight and done with the drama, I waived my rights to spousal support.

At the very least, I assumed my ex-husband would be amiable when it came to opening his home for family birthdays and other special occasions. Yet he never allowed me to step foot in his house for any celebration, not even Christmas. All of the holiday photos and birthday memories with my children that could have been, are only an empty page of time lost.

That October day in 1990 was the beginning of my emotional 9/11. It was the day my family "died." It changed me forever. Too shocked for bitterness to overtake me, an aching hollowness gnawed at me from the inside out. Without my kids or a dime in my purse, I had nothing left to live for.

On a rust-stained mattress in the center of my room's puke-green shag-carpet, I try to wish myself unconscious. Across the hall, into the kitchen, the refrigerator mocks me with its loud hum. Oh, and if these walls could talk, perhaps I wouldn't be so lonely. This was the worst part of being at the mercy of my own mind. I pictured a rope in the storage shed, the one I'd been thinking about for a while—how it could end my misery once and for all by one easy slip of the knot …

CHAPTER 37

GRIEF, LONELINESS, PEACE, & TRANQUILITY

Better to hang myself, I murmured, *than go on like this. I have plenty of rope in the shed. Why not?*

Grief grew a garden of dark thoughts, poisoning my mind with noxious weeds. The more I watered the garden, the more temping the rope became.

When night fell, Loneliness turned up the sound of my eerily quiet walls and added extra reverb to the mocking sound of dead space. Even with my pillow over my ears, I couldn't snuff out Its loud cackles. Oh, how I missed our home's sun-filled windows along with chirpy little Drew's sweet hugs—two light sources that I didn't get nearly enough of. I kept a stash of Ding Dongs under my bed for times like this.

One morning, I went to use the bathroom and almost screamed in horror. A cockroach the size of a small child was sitting on the edge of my toilet seat, peering up at me, rubbing its threadlike antenna as if it were marking its territory. I imagined it mocking me: "This is what you get for not having enough money for a nice apartment." *Was there more?* I tip-toed into the kitchen and carefully creaked open the cupboard, when all at once, a four-generation family of roaches ambushed me, nose-diving onto the countertop—most likely a long-established military tactic to raid what little food I had. I just stood there shrieking in horror.

To add to the disaster, the fickle flapper in my cracked toilet decided it was the perfect time to flood my bathroom. I was now at the mercy of my present slumlord which meant it would never get fixed. *Forget the rope. Where was a gun? With one bullet I could get this slow death over with.* What did I have to lose? I had already lost everything. My dark thoughts multiplied daily. Grief, Loneliness, Despair, Self-Pity, they soon took over.

Then, one day, when at the end of my tether, I knelt in front of my feather-leaking sofa pleading with the Lord to give me strength. That's when I heard it. A melody with words—The Lord was singing to me, comforting me with a song that echoed through me. I couldn't grab my portable tape-recorder fast enough. As I sang into the mic, the spirit overwhelmed me. I ended up in tears. If this wasn't enough proof the Lord had my back, nothing was.

That beautiful, spiritual experience saved me from going under that day. Heavenly Father helped me to know He would always be there to see me through. He told me that I was capable and strong and invincible. But most of all, loved. The lyrics are as follows:

HE'S ALWAYS THERE

As I kneel to pray, I close my eyes to see
His loving arms reaching out to me.
I know that He is near, to hear my every prayer.
When I walk in faith, He's always there.

When I'm feeling all alone and have no one to turn to
He will be right there; He will hear my prayer.
Tenderly He whispers to my soul, and within my heart, I know
That He is always there.
When I'm sad and lonely, He comforts me.
He whispers softly to my heart with a warm and gentle tone.
Through my joy and sorrow, He laughs, and He cries,
And I know I'm not alone …

Loneliness and Grief moved out that day. In the weeks that followed, I was visited by Peace and Tranquility and blessed with a kind of strength I had never experienced. My outer world came in second place to the world where my music was created. I held my head high and faced each day with a smile instead of choosing to hang myself in my closet.

For the first time, I saw the advantages of divorce. I was finally free from the clutches of abuse—the kind of freedom that rushes through you when you're perched on a mountain ready to make the first run and your gazing down on a soft, white blanket of snow. In my mind's eyes, the expanse of mountains and valleys in all directions was breathtaking. Ahead of me, my new life was calling. Caught up in my rush, I chose to see it as a challenging adventure. I almost forgot I needed a monthly income to survive. And although the workforce was foreign to me, I chose to power through the discomfort and jump in with both feet.

On the bunny slope of life, as I tried to keep my balance and stay above ground financially and emotionally—I believed there wasn't anything I could not do. For the Lord had blessed me through His warm, fuzzy lyrics and comforting melody. He reminded me that I was not alone. He would be my anchor through the storm. I believed I could even change the world if I wanted to.

In no time, I landed a part-time gig as a teacher's aide. I was chosen out of thirty applicants. Gary had me convinced that I was dumber than bean straw. After I got the call, I scratched my head, wondering if they had made a mistake. But then I remembered that exquisite song that rained down on me from heaven. The Lord had never left my side.

I proved to be quite good at my job. Yet like any human, I would occasionally fall back into my depression, singing the blues behind a plastic smile while earning a whopping $6.38 per hour. I needed a side hustle, so in the afternoons, I'd canvas nearby neighborhoods promoting my piano-lesson services, a low-profit, thankless endeavor. Still, my daily pep talks encouraged me to keep pushing forward.

Although my parental visitation rights were limited to every other weekend, Gary would sometimes allow me to see the children a few weekends in row with some random weekdays in between. I was grateful for every day I got. The good part about this arrangement was that it helped lessen the tension between Zach and me. Spending more time with his dad and Grandma seemed to be beneficial for both of us.

One of my most precious memories was when Zachary, Drew, and I threw on our skates and zig-zagged beneath a canopy of old oaks, vibrant with leaves of amber golds, ruby reds and nutmeg browns. The air was dewy fresh as we crunched through dry leaves that decorated the sidewalks with an assortment of colors. With his coppery curls tousled in the autumn breeze, nine-year-old Zach was particularly pleasant and didn't throw one tantrum. The three of us laughed and giggled till the setting sun painted the sky with streaks of magenta.

My regular visits with six-year-old Drew kept my dark, self-destructive thoughts away. He missed his mommy as much as I missed him. I lived for his playful butterfly kisses and his high-piping, little voice telling me stories. Not having the rights to full-time mommyhood cut me to the core, but it also enhanced the joy of every precious moment.

After a playdate, Drew and I would often curl up on a throw rug next to my smokey wall furnace and read funny stories. Sometimes I'd squeeze him so tight it would take his breath away. Being that "weekend-loser mom" who had to fight like hell for holiday rights really sucked. It was bitter-sweet with my youngest son. Tears would often well up in my eyes while we cuddled and talked. I'd try my darnedest to fight them back but just couldn't.

Little Drew was very perceptive. He sensed the sadness behind my smile. He'd pat my shoulder to comfort me as the furnace coughed its warmth around us. My precious son inspired me to be grateful for the little things in life. Essentially, I had a throw rug, a crappy but functional wall heater, and a beautiful little boy who loved me dearly, even though I couldn't do for him the daily things mommies do.

When Gary came to my door to pick up Drew one evening, I noticed a woman waiting in the car. It had only been six weeks since our separation. *Was he already seriously dating someone?* Mormons are taught that marriage in the temple is critical to one's exaltation in heaven. Was Gary getting ready to take a new woman to the altar? Whoever she was, it caused a wrenching pain in my gut. To think that after fourteen years of marriage, I was that easily replaced.

Grief and Loneliness—I thought they had gone for good. But they came back and had me binging on Ho Ho's this time.

CHAPTER 38

QUIT GIVING MEN PODIUMS

Before long, I found out that my soon-to-be-ex-husband was seriously dating. He met that new girl at an LDS singles dance. They were already discussing marriage. So much for Mr. Perfect obeying church rules about not dating before his divorce is final.

Like Gary, I had already checked out several LDS singles groups in the area and fancy this—despite his claim about an endless supply of eligible bachelors, I had yet to meet just one worth pursuing. *Why do men have all the luck?* There were literally dozens more single women than men. Most single guys in the San Joaquin valley were nearly dead widowers who sported a spinster on each arm. If there was a man or two my age, they were clearly not hot real estate. Even in a seller's market, their sad little sign would remain forever on their dying lawn.

One foot in the married world and one foot in Divorce Land made me feel like I had been captured by aliens and carried off to Pluto. Oh, how I wished the Lord would magically produce a song in my heart at every struggling turn—that Tranquility would flow through me continually. But I wasn't always in a state of grace. There were days when the music stopped. On those days, I needed to find some good female friends. And I knew just where to find them.

There was big talk about the Modesto Singles Sunday night firesides. I felt weird about attending the meetings because my divorce had not yet been finalized. The church had strict rules for those of us living in limbo. To avoid Sunday gossip on the pew, upholding the letter of the law was of utmost importance. What better person could I talk to about my dilemma than Bishop Turley, the bishop of the ward who oversaw the singles fireside gatherings. Surely, he'd properly guide me to find my place in the world.

A week later, as I sat down across from a bespectacled, silver-haired gentleman, I wasted no time. I leaned forward in my chair and blathered on about my separation, how I missed my children, along with my deep need for female friendships and a chance for connection with those who shared my same struggle. I guess I was just looking for validation. I assumed he would encourage me to step across the threshold beyond my grunge-yellow walls into a haven where single, divorced women could help support me.

After I had finished talking, I searched Bishop Turley's face. He had an alertness in the eyes behind the glasses that sat crookedly on the nose. His sagging jawline and discolored skin told the story of a man who lived long enough to have all the answers.

That's why I was taken aback when he advised against me attending any and all singles social events. I actually saw it going differently. I mistakenly assumed he would strongly encourage me to attend the meetings. It didn't make sense. But then it got weirder.

"What if you happened to meet someone at a gathering," he said, "and you end up falling in love. Then what?" Wow. I wasn't prepared for that. I just sat there wordless as he warned me about the woes of sexual temptation. He went on to tell me that preserving my virtue would far outweigh the benefits of fitting in somewhere. I really couldn't believe what I was hearing. Yet, when it came right down to it, I found it rather sweet that he was genuinely concerned for my salvation. *But why bring up sex?*

Did I just say "sex?" If I wasn't thinking about it before, I sure the heck was thinking about it right then. Why did he have to put sex on centerstage with a microphone, yet be so blind to all my other unsurmountable issues—the need to be with other people who shared my same values, the need to get out of the house, the need to figure out where I fit in the equation?

Decades later, as I think back on my visit with Bishop Turley, I can't blame him for his narrow focus. Instead, I blame the church's hierarchy. If the issue involves sex, generally, "The Brethren" are the world's cheerleaders for chastity. They are also the Virtue Squad. The Purity Police Force. This is what happens when we give men podiums.

Take President Kimball's focus on masturbation for example. I lost count of all the talks he gave on the topic. I mean, how can a person maintain clean thoughts when "The Brethren" keep reminding us of the forbidden?

I remember a survey that said the typical man thinks about sex every 1.26 hours. Bishop Turley was a man. I, a lonely attractive woman went to him asking for guidance. I can't help but wonder if the puritanical head-hammering made it impossible for him to give me healthy, balanced, spiritual advice without bringing up sex.

As my God-fearing, virtue-focused leader continued to warn me of the atrocities and destructiveness of sexual sin, I threw him off course by asking if he had taken a good look at the unclaimed males out there.

If these guys were the only fish to be caught in the valley's waterholes, my salvation would remain bulletproof.

When all was said and done, I didn't take the bishop's advice too seriously. Starving for some spiritual nourishment, I needed those uplifting Sunday devotionals as badly as I needed air. It was either get out of the house and mingle or turn into a whipped-cream gorging couch potato whose fallow fate was a life of recycled TV dinners followed by guilt-ridden masturbation.

I couldn't afford to turn into a sloth. I believed that those spiritual meetings could start me on a healthier path. I also knew I needed therapy. The Church offers professional therapy to its members who need it but can't afford it, as well as food and other basic needs. It was time to see my bishop again. Time to swallow my pride and ask for church assistance.

CHAPTER 39

RUTHLESS SHEPHERD

Marvin Mason, "the father" of my ward, was the kind of bishop … Well, let me start from the beginning. It had been only a few months since my separation, and even though I had some amazing personal revelations and had grown closer to the Lord, there were still days when the storm would not let up. On those days, I wanted life to end.

When I lost my family, I switched wards to escape my soon-to-be-ex on Sundays. I didn't know Bishop Mason other than from his talks at the pulpit and handshakes in the foyer. Even so, I had faith that this wise, kind shepherd would not hesitate to leave those ninety-nine others to rescue that one lost lamb.

I was that lamb who needed rescuing. Everything about me was amiss. I went from being part of "a family forever" to being totally alone. I longed to be loved by a good man, and I fiercely missed my children.

Fourteen years as someone's wife, then suddenly, I had no identity. On my wedding day, as I buried myself in all that temple garb, I buried my soul as well. When married, I had never learned to be my own person or make my own choices. I'd always been my husband's little girl. More than anything, I wanted to prove to Gary—prove to the world that I was a talented, competent, independent woman. At times I felt invincible. At that moment, I was falling apart.

If anyone could lead me to green pastures, I knew it would be my shepherd, Bishop Mason. He was a military Air Force veteran, and it frightened me a little. He was known to march around the meetinghouse with an ostentatious air, executing orders as if he were still in the service. Yet, those who knew him well claimed he was a big bowl of mush, the warm fuzzy teddy-bear type that gives out lollipops. *How could I go wrong with mush and lollipops?*

I studied him intently from the chair across from his desk as he shuffled a tall stack of paper then set it aside. His stern look, buzz-cut, and imposing frame put him in the rank of a "Dare to Be Dangerous" Wilderness survivor.

"What brings you here, Sister Wilson?" Clearly a military man, he was frank and to the point. But a slight hint of a smile gave him just enough humanity to help me feel at ease. Since he knew about my recent separation, I felt relaxed enough to share about my crappy life, including my depression. I couldn't help but notice an unspoken compassion in his large camo-green eyes as they moved to the rhythm of my words like the bouncing ball on the 1958 "Sing Along with Mitch" TV series.

After a slight pause, I sat up straighter in my chair and cleared my throat. I knew I had to say what I came to say or perish. The last thing I wanted was to have him see me as pathetic. Yet what choice did I have? I was dirt broke and in dire need of some counseling. Asking for a handout is humiliating, but as a faithful church member, I had paid ten percent of my income to the church all my life. I had done this willingly, having been taught that tithes were used to help the needy.

Here I was, unexpectedly on the other side of a tithing receipt. I was definitely needy.

So I asked him—I asked if the church could help finance some badly needed therapy. Then we just sat there. The silence in the room was nerve-wracking. It gave me more time to squirm. As Bishop Mason drummed his thumbs on the lacquered walnut desk, I let out a slow, wobbly breath. As I gazed up from his rolling thumbs to look at him, his eyes turned a shade darker. Still, I remained hopeful, anticipating that any moment, I'd see that warm, fuzzy teddy-bear grin.

Instead, a dark shadow eclipsed his once cheery countenance. He even looked as though he was sneering at me from where he sat, his large, white teeth clenched like a pit bull's, clamping hard as if they had been trained for a "hold and shake" bite.

I could feel my insides rattling and my heart thumping louder in my ears as my so-called shepherd leaned forward in his chair. He peeled off his glasses to wipe his eyes, then squinted at me disapprovingly. "I'm sorry," he said flatly, "but because you left your husband without a cause, I'm afraid the church can't help you."

What? WITHOUT A CAUSE? I felt my entire body contract into one large tight knot. The antithesis of how I expected this to play out had me dumbfounded. All at once, a slow, whirling nausea settled in the pit of my gut. *Who was this man?*

My bishop in the East Bay had reported Gary's abuse on church records. When I inquired about the history of abuse that should have been noted on the record, Bishop Mason said he knew nothing. Perhaps my supposed "prophet-material" soon-to-be ex talked someone into removing the report?

When I thought it couldn't possibly get worse, he had the audacity to ask if I was having an affair. *What!* I was so outraged by his insulting question that I couldn't find my voice. My eyes stung with tears that threatened to spill over. I swallowed hard, then raised my quivering chin, mustering the courage to speak. *Come on, Jennifer. You can do this.*

I felt my voice shaking when I straight up asked him where he'd heard this false rumor. By the look of distain in his eyes, I could tell he didn't appreciate my indignant candor. He just rolled back in his chair, resting his hands behind his head, firing a volley with a sanctimonious eyeroll.

That's when it hit me. In my absence, Gary must have fed him a bunch of lies that he ate up without question. Gary's parents, who had been members of the ward for years, most likely colluded in those lies. Of course. They were desperate. They needed to save face. They couldn't possibly have the bishop or the members of the ward see Gary as a monster.

It infuriated me that Bishop Mason didn't even press this issue to see what the truth was or wasn't. Because he didn't know me well, he formed a prejudice against me based on hearsay only. *What about assuming my innocence before pronouncing a guilty verdict? What an arrogant, misogynist ass.*

I typically never called people an "ass." Especially when referring to my leaders. But I was majorly pissed. I'd repent later, but at that moment, I wanted to kill.

Mean-spirited Mason opened my eyes to the cold hard truth that short-sighted, misogynistic men like himself can slip through the cracks when being interviewed for church leadership positions. I went to my bishop, desperate and downtrodden asking for help. Yet rather than leading me beside still waters, he threw stones and crushed me with them.

Not only had I been a loyal member of the church for thirty-five years but had donated thousands of dollars to its cause. Yet when going through the worst crisis of my life, I was not only judged and condemned but turned away. After that unexpected blow, I couldn't help but look at the church differently. It made me wonder why bishops weren't required to have an education in psychology. Pastors of other denominations were expected to spend years training for the ministry. *Why should LDS leaders be any different?*

The Brethren admonished members to respect their local leaders, to be meek and patient and forgiving, no matter how badly offended. They should have also taught their bishops to be compassionate, forgiving, and a heck of a lot more helpful.

Meanwhile, this awful man remained doggedly prejudiced toward me. He never budged. Soon, gossip and cruel lies about my so-called affair rapidly disseminated throughout the ward. But I held my head high.

Many members of the ward were convinced I had abandoned my kids and run off with another man. That's what happens when you're a newcomer to a community and your old-timer in-laws have had years to earn the trust of their fellow congregates. To preserve their own reputation, they did the only thing they knew how to do—tear down mine. Since my ward family already saw me as a slut, I was sorely tempted to become one. Think of the heads I could turn if I walked into church one day with a nice "tall drink of water" on my arm.

In the end, I was alone, misjudged, and misrepresented after a lifetime of obedience and dedication trying to be everything the church wanted me to be. Without a support system, I became a wandering, aimless nobody seeking love in all the wrong places. Or perhaps … just perhaps, I was in the right places all along and just didn't know it.

Fat bishops,
Thin bishops,
Happy Bishops,
Grim bishops
You are there to guess
Which ones will love and bless,
Or make your life a mess.
Jolly, fun, and free bishops,
The kind that shouldn't be bishops—
Heartless, cruel and shaded.
Grossly overrated.
Wash them down your basin
Like ruthless Marvin Mason.

CHAPTER 40

WE ALL WEAR MASKS

Having been taught that temple marriage is the pinnacle of a women's existence, I was completely clueless about how to live my life without a husband. That dangling carrot of marital bliss was something I had to have, not simply for the bliss but for the blessing of eternal exaltation. I could not reach the top tier of heaven without it. As a premature empty nester, my loneliness further compelled me to find my elusive future spouse.

✳✳✳

Sitting in church makes my mind wander. I haven't had sex for six whole months and I'm going crazy. The deacons, boys ages twelve and thirteen, gather their shiny silver trays at the white-linen-clothed table up front. Now they're walking up and down the aisles to serve the Sacramental bread and water to the congregation.

I take the bread which represents Christ's body while I'm thinking about sex. Not feeling too holy at that moment. I feel like it's been forever since I've been touched, been loved. I can't believe Bishop Mason refused to provide financial assistance for my therapy sessions. I see him glaring down at me from the pulpit. *You're not a good man, Marvin Mason!*

I watch the church organist as she moves her hands across the keys like a slow-ebbing tide. I used to be in her place. Between hymns, I'd often glimpse down and wink at my kids who sat on the front pew. Now Gary and the children attend meetings in the mornings. They have their Sunday routine going with their friends and teachers. I attend the ward that meets in the afternoons. Alone.

For a half a year I've been a weepy, hormonal mess hunched over on the back row looking like I could use a double shot of Jack Daniels. Now I deal with my loneliness by sitting near the front so I can get a better view of Brother Downing. First counselor to the bishop, he sits on the podium in his perfectly tailored suit, where he can be admired by all the women. *Ahem … What a fantastic jawline.*

Now the water's being served. I grip a paper cup, smear my lipstick along its rim, take a sip, and drop it in the tray. When drinking the water, I'm supposed to be thinking about the blood my Savior shed for me, but instead, I fantasize about borrowing Brother Downing for a day and making him mine.

Oh, how I would love to have my way with him on the back pew. *Who am I turning into?* As a lonely, broke, weekend mommy, I have to face the grim reality whether I like it or not; fantasizing about Brother Downing makes my lonely life more bearable.

Now little Goldilocks is at the pulpit. The bishop is adjusting the step stool and microphone for her. Our church is different than most in that they let kids speak in sacrament meetings. She's giving a talk about virtue. *What would she know about that?* She can't be more than seven. I'm deep in my reverie. *Why is it so hard to find a decent guy?* My ex-husband found another wife. I just happen to be the wrong gender. After age thirty, they say men are like parking lots. The good ones are taken, and the rest are handicapped.

Goldilocks finally sits down. The tension leaves my body. Now I have the chance to be restored to normal boredom. *Wait. Is Brother Downing looking at me? I think he's checking me out.* I immediately glance away and feel a fever in my cheeks. From my lonely spot, I scan the congregation and wonder if I'm the only one with naughty thoughts.

Although the Church expects us to be perfect, I can tell you one thing: no one here walks on water. Sitting alone on the pew amid the "happy" families has somehow switched out that bulb in my head from a nightlight to a floodlight. I've come to believe we all wear masks. I think it's human nature to fear disappointing others. What better place to hide our insecurities than behind our sparkling Sunday smiles?

I try my best to block out all that sappy noise from the pulpit about family unity, family prayer, family scripture study. Family, family, family! Screw family!! But I can't. Although half of me wants to, the other half whispers, "If you quit going to church, you'll never find a man who can take you to the temple."

Although I'm divorced, my bishop reminds me that my soon-to-be ex-husband and I are bound together in heaven for "time and all eternity." It doesn't make sense. Gary is a bully. I'm told the only way I can "break the sealing" is by hunting down and marrying another temple-worthy candidate. The thought of being joined to the hip forever to a hostile, vitriolic man motivates me to stay on the husband-hunting trail.

Yet how can I attract someone when I can't even pay my bills? With no monthly alimony check and little job experience, I'm destined to live under a bridge. But it gets worse. To maintain my "temple-worthy" status, I'm supposed to be contributing ten percent of my monthly income to the church. Yet I'm told by my leaders to avoid debt. *Will they make up their minds?*

CHAPTER 41

THOU SHALT PAY TITHING IN EXCHANGE FOR BLEACHED BREADS

I'm sitting in a chair across from my bishop who is all thorns and prickles. But it's not like I'm playing chess and can kick him off the game board. I need to talk to him about tithing. Being dirt poor has whittled my faith down to a grain far tinier than any mustard seed. I'm sure the Lord is displeased with me for not wanting to be generous regardless of my impoverished state. I need to please Him. I want to be temple worthy so I can remarry someday. That means I have to follow the rules.

With legs crossed, I glance across the desk at my leader, the corners of my lips turned down into a frown, my eyes blinking nervously. I'm distressed. I need a rational explanation as to why this austere man I'm required to call "bishop" insists that the church needs a portion of my hard-earned money.

Clasping my hands, I stretch my arms with locked elbows as a hard rippling crack breaks the silence. So unrefined, I know. But the bishop is busy writing something on a piece of paper and doesn't look up. I clear my throat and ask my question: "But Bishop Mason, how can I pay tithing when I can barely afford my rent?" My bishop finally sets down his paper and shoots a look over the top of his glasses, answering my question with a question:

"How can you afford *not* to pay your tithing? Give the Lord what is his, and he shall provide."

Sounds simple in theory, I muse. *But if I come up short at the end of the month, will my fairy godmother slip a bundle of Benjamin's under my doormat?*

Today the LDS church is a multi-billion-dollar corporation. Still, all members, even those in abject poverty are required to pay tithing if they want to remain in good standing. It was no different in 1974. Although I'm barely able to make ends meet; to remain in good standing, my bishop tells me that paying tithing will teach me unselfishness and deepen my gratitude for all my blessings.

All my blessings? I'm just trying to survive. The mere thought of handing over a portion of my insufficient pocket change to the bishop compounds my anxieties. Especially when he has refused to foot the bill for some badly needed therapy.

To be a full-tithe payer, would I have to forgo my evening's Spaghetti-O's? The only blanket I own almost caught fire when I fell asleep in front of the wall-furnace one night. *What kind of greedy God would take my last cent and let me freeze to death?*

He tells me to go home and turn to the last book in the Old Testament. In Malachi 3:10, I read: "Bring the whole tithe into the storehouse, that there may be food in my house." I had never seen any food in the chapel or the temple. I don't understand the meaning of the scripture. Still, I follow the rules because I believe it's the right thing to do. In no time, I scribble out a tithing check and pop it in the mail. I convince myself it's the Christian way to show gratitude no matter how crappy my life is.

A month later, I'm back to eating Top Ramen and have turned my thermostat down to forty. Soon, I'm crawling on my hands and knees to the bishop asking for church assistance. "If you continue to pay your tithes," he said, "we will help you with your monthly grocery bill."

Sounds good, I say. I continue to give the Lord my tenth in exchange for bleached breads and thickly marbled meats from the Deseret food truck. It rolls into the church parking lot every second Tuesday of the month. If I don't want to go hungry, I must be there to greet it. But if I keep depending on this food, my chances for a stroke or heart failure will increase one-hundred-fold.

I discover that whole-grain anything is not offered, but high-carb everything is. I stand in horror as over-ripe fruits and vegetables grow faces and scream from their smelly crates, "You don't deserve anything better than us!" Just another slap in the face. But there's one more slap around the corner.

One of my wasband's friends, Brother Schmidt, happens to be there as a volunteer. I'm loading my goody bags into the back of my truck when I turn to see him approach me with another bag. After I thank him, I watch his lips curl over his teeth in disgust. He mutters an accusation under his breath, but I hear him loud and clear. "You're a loser," he deadpans. After rolling his eyes at me, he turns and walks away.

Did the old gizzard just call me a loser? My skin begs me to rip it from its bones and throw it at him. It doesn't take long for me to figure out that Gary probably got to him as he did several others, making up stories that I'm some crazy lady who abandoned her kids. Too shocked to know how to respond to such cruelty, I jump into my truck, throw it into gear, and cry all the way home.

Why can't people get it? Why do they have to be so bitingly cruel? What happened to kindness, empathy, and understanding? To think I had donated tens of thousands of dollars as well as my time, talents, and energy to the church for over two decades only to be treated like a panhandling loser-druggie on the street.

Emotionally starved and financially bankrupt, the only advice my church leaders offer me is to get back on the manhunt trail. They remind me that remarrying is a worthy endeavor, even more eternally consequential than a career. I've been conditioned far too long to consider how backward their advice is. In the world of Mormonism, it's all I know.

Once again, I'm sitting in church with my wandering mind. I'm staring out into the foyer, hoping a newcomer will walk through the door any moment—someone around my age, single, and much kinder than my husband. Another adorable Brother Downing perhaps?

Until I meet him, my life is on hold. Why do I feel so stuck? *Is it because I've been taught that this elusive thing called marriage is everything? Or is it because everything I've been taught about marriage is elusive? Or perhaps both?*

CHAPTER 42

LOVE STARVED

Since puberty, I had been conditioned to repress my sexual self. When my peers were sleeping around, I made great strides to disown that sexual part of me. I rejected men who didn't share my values. I married as a virgin. My obedience was all that mattered. My obedient self would steer me toward salvation. It was the good self. My sexual self was bad.

After emerging from a failed marriage at age thirty-five, my therapist told me I was love starved. And because I couldn't afford ongoing counseling, I was left on my own without a roadmap to figure out how to navigate the dating world in hopes to find connection and perhaps love.

There was no quick fix for a girl like me who had spent most of her marriage cornered in the kitchen and bullyragged instead of cornered in the kitchen and kissed. My larger-than-life personality had been beaten down bit by bit. "Love starved." It made sense. I needed sanctuary; a friend who had my back.

In my singledom, survival mode didn't offer much time for a social life. As it was, girlfriends were scarce. Most were buried in their church callings and raising families. I worked three jobs in order to stay afloat. In the mornings I was a teacher's aide at McSwain Elementary. In the afternoons, I taught piano lessons in my home. After months of struggling to make ends meet, I came up with a plan to become a traveling piano teacher. Sometimes, I'd teach in students' homes till late evenings. I eliminated the competing piano-teaching market by not charging my students for my gas, milage, or travel time. Collectively, my three gigs brought in the necessary income to pay my bills with a smidge leftover to save for a rainy day.

Caught in the underbrush of dating after divorce, I didn't know which way was up when it came to men. I innocently trusted guys I hardly knew and was a sucker for a friendly smile. In my extremely needy state, I yearned for masculine energy, basked in the scent of men's cologne, and reveled in the vibrato of deep, male voices. If a hot guy accidently brushed up against me in a grocery checkout line, I'd get goosebumps. It felt as good as sex. Skin hunger (touch starved), love starved. My therapist nailed it.

My love language has always been connection and affection. And because I was lonely, I looked forward to engaging with random strangers in the produce section. This was a godsend of guiltless adult interaction. I wasn't greedy. I didn't need long conversation. "Gimme what you got, gimme anything—a few words, a friendly nod or smile and I'm good to go." It didn't take much for the darkness within to dissipate. Amazing how something so effortless from a stranger fueled me throughout the day. "One moment at a time, baby." That's how I survived.

To be deserving of a righteous man, I worked hard to suppress my high libido. And when I occasionally took care of my sexual needs, I ended up crying. Not because I was happy. Not because I was able to relieve tension, but because I felt ashamed. Shaming myself for wanting an occasional release on top of my desperate need for good company served to further intensify my anxieties. I was a taut thread, bound to snap at any given moment.

No longer under my husband's control, I needed to take advantage of my freedom to expand my horizons, live a little—take care of Jennifer for a change. *But who was I?* My identity was always tied up in serving and pleasing Gary. *What did I want? What were my needs?*

Because I had the kind of figure that guys noticed, even when wearing loose sweaters, I could never tell if men liked me for me or for my body. It never entered my head that they could admire me for both. Being raised in a purity culture had me confused. Love starved, sex starved, friend starved, I'd been running on fumes for quite some time. How was I to change my situation? *Were all men dogs like my mother said?*

In the ensuing months, I dated Mormons and non-Mormons alike. I needed a comforting hand. Perhaps a kiss. *Would a backrub be okay?* My dates were a disaster. If guys became a little touchy feely—which happened mostly with LDS men since they were hungrier for "the candy" — I'd panic and boot them out the door.

Then one day, I figured out a safe way to get a little affection without getting into too much trouble. Whenever I had a guy over, I'd put on my catsuit, the one I bought at Penny's for the purpose of exercising. My clingy, spandex neck-to-heal outfit had no easy-access zipper. Yanking it off my shoulders and down my arms proved too challenging for most guys. My breathable dance wear made me feel sexy, allowing for harmless petting without Guilt. No question—this jumbo-sized condom kept me safe and protected.

My divorce was finalized at the beginning of 1991. I was certifiably single five years before match.com, and fifteen years before social media posts and smart phones. *And* I lived in a little country town. My chances of finding a virtuous LDS man with all his limbs and vital organs was next to nil. But I was a good girl who held tight to my values and kept my clothes on.

There were hundreds of haystacks in the San Joaquin valley. What were my chances of finding my perfect prince endowed in sacred underwear amid all that hay? Love starved. *Would you blame me if one day I suddenly cracked?*

MADMAN MANFORD

I spotted Manford at an LDS Singles game night. I soon learned he was a newcomer to the valley. Manford was handsome, and his trimmed mustache made him look distinguished. Eye-candy didn't typically come as a perk when attending these dreadful middle-age single events, so I couldn't help but notice him from across the cultural hall. I studied his gestures as he chatted with a handful of old spinsters.

Game night was all about mingling, so when it was time to switch tables, I deliberately sat across from him so I could get to know him. Perhaps he wasn't aware of it, but Manford made himself front and center of the conversation, hardly allowing anyone to talk.

In a matter of seconds, I learned that this hot-looking prattler was madly in love with three things: missionary work, the LDS institute program, and himself. As he jabbered away, he hardly asked anyone at the table about themselves. He seemed to be on an urgent mission to save the world. "There's nothing more important than missionary work," he'd say with a gleam in his eyes. I bet he believed that heaven had missionaries too. At least he was spiritual. Yet would he be able to put a woman first in his life, or would she always have to walk in the shadow of his extreme religiosity?

I was yawning through most of his yapping, so when he tapped my hand and asked if I would like to attend the Wednesday night institute class with him, it threw me off balance. I hadn't shown nearly as much interest in his sermons as the other ladies. But with his striking good looks, how could I say no? Attending a religion class with him would be far better than watching Magnum, P.I. reruns. To land a guy who was both hot and spiritual? *Perhaps it wouldn't be such a bad thing.*

I went to the class with him and could only describe it as the perfect sleep aid for insomniacs. When Manford invited me to his home afterward for a root beer, I figured that any kind of company was better than being alone.

After we sipped on our sodas in his kitchen, he asked if I'd like to check out his bedroom. Following him down the hallway towards the door, I wondered what he was planning. *A little make-out session perhaps?* While I was envisioning his full lips on mine, he stopped in front of his bedroom doorway then turned to face me. This was my moment. As Manford placed his large, masculine hand on my shoulder, my heartbeat quickened.

My eyes were halfway closed, waiting for that kiss when he set another hand on my other shoulder and gently turned me to face the opened door. That's when I peered into his room. *What the . . . ?* I stood with my mouth agape, then blinked a few times in hopes that the nightmare before me would disappear. But it wasn't going away.

Giant-size posters of the church's prophets along with LDS temples covered every inch of his walls. Newspaper clippings on missionary work and LDS conferences managed to fill in all the gaps. I wondered what color his walls were beneath all the mishmash.

Manford excitedly bade me to follow him into the room then plunked himself down on the bed and patted a place beside him ushering me to sit. I warily followed, eyeballing all the weirdness around me, then cautiously lowered myself to the mattress. It was as if I were sitting in front of a psycho killer's mood board. I'm surprised my photo wasn't up there.

Shifting my eyes from one wall to another, taxed by visual strain, I almost ran for it when he rose from the bed and closed his door. That's when I saw Uruguay. It occupied every inch of the wood except for the door handle. *What was he planning to do?* Whatever it was, I knew there'd be no chance for escape. I shuddered at the thought of dying at the hands of a religious fanatic, and no one would even bother looking here.

Manford grabbed a pointer stick from off the bed and slapped it across the map. He smiled an almost ghoulish smile as he smacked his stick on the places where he served on his mission. They were all highlighted in yellow. Of course they were. As he proudly hummed on about his Uruguay experiences, I tried to plan my escape. Although he didn't fit the profile of a serial killer, he sure killed any interest I ever had in him. I glanced over at the trumpet that sat on his dresser. *Did he climb up a temple pinnacle and steal it from Angel Moroni to add to his room's theme?* I should've grabbed it to blow away his self-adulation.

Remarkably, during my single years, I met dozens of Manfords—some stuck in a fantasy world, others stuck on themselves, and then there were those who were just plain stuck like me. Rushing in, trapped in that same cycle, I never took a moment to ask myself what part I played in attracting these types of crazies. I figured my excuse was lack of opportunity. After all, I didn't live in a big, cultural city. I was surrounded by farm boys, cowhands, and anglers—not exactly the kind of men I was interested in. *But who was my type?* Perhaps my issues went beyond lack of opportunity. I mean, how well, did I truly know myself?

CHAPTER 43

EYE-CANDY RANDY

"You better hurry and find someone before you lose your looks." That's what he told me when we split. I still remember his urgent tone, and me, trembling before the bathroom mirror in fear that my face would dry up and wrinkle like the year-old prunes in my pantry.

Gary's grenade shook me into panic mode. I was 35 years old. In five years, I'd be 40. Would anyone want me if I were still single then?

His warning was meant to serve no one but himself. "If you act fast, you can find a husband." Yea, right. There were no men in the valley. It was just his sneaky way of encouraging me to marry and forever end the possibility that he'd have to pay me alimony.

At that time, I worked as a teacher's aide and was gradually accumulating piano students. It was tough to stay afloat. I had always dreamt of a career in music yet wasn't sure where to begin. Suddenly it dawned on me that working at a music store selling pianos and teaching in-store piano lessons would be the perfect job. I soon found myself heading north on highway 99 toward Modesto, checking out the music stores along the main drag.

I tell you—stepping inside Barker's Music was like taking an antidepressant. The wailing guitars, keyboards with symphonic sounds, everyone demoing at once—I felt at home with this gloriously chaotic setting.

Wait. Who was that hot guitarist in the back corner? He was all Fender. Fender hat, Fender shirt, Fender Strat, and a pair of acid-washed ripped jeans. I imagined him as the kind of rock and roller who'd have his cigarette stashed between his guitar's tuning pegs if we were in a blues nightclub. But this was a music store. As I studied him, I got caught up in my reverie.

Everything appears in slow-motion …

Rich tobacco curls swirl past his shoulders like a beautiful eddy of water as he rocks his Stratocaster, tearing into some Jeff Beck blues licks. As the hard-driving beat propels his fingers along the frets, his whole face contorts. He has a muse, and he isn't chasing it. He's devouring it. His muse is his music. I shake my head in awe and let out a slow wush.

"How may I help you, Miss." I was so deep in my reverie; I didn't notice his approach. This fair-skinned kid with ebony hair stood about five-foot-ten, and his name tag was staring me in the face. "Randy: Assistant Manager." He was probably no more than twenty-four. I tried to be coy, tried to not give off that "giddy-in-love" schoolgirl vibe when asking him if Barker's was hiring. When he told me they weren't, I changed the topic to show interest in his talent. From there, our conversation seemed to take on a natural rhythm, like we were on the same frequency, sharing the same light-bouncing vibrations.

I felt flattered when he couldn't seem to take his eyes off me. Was I simply imagining a connection because of my dire need for male attention? Just thinking of his young, hot lips floating down my bounteous cleavage stirred my loins like nothing else had before.

He wrapped up our conversation by handing me his business card. Up close, his small nose was peppered with freckles. And his eyes, a shiny silver-blue, speckled with gold reminded me of my childhood days on the beach when I would look at a beautiful abalone shell. I couldn't stop staring.

As we exchanged smiles, I immediately felt the blood rushing up my neck into my cheeks. *How was I to read this young, hedonistic male alien creature? What were his intentions? Did he like me, or did he just feel sorry for me because I needed a job?*

Back when I was married, if a guy flirted with me, I enjoyed it, yet I stayed guarded and kept my boundaries. Now that I was single, the sky was the limit. *Or was it?* Resisting all manner of temptation has been my firm mindset since puberty. And because I had never actually crossed the line, what would happen if I did?

After arriving home, I examined my face in the bathroom mirror. "You better hurry and find someone before you lose your looks." This time, I paid no heed to Gary's warnings. After meeting Randy, I felt very much alive with no thoughts of racing against the clock or living on borrowed time.

"Remember, all men are dogs."

Huh? ... is that you, Mother? ...

CHAPTER 44

BEYOND THE BLACK & WHITE

Randall Carr

Grunge Metal

STONE THONG

(555) 784-2360

At the kitchen table, I picked up Randy's card, stroked the embossed letters of his name, and wondered if he was the marrying type. At the store, he informed me his band, "Stone Thong" would be playing at the Clunk House, Saturday at 8:00 p.m. *What's with all the funky names?*

Although I'd never been to a nightclub, I just had to see him again. New to the dating world, I couldn't tell the difference between a solid guy and a player. *Was he truly interested in me?* I had to find out.

With my head cradled in my hands, I got lost in thought, imagining what a date would look like with this young, talented musician. I tried to have pure thoughts; I really did. But even my scripture-affirming sticky notes on the kitchen fridge couldn't keep me from having naughty impulses.

Soon, a warm current spread through my veins and filled me with an overwhelming desire to head toward the bathroom. In my aroused state, my pulse pounded in my ears as I gingerly removed my top. Through the mirror, a pretty woman clad only in a shiny periwinkle bra stared back at me with mischief in her eyes. I imagined Randy standing beside me, watching me admire myself through the glass. He looked at me with a flame in his eyes as he edged closer and began to unfasten my bra. Both straps fell off my shoulders and down my arms. When I slowly removed my bra, Randall couldn't take his eyes off me. I pulled back my shoulders to maximize my assets and admired my statuesque shape. I turned sideways and lifted them high, then faced front again. I gently touched my nipples and shivered.

Of course, Guilt and Shame were opportunists. Shame jumped right in and trash-talked me; told me I was nothing more than a disgusting floozy. "Repent!" Guilt roared. "You're going down the wrong road." Perhaps I was. But I missed having a man in my life and craved attention.

I laid down in the tub, grabbed my new shower hose and satisfied that sweet spot in no time—as in way too fast. It went flat before I had a chance to my build my momentum. It had been far too long since I had "taken matters into my own hands."

THE CLUNK HOUSE

The following weekend, on a cold foggy February night, I parked my faithful old clunker between two large cars on the main drag across the street from The Clunk House. Stalling a bit, I blew air into my hands as I eyed the young, trendy crowd sifting through the dark door to Hell. I had never stepped foot in a nightclub before. I guess there was always a first.

As I watched the funneling crowd grow smaller, I had to believe there was a more prismatic world out there—a world beyond the black and white teachings of the church—a place of multidimensional thought and endless possibilities. *Would I find it in a dirty, low-lit roadhouse?* So far, there weren't any respectable, age-appropriate LDS men in my black and white world. They had to be somewhere. *Would I find them here?*

Before talking myself out of the whole thing, I leaped from my truck and clicked my stilettos across the misty sidewalk toward the clubhouse.

The minute I stepped inside, dense cumulous clouds of smoke singed my eyes and nose, and haunting ghostlike figures drifted in and out of shadows. *Why all the smoke? I could barely breathe. And why did it have to be so dark? Were people ashamed to be here?*

I felt so silly and out-of-place, a squeaky-clean mother of three amid the young, hedonistic crowd. As I coughed my way through the clouded stench of Newport menthols and Camel Non-Filters, I noted all the trendy wear—tight denim skirts, everything jeans, and of course trendy DOC Martens. I tried my best not to wobble on my three-inch heels as I made my way toward the bar.

After a few more shoulder smacks by random patrons, I finally reached my destination. I was in front of the bar. Feeling self-conscious, I fidgeted with my loose, crinkled top, bunching it up, trying to fit in with the fashion. *Now what? Perhaps holding a drink in my hand would help me to blend in?*

Beyond a dusty Heineken mobile there was a mirrored shelf lined with multicolored bottles of spirits, the place where most people lost their souls. *How does one order a drink? Am I supposed to reserve a stool or pick a number like at a CVS pharmacy? Or perhaps I can flag down that muscle-bound guy buzzing around behind the counter? Or maybe the best way to get attention is to flash my pearly whites?*

I fiddled with my blouse while breathing in the rancid smell of soured beer and liquor reeking through the floorboards, when at last, the bodies in front of me cleared. I needed to calm my nerves. So I crept up to the counter as if I were on a clandestine mission and ordered a stiff Shirley temple.

As I stepped away from the bar with drink in hand, I got swept into a torrent of people who were fighting their way into the dance hall. The sound of a few rumbling guitars lured the crowd in.

That's when I spotted him. Out of nowhere, Randy sprang onstage and into the spotlight followed by three other band members. I watched with rapt attention. Everyone in the club was going nuts—high-pitched cheers, flailing arms, boots crushing the floorboards.

As a faithful churchgoer, I'd never seen or heard anything like it. Compared to this gang, I was a tame kitten. I grew up purring to the sound of Lawrence Welk, Bread, The Association, and The Mormon Tabernacle Choir. I'd never taken a liking to hardcore music. Yet there I was. Funny how longing to be loved by someone, anyone, can make you do almost anything.

My church leaders had always referred to loud music as the devil's tool. *Was it?* The throbbing vein in my right temple reminded me just how low my threshold was for head-banging rock. Still, Stone Thong Boy had my full attention as he yanked the mic-stand toward the floor. *Is this what grunge metal looks like?*

Now he was on the floor, convulsing in circles as his out-of-control fans sprang to the stage trying to touch him. I could only imagine my bishop witnessing this whole scene. No doubt, he'd deem my friend "possessed" and suggest a prayer to remove the demon. I honestly would have never guessed my friend to be so popular.

Admittedly, it was kind of a turn on. He was putting on a damn good show if you liked heavy metal or grunge or whatever it was. Yet, most surprising, here I stood on Lucifer's property, and it seemed to have no effect on my salvation. Not one lightning bolt. All was copasetic.

As soon as the band dispensed, I locked eyes on Randy, never losing contact as spiked-purple-haired kids half my age high-fived and pogo-sticked around me. As he moved closer, he caught my gaze, and in my mind's eye the loud driving bass melted into a romantic song, and the bustling crowd parted like the Red Sea as he made his way toward me.

When he placed a warm hand on my shoulder, all the discomfort and unpleasantries of the night dissipated. Especially when he told me how great I looked and asked for my phone number. With all his swarming admirers, he chose me. *Perhaps I was more than just a piece of meat to him?* All too soon, he was swept away into the crowd.

When I arrived home, I kept replaying the tape in my head of that moment when he came up to me on the dance floor. *Surely, he wouldn't have gone through all that trouble to seek me out among all those girls and retrieve my number if he wasn't interested. He had to call ... he just had to!*

CHAPTER 45

DELULU LOVE IN A SHAGGIN' WAGON

A long, grinding week had passed since Randy's band performed at the Clunk House, and I still hadn't heard from him. My world was coming to a crashing halt.

Then, a few days later, while I was staring blankly into the TV spraying whipped cream into my mouth, my phone rang. It was Fender Boy. He invited me to his house party. I couldn't believe it. I immediately came to life, leaping into a heel click, then landing on my butt.

As his deep, smoky voice soothed my racing heart, I tried to imagine how a house party would look—kids half my age with blue mohawks stumbling in and out of his home, stoned out of their wits, having sex in the back room. All those things I had so carefully avoided in high school. Sounded perfect.

Randy met me at the door that night and offered me a soda when beer was served. *Did he know I was Mormon?* He then immediately led me into his bedroom and shut the door. I didn't see that coming. Crammed with a synthesizer, sounding board, and a crapload of amps, you couldn't even see the bedroom carpet. Artistic, messy, disorganized;

this had to be fate. We were destined for each other. It never once occurred to me that he might not be relationship material.

Randy flipped a button on his synthesizer and was sharing his latest song with me when one of his groupies opened the bedroom door and wandered in without knocking. "Hey, why didn't you ever call me?" She looked no more than seventeen. Her dark eyes flashed with annoyance as she peered up at Randy, her brindled hair straggling across her cheeks.

The girl appeared to be sloshed and angry. I wonder what happened between the two. I looked at him quizzically. He didn't have much to say. He just walked over to his bed, picked up his guitar, and plunked out a funky tune. I guess it was enough to appease her. Either that or she was too stoned to remember what she came in there for as she pivoted full circle and stumbled away. Even though the whole scene was a little weird, I chose to ignore the red flags. All I saw was the potential for a budding romance.

When we were alone again, Randy set his guitar on its stand, snatched a photo of his three-year-old son from the dresser, and proceeded to tell me about him and about his recent divorce. I felt incredibly honored that he would share something so personal. He was a daddy. And he'd been married before. That meant he wasn't afraid of commitment. My heart danced with merriment. *Was that the reason he was pursuing me? He needed a stepmom for his little tyke? And a wife too?* In my delusional state, I convinced myself I wasn't just any girl. I was his soulmate. Even better I was LDS. I'd make a perfect mommy.

After the party, Randy and I hopped into his '60s shaggin' wagon and took a ride to the local market. It was way past my bedtime, and raining outside, but this was a cougar's fantasy.

In the grocery aisle, he playfully skittered ahead of me, did a vanishing act, then popped his head around the corner to create the element of surprise. *How did he live so completely in the moment?* I told my friend he was nuts. He responded with a playful grin, then opened his arms, wrapping me in the warmth of his gray trench coat. Wow, I was glowing inside his coat and couldn't have felt more joyful than at that moment.

In the back of his VW van, his blowup mattress beneath us hissed its way toward deflation. *But did I care?* My date was lying on his side, his head propped up, smacking on two Starbursts at a time, flicking them back and forth through his teeth, making slurping sounds. A wee bit immature, but I'd take that over being abused any day.

Gorgeous and crazy-fun rolled into one, Randy outclassed all the LDS single losers I'd met thus far. But would he be willing to become a Mormon?

In 1988, three years before my divorce, the Church's prophet, Ezra Taft Benson, warned single women like me to not trifle away their happiness by involving themselves with men who did not possess temple-worthy attributes. I feared that if I got serious with Randy, I would find myself outside Heaven's gates for eternity.

Now, at the crossroad where I sat, on a sinking mattress in a van looking into the eyes of the sexiest guy I had ever met, I was suddenly burdened with the thought that Randy may not ever convert. But wasn't it okay for me to just want to feel normal? *What about just wanting to feel less lonely?*

As Randy munched on his Pringles, I focused on his full lips. And his hair. My loins quivered as I reached out and caressed the rain-soaked curls that draped over his eyes like Morning Glory. Oh, how I wanted him more than anything. But Shame beat me down.

Why did my thoughts have to fill me with so much shame? Why was thinking about sex so wrong? *Where was my faith?* Perhaps the Lord wanted me to be with Randy? Didn't He say that His thoughts are not always our thoughts, nor are our ways His ways? Perhaps my young, hot friend was a curve ball? Maybe this was the real deal? Or maybe I just wanted it to be. Isn't God in his omniscience occasionally allowed to surprise me with something grand?

The crackling sound of my friend's Frito bag intercepted my thoughts as he crumpled it into a ball and tossed it on the floor. He was looking at me with a sphinxlike smile—a side of him I had not yet seen. His Lapis lazuli blues had me perfectly confused. *Did he want me as much as I wanted him?* I breathed in his earthy scent and had to catch my breath as he leaned in and fiddled with my silver earring stud. I wanted to devour him.

The rain-soaked parking lot was deserted now, and as beads of water trickled down the windowpane, Randy slowly cupped my chin in his hand and drew me in for a kiss.

In the span of five seconds, my world shifted, and somehow that straight-gated, narrow way toward heaven had lost its appeal. I didn't care if a rotten-apple-core, stale-potato-chip odor seeped from the carpet as his lips warmed my neck. I was in a hippie van with a twenty-four-year-old headbanger. *Perhaps I was going through an early mid-life crisis? Or maybe I just never knew what real love felt like? Was this it?*

Outside, the rain suddenly stopped. No more drumming like a tin can on the dented metal doors as the silence descended. The only sound was that of my heart thundering in my ears as Randy's hand slipped beneath my blouse and wandered up my back toward my bra strap. He had no idea about the almost impossible task ahead—to unclasp a half dozen very rigid, stubborn bra hooks.

I shivered as his large, adroit fingers crawled along my midback. I couldn't wait to be rocked into a world of youth, artistry, stage lights, and Grunge Metal magic. Still, I knew I had to be the one in control. That's what my mom taught me. "Why buy the cow when they can get the milk for free?" She quoted that idiom to scare me into being a good girl. She told me that if I give myself away before marriage, a guy would lose interest in tying the knot. Honestly, she made sense.

While I contemplated my salvation, Randy had already managed to undo two bra hooks. I hadn't given him enough credit for his expertise with these types of things. Especially when my bra size involved more digits than tuners on a twelve-string guitar. As I felt his fingers fiddle with my strap, a feeling of excitement jolted through me. My dancing vagina spoke far louder than my mom's warning which was now a mere whisper.

After Randy unclasped the third hook and was halfway there, I suddenly pictured us kneeling at the temple altar. *Was it a premonition?* If so, in spite of the aching in my loins, I needed to stop him before this went too far. I had to leave his van at once. It wasn't too late. Perhaps I could even convince him to take the missionary lessons. But before parting, perhaps the Lord would understand if I let loose a little? *There was always repentance … Right?*

Come to find out, Randy was a pro with large, stiff hooks. With five down, he had only one left to go …

CHAPTER 46

LEGS CROSSED, HEART OPEN

Randy gently leaned in and flicked his tongue on that sweet spot right below my earlobe. I sucked in a breath as chills ran up my spine. Perhaps I could stay put a little longer. *Maybe another minute? Maybe two?* Then just like that, I felt my bra strap spring loose.

With my blouse still on, I suddenly sat upright cupping my breasts so my bra wouldn't fall off. I just couldn't do it. I couldn't go any farther. Leave it to me and my lousy sense of timing to buzzkill a boner. Randy didn't see it coming, nor was he the least bit agitated. He always had a perpetual smile on his face. *Was he high?*

At that moment, I knew I had to leave. Not because he was high, but because I was not that woman who would sell her soul for a quickie. I figured that if I kept my legs crossed and heart open, (instead of the other way around), this laid-back musician would be hunting me down in no time. He'd soon realize I was different than the other girls. He would see me as a rare jewel.

It was 5:00 a.m. when he drove me back to my car, and even though we hadn't even gotten to second base, I smiled all the way home. In my innocence, I asked myself if I had finally found a lasting love.

To escape my deep loneliness, I lived in a fabricated paradise—a place where I believed Randy would one day join the church and marry "delulu little me" in the temple. I saw him as a daddy who was looking for someone more mature like me—someone who could nurture his son—the type of guy who would get easily bored with an aimless twenty-year-old. So when he never called, I was devastated.

Too busy living a fantasy to pick up on his player vibe, I missed all the obvious signs, like the mob of girls that crowded the stage to touch him at the club, and that one pissed-off chick who barged into his room while he was serenading me.

Along with my religious reasons to marry, there was a popular saying that captured the zeitgeist of the '90s, instilling panic and fear in the hearts of girls everywhere. It claimed: "A woman over age 40 has a better chance of being killed by a terrorist than of getting married." If that little adage was true, I had about five years max, then I'd be damn out of luck.

After losing Randy, I had lost all hope of ever finding anyone. With each passing year, I envisioned the onrush of time as if it were fading away like the colors of the setting sun, soon to go dark. Presently at age 35, I saw a yellow sun. But with every birthday, I intuitively knew that the sun would morph through all the colors of the sky at sunset. On my 40th birthday, it would be crimson red—a color that would remind me of one last chance to marry before it slowly dipped below the horizon. After that, my chances were minuscule. If I didn't have a ring on my finger by then, I fretted I would spend eternity as a spinster—totally alone and celibate.

Other than one very busy friend who rarely had time for me, there was no one to turn to, no one who seemed to understand my loneliness. Broken down and beaten, with no roadmap to navigate my new world, I simply allowed my delusions to alleviate the pain.

In the end, the memory of making out with a young, hot local rock-star in a shaggin 'wagon served to help me survive another day.

CHAPTER 47

A THOUSAND CHA-CHINGS BUT NO WEDDING RING

Around August of 1991, eight months after my divorce was finalized, I finally decided to embrace solo play. Since I vowed to be abstinent while single, it made sense to choose "the lesser vice." Besides, walking around with all that pent-up energy just didn't seem healthy. There was nothing like "taking matters into my own hands" when the tension mounted. I was no longer a taut thread ready to snap at any given moment. At last, I found a way to calm my mind and relieve stress.

Abstinence, however, was a different matter altogether. I couldn't afford to slip. Fornication was a huge no-no. I was still after that pie-in-the-sky promise of a magic kingdom.

After a failed marriage, the chance for a "do-over" kept me committed to the hunt. My next spouse would be the opposite of a villain. He'd be warm, fun, and engaging. *The best part?* Death would not divide us. Sex would be endless and eternal. Now that's a heaven worth aiming for. And if my new guy chose to practice polygamy in the afterlife, I wouldn't even care. If time and sex were infinite, why would I?

Since I had a healthy libido, to stay out of trouble, I knew I needed to meet a church member who was more-liberal minded like I was—one who didn't feel the need to run and confess to his bishop every time he pleasured himself. But so far, I wasn't having much luck finding anyone. Dating the local yokels was like shopping at a thrift store. They had already been picked over and reduced in price. Even at eighty percent off they were still no bargain.

Yet, at age 36, I was no Louis Vuitton purse. I had a lot to work on. I summed it up to not being lucky in love, but truthfully, delulu little me had zero self-awareness. I saw myself as a self-enlightened guru and believed I was a dream come true for any good man. After all, I was spiritual, kept myself fit, and loved sex. *What more could a good Mormon man want?*

As a BYU coed, I didn't date all that much for a reason. What classy guy would want a girl who knows nothing about what's going on in the world?

Try to imagine this, because it's true. I had never heard of the Twin Towers until 2001, when 9/11 occurred. I was a substitute teacher at the time and happened to show up at El Capitan Elementary on a day filled with consternation and fear. The staff intercom echoed, "Twin Towers this, Twin Towers that" as if it were some secret passcode. They were deciding whether to shut down the school. *Why was everyone so neurotic?* I had given up watching TV and didn't subscribe to the daily news. God came first, and while at home, I was diligently buried in His word. When two hijacked airliners deliberately crashed into two of New York City's most prominent towers, killing thousands of people, I was writing songs about peace and love.

Despite my ignorance, or perhaps because of it, I believed I needed a guy like me—one who was a little off-center and strong in the church. *But how would I find him?* In 1991, dating sites were still in the incubator.

Luckily, I got wind of an upcoming LDS singles conference that would take place in the beautiful northern coastal town of Eureka. The conference was well-advertised, and I had a hunch this all-day event with workshops, dinner, and a dance was going to be huge. I immediately called Chloe, my church friend who was just as desperate to land a husband as I was. We planned the trip together.

When the eventful day arrived, we were exhausted from the previous day's six-hour trip and groggy from a fitful night sleep at a friend's cabin. That morning, we strolled into the Eureka meeting house half awake—I, in my red dress and Chloe in her blue. For the first time in my life, I desperately wished that Mormons served coffee.

Three greeters sitting at a foldout table in the foyer cheerfully handed us our name tags and pointedly reminded us we were thirty minutes late. They also told us that we could choose one class out of the three offered, and that every hour, we could switch classes if we wanted to hear a different lecture. But we weren't there for the lectures. We were there to find our eternal companions.

After we pinned on our name tags, Chloe gave me "that look," and I knew what that look meant. We would start by checking out each classroom to see which one had the most guys. We made a beeline for the carpeted hallway; then we peeked in each door, counting the male inventory.

All three classes were packed with wall-to-wall women. We counted around five or six men in each room. That meant there was a total of fifteen to eighteen guys tops. Normally, that number would be okay.

221

But there were a lot of women. What were the chances of snagging a good guy with so much competition?

When dinner was served in the cultural hall, I looked over at Chloe. There were fewer men attending the dinner than the classes. *Where did they all go?* As we chewed on our $20 overcooked meatloaf and soggy macaroni salad, I glanced up and saw him. He was sitting at another table across from us—a captivating, mysterious looking gentleman with nutmeg bangs falling across his eyes. He had a somewhat enigmatic appearance. A rare specimen in a room teeming with mediocrity. He tilted his head in my direction and smiled at me. I immediately let out a sigh and quickly clutched onto Chloe's elbow. "Check him out," I whispered.

I told her that if a face could paint a thousand words, by reading this guy's, I could tell he had a good set of moral values and was not likely burdened by religious OCD. Chloe believed in my intuition. She claimed I was more gifted than a licensed palm reader. Yep. His smile said it all. I prayed with great fervor that I would run into him at the dance.

At 9:00 p.m. sharp, my friend in her sapphire earrings, and I in my ruby sparkles, headed toward the dance floor, ready and eager to meet our Mr. Wonderfuls. But as we scanned the low-lit multi-purpose hall from left to right, we dropped our heads in disappointment. This was an all-too-familiar carking chick-fest. Even with a blindfold on, you would know it was a Mormon dance just by breathing in the predominance of girly fragrances.

An hour later, about a half dozen stragglers entered the hall—two Big Hunks outnumbered by a handful of Sugar Daddys. The Big Hunks knew they were hot items (even though they were only worth a nickel when I was a seven) and strutted around the dancehall with fat egos and delusional expectations. Convinced that they were Greek Gods, they would more than likely end up alone until the end of time. As attractive as Chloe and I were, we were fortunately dressed too modestly to attract these lowlifes. Or perhaps we were two conspicuous wallflowers with that urgent look in our eyes as we occasionally chewed off a nail or two.

Mr. Dinner Hour was different from the rest. I felt it in my bones. I wanted to kick myself for not having the courage to introduce myself to him when I had a chance. Apparently, he was the only smart one who chose not to show up here.

To kill time, I studied the disco ball that hung slightly off center from the ceiling. It neither sparkled nor reflected light. They must have found a thrift-store reject. I turned back just in time to see Chloe being pulled into the crowd. Some guy had asked her to dance. I waved a tiny wave as she flashed an impish grin from afar. *Traitor.* Now I was left all alone to fend off a couple of Bronx thugs who appeared out of nowhere and had nothing better to do than invade my personal space and stare down my blouse. I was donned in a modest dress with a lower-case rather than an upper-case v-neckline. But with my large bustline, as hard as I tried, I couldn't seem to hide my endless cleavage. *Dogs.* I murmured. *Just like my mom said.*

With each passing minute, the refreshment table was looking better than ever. Out of sheer boredom, I wandered closer so I could breathe in all the yummy buttery smells. *Homemade chocolate-chip cookies? Oh, what the hell.* I wolfed down two then licked the chocolate off my fingers. *Ummm.* I was working on a brownie when I felt a light tap on my shoulder.

"How are they?" the stranger asked.

"Huh?"

"The refreshments? Are they good?" I had a spy. A spy who had the worst timing ever. *How dare he approach me the moment I make a pig of myself.* Said his name was Bobby. His shirt was so bright I had to shade my eyes to look at him. The part down the center of his hair was a jagged lightning bolt of pale scalp. I wondered if he dyed it to cover his premature gray. The whole look inspired me to finish my brownie. When he tried to engage again, I didn't hear a word he said. I was too busy chomping, and my jaws were an echo chamber inside my head.

The second I let my guard down, Bobbie the Weirdo grabbed hold of my arm and dragged me into the crowd. I downed the rest of my brownie while Ring-a-Ding Crazy clumsily flailed his arms in circles to the music like a puppet tangled in strings. *Was he listening to the lyrics?* This was "Right Here Waiting," Richard Marx's most romantic song. I couldn't help it. I covered my mouth to stifle my laughter as Bobby eddied around me doing the chicken-mating dance.

As soon as the song ended, another began. This is when he seized the chance to whirl me into his arms and spin me in circles, Wow. He was light on his feet. Close up, he had a cute little button nose that scrunched like a bunny's every time I said something funny. There was an endearing merriment about him. He was so upbeat—the way he chuckled frequently and threw his head back. This kook was growing on me.

Once the music slowed, I had a chance to gaze into his pale sea-green eyes, and suddenly felt what I wanted it to be—a soul-to-soul connection. Maybe this puppet on strings was more than meets the eye? *Could he possibly be the one for me?*

Okay, I confess I was feeling some urgency. It had been seven months since Grunge Band Boy had disappeared from my life. And I had celebrated my thirty-sixth birthday three months prior to this dance.

In my mind's eye, I saw it—the sun's color had faded from yellow to pale orange and was in the far corner of the sky. If I wanted to find a man, I didn't have much time.

As the evening progressed, Bobby managed to slow his pace and dance the entire night without tripping over my feet. "Cha-ching." He racked up one hundred points. His breath didn't smell like a raccoon's butt, and he listened when I talked. "Cha-ching," another two hundred. He talked a-lot about his love for God and family. "Cha-ching," three hundred points. In three cha-chings, it seemed as if all my troubles were over. Maybe I could get him to change his wardrobe. His bright lime-green shirt was critically over the top. Other than that, my future looked promising.

When the dance let out, he walked me to my car. I had no idea where Chloe was, but didn't care. Ahead of us, he noticed a piece of broken glass and chivalrously took my hand, escorting me around it. He was sure racking up those cha-chings!

When we arrived at my truck, he asked if he could kiss me. I know. We hadn't even had our first date yet, but our spiritual connection made me want to sing a hymn. And because I was starving for affection, I yelled out, "Yes, please!"

My eyelids quivered as he pressed his lips against mine. Wow. "Cha-ching! Cha-ching! Cha-Ching!"

But as my eyes slowly opened, I looked straight into the face of terror. "Oh my gosh!" he exclaimed. "I shouldn't be with you. I need to get out of here. I just jizzed in my pants!"

You what? I backed up a step then slowly shifted my eyes down just in time to see the crotch of his jeans turn dark blue. *Wow. He wasn't kidding. The guy really jizzed his pants!* I flipped my head around to see if others had witnessed this and was about to yell out, "Clean up on

Parking Lot 3C," but when I turned back, Bobby Bright was nowhere to be found. He had disappeared into the dark never to be seen again.

Why did he have to be such a do-gooder and ruin everything? To think we could have been married within a few months if he hadn't been so uptight.

CHAPTER 48

FEVER ON THE DANCE FLOOR

After recovering from the Eureka Singles Conference, I quickly learned about the happenin' singles dances that took place every third Friday at the East Bay Stake House on Orchard Drive in Danville. To join in on the Techno and Electric Slide every month, I drove my old beater down highway 580 through the turbine–covered hills of the Altamont Pass. From San Joaquin Valley's water holes to the Bay Area estuaries, my goal was to catch bigger and better fish. Then I met Oliver Huxley and foolishly believed I had snagged a bluefin tuna.

I stumbled across him one night when entering the Danville meeting house. Oliver was sitting on a stool in the corner of the foyer softly strumming an acoustic guitar. I instantly became an enraptured fan. His smooth-as-velvet voice with a raspy edge caught my attention. I had to buy his cassette, that's all there was to it. That's when we had our first exchange.

Shortly after that, he seemed to pop up everywhere. It didn't take long to learn about Oliver's reputation with the ladies. He spent a good portion of his time traveling the LDS singles circuit promoting and selling his music, picking up a girl or two along the way. At least that's what I had heard.

Second-hand stories don't hold much weight, but when I became a prime witness to Oliver's snuggling habits on the dance floor, it was time to yellow tape the incident location. In my sanctimony, I judged him without knowing him. Why would I have to know him? I knew a smooth operator when I saw one, and I had convinced myself that Oliver was as smooth as they come.

As his smitten female groupies circled around him like vultures waiting for him to pencil them in on his dance card, I neither stared nor gawked, nor bothered to pretend I was halfway interested. I saw Oliver as none other than a wolf in sheep's clothing who slept with dozens of girls a month, maybe hundreds. I relied on my sixth sense to avoid becoming the wolf's next free meal.

I often wondered how a bad boy like him managed to remain in good standing with the church. Maybe he stayed up all night doing penance? Or perhaps he simply knew how to play "good Mormon boy" in the presence of his bishop?

In my smugness, I believed I was more righteous than this showman. Instead of succumbing to my sexual urges, I fought them. My desire was to please the Lord and to remain in good standing with the church—all while secretly envying Oliver's free spirit.

I was a girl with high everything—high energy, high emotions, high volume, high libido. You take an average person with average feelings and then add a couple of exclamation points to everything—that's me.

My bishop instructed me to shut down my libido. How was I supposed to turn it off, just like that when I'd been a sexual adult for the past fifteen years? No one ever explained to me how to do it. How was

I to extinguish the blazing fire inside of me? Especially when running across a hot guy? I had skin hunger. I was emotionally and sexually starving. Even though it looked as though Oliver was getting plenty of personal attention, perhaps he was starving for love too? *Was I in a place to really judge him?*

Most LDS singles in my age bracket had been previously married for a long time. I'm sure nearly all of us were struggling with the abstinence requirement. How do you go from being a sexual being to absolute celibacy? My LDS therapist told me that once you've been used to having sex, living without it is like going without sleep.

The cool thing about Danville was that besides the singles dances, the city had an entire LDS singles ward, which was rare. I occasionally drove a hundred miles on a Sunday to attend the singles sacrament meeting. It gave me a sense of belonging. It helped me to fit in somewhere. Oliver belonged to the ward, but I intentionally snubbed him. I had no desire to be just a name on his list of conquests.

A few months after I met him at the dance, my friend, Margo and I, drove over an hour to Antioch to attend another LDS dance hoping we'd find new faces. It didn't take long to spot Oliver. He was everywhere. All you had to do was follow his gawking fans, and he'd be in the center of them sporting a freshly starched shirt, black blazer and jeans, and his signature diamond-beveled Rolex. He certainly didn't look like a "starving musician" —more like a "drunk on attention" musician if you asked me; a shorter, beefier, not-as-graceful version of John Travolta as he created a fever on the dance floor in front of his enamored female entourage.

Around 11:00 p.m., near the end of the dance, I spotted "the player" swaggering my way. I knew exactly why he was heading toward me. The disc jockey had offered one last slow dance. It was Mr. Huxley's final chance to gobble up his dessert after enjoying a five-course meal of dumb platinum blondes. I suspected curiosity, not genuine interest. I was the one cold-shoulder that hadn't warmed up to him and he had to find out why. To him, I was neither tiramisu nor creme brûlée. I was a mystery dish he was curious to try, then enjoy or toss out according to his tastes.

Still, I couldn't help but notice some hopeful twinges in my nether regions as he inched closer. I had a habit of listening to his cassette almost nightly, and the unique timbre of his voice lulled me into X-rated dreams.

It wasn't very long before I felt the presence of Oliver's shadow behind me. When he tapped me on the shoulder, a thrill coursed through my body. *Ummm. Why did he have to smell so damn divine?* He smelled like fresh cedarwood, and did I smell a hint of rosemary? His scent would be the death of me. What woman in her right mind would turn down such a manly fragrance?

It happened in a flash. One moment I was standing there; the next we were slow- dancing out in the open. Engulfed in his bearhug, I began feeling woozy. I was convinced he was a master manipulator, but his cologne whispered things even Oliver wasn't clever enough to say. It certainly didn't mix well with a sex-starved, love-starved sleep-deprived divorcee like me.

As we danced, this lady charmer with a divine tenor voice didn't appear to be as shallow as I judged him. He showed genuine interest in me. Or at least he appeared to. As a soft, romantic song with far too much bass vibrated around us, he snuggled in closer, and although I was guarded, I felt weak in the knees. The coolness of his breath skated softly down the back of my neck causing my skin hairs to stand on edge. *"You feel great,"* he whispered, squeezing my waist a little tighter. *Uh-oh.*

When Margo, approached me about wanting to leave early, Oliver ended up offering to take me home. The thing was, Mr. Smooth Operator lived in Danville. He would have to drive ninety miles out of his way to drop me off in Merced, the town I had recently moved to. I wasn't stupid. I knew what he was up to. But I was lonely. I mean, really, really lonely ...

CHAPTER 49

NIGHT WITH A "BAD BOY"

Unlike his other fans, I was far more impressed with Oliver's Krispy-Kreme voice and fresh, woody cologne than I was with his charm. He didn't have to convince me to go home with him. The cologne made the decision for me.

All my life, I often fantasized about meeting a bad boy. Not a real bad boy, but the kind of guy that would be wicked if he had the chance to be. I didn't want to sleep with just anyone. Or did I? I was pretty hard up.

Halfway to Merced, my bad boy said he was too zonked to continue driving. Of course, he was. When he arranged to check us into a hotel, in my weak and desperately lonely state, I went along like a happy little lemming bounding toward a cliff.

At 2:00 a.m., my friend and I found ourselves sitting together on a double mattress donned in only our temple garments. Both Oliver and I had been married in the temple and divorced. This meant we were required to wear our sacred underwear day and night. The garment, we believed, served as a protection to help us stay clean and pure. *How could it not protect us?* It was anything but sexy. I noticed my friend fumbling beneath the sheets removing his garments, so I followed suit. Our "purity protection" lay in small heaps on the floor.

Sitting on the bed with a sheet tucked under my arms, there was an awkwardness in the air at first. We were practically strangers, and we were both naked under the sheets. I wasn't sure what he was thinking. Maybe he just liked talking in the nude. But whatever it was, I had no doubt he could make feeling lonely feel better.

My pillow partner and I chatted for a bit. Then Oliver suddenly jumped out of the sheets in his birthday suit to fetch a glass of water. *Ahem.* When he climbed back in bed, he asked me in a husky voice if I liked his "package." *What? Really? Was he reliving second grade "show and tell?"*

I was having second thoughts about all this. Choosing to spend the night with this guy was a dumb idea. Now he wanted my opinion about his penis. I sure knew how to get myself in awkward situations, but I certainly didn't know how to get out of them. If I were in my right mind, I would have spoken up and said, "What's your problem? Put that thing away!" But if I were in my right mind in the first place, I would have never agreed to camp out for the night in a motel with him.

When Oliver started talking about his music, I suddenly saw him in a different light. He was most likely a lost soul like me—just a less lonely one. Being divorced after age thirty is kind of like being in a fishbowl looking out into the real world, envying those outside the glass who are settled and happy, wishing we could breathe their air. Spinning in circles in the dating pool can turn you into desperate, disoriented floundering … fish?

When my new friend leaned in to kiss me on the cheek, I really liked it. Then he kissed me slowly and deliberately on the mouth. As we got caught up in our passion, I allowed one of Oliver's songs to play in my head to ease my nerves. His gorgeous tones made the kiss more magical. The curl of his upper lip as he winked at me, the movement of his fingers through my hair—he seemed to have a natural rhythm about him, even without music. *Was it all rehearsed?*

"You're so gorgeous!" he said in a hushed tone. Even his whisper had melody. But I wasn't born yesterday. My guess is that he used that same line on all his victims. I didn't want to be just one more of those gullible girls. The uncertainty of it all made my head spin.

What he did next surprised me. That sweet, laid-back musician whom I clearly misjudged, sprang from the bed, fetched some blankets out from the dresser, and covered my nakedness. I let out a slow breath as we contentedly spooned in the quiet. Quite honestly, not having sex with him that night possibly saved my sanity.

As we snuggled together, his warm-blooded masculine presence filled my gnawing emptiness. It was exactly what I needed, but I knew my church leaders wouldn't agree. We were like Adam and Eve in the garden without our fig leaves. Too many talks from the pulpit had convinced me that getting too close and cuddly outside the bounds of marriage was dangerous. Cradled in the cozy arms of a gifted artist, I wasn't sure what I believed anymore. To have a handsome showman softly purring beside me, certainly did not seem to fit the category of "dangerous."

At around 3:00 a.m., I lay awake gazing through the thinly woven curtain into the moonlight. After almost a year without being touched, my longings had been deeply satisfied with a practical stranger. The sheer irony of it forced me to realize just how broken I was. I didn't know what he ate for breakfast. I didn't even know his birthday. Yet I felt more content than I had in years.

Other than his need to go Full Monty and request an assessment of his male appendage, Oliver showed tremendous restraint by choosing cuddling over sex. *Could he be the one for me?*

The next day, I awoke to a sexy man in a black blazer and Perry Ellis jeans standing by a minibar, stirring a package of powdered cocoa into a mug of hot water. *Is my mind playing tricks on me?* For a moment I couldn't recall the previous night's events. I instantly sprang from my pillow and snatched the blanket to shield my chest. I felt like a slut even though I was guilty of nothing more than naked cuddling.

Oliver was sitting in the armchair across from me sipping a cup of cocoa, his gunmetal blue eyes branding his monogram on my heart. After a prolonged silence, he began to talk. All at once, he spilled out everything as if he were in church court, sharing all about his promiscuity with some of the Danville ladies—said he'd been warned by his bishop to cool it.

Wow. I didn't know how to respond. Before he shared his history with me, I was ninety-nine percent convinced he was guilty as charged. But now I knew it. *He really was a bad boy!* I saw him differently after that. It takes guts to admit you're a scoundrel. I actually felt honored that he felt safe enough to share his vulnerabilities with me, and that he chose to respect me by using restraint.

As I listened and nodded intently to his every word, his cheeks flushed, his eyes bluer than ever, all I could think about was wanting to chuck any cuddling and consummate our friendship in bed right then. His candid honesty was a turn on. But the bed was made, and it was almost checkout time. And I wasn't the kind of girl who'd make the first move anyway.

As he dropped me off at home that morning, and we said our goodbyes, I had a hunch I would never see him again—that it had been a one-time deal. But I was okay with it.

Today, I look back at that night for what it was—a beautiful moment when two faltering, lonely adults came together to make their desperate worlds a little more tolerable. For him, it may not have been what it was to me, but it doesn't matter. It's a memory that serves to put a smile on my face.

But back then, it didn't take long until I fell prey to what I'd been taught: that lasting happiness doesn't find a place in casual hookups, or rest stops, or hotel sleepovers where two people use each other to mend their brokenness. So Shame took over with hellbent determination to slay any self-love I had left.

CHAPTER 50

CONFESSIONS OF A NON STRATEGIST

Although it had been weeks since that night with Oliver, Guilt and Shame would not let up. Shame convinced me I had less value than the gritty residue at the bottom of a coffee-cup. Guilt was the good guy, and a concerned friend. It nagged me to change course when I veered from my own values and goals. It gently reminded me that if I kept going down the road of sharing intimacy with guys I barely knew, my path would lead to a place that was so far off course, I'd never find my Mormon prince.

I had a hunch that Oliver Huxley never gave our sleepover a second thought. Why couldn't I be more like him? He had a certain finesse and type of confidence that left no room for self-blame or low self-esteem. *Could that be the reason he only got a slap on the wrist for his transgressions?* No question. Hands down, Oliver was a better strategist.

Yet to be like him, I'd have to kill my conscience. Mr. Smooth Talker seemed to be born without one. He appeared to know and say all the right things to get out of damning situations. When it came to playing a strategic game, I was the exact opposite—genuine to a fault and pathetically self-blaming. There wasn't an ounce of guile in me. Instead of shooing away Shame, I embraced it.

Imagine a world where you had family and friends and church, then suddenly you were cut off from everything. After my divorce, I had no one to talk to when I desperately needed to hear a comforting voice on the other end of the line, except for a friend who lived in the Bay Area, which required a long-distance call that I couldn't afford.

I had no ward family to speak of. Divorce tends to scare everyone away. It's messy and complicated. My former friends didn't want to get involved because they were afraid of taking sides. So they left me alone to figure things out on my own. By default, I was ostracized by everyone but the bishop's wife. And she was so busy with her eight kids, she rarely had time to talk.

Meeting up with men at the church dances and sharing intimacy was the only way I knew how to survive. Because I couldn't figure life out on my own, I thought it would be wise to seek counsel from my church leaders. Guilt was prodding me in that direction, steering me toward a confession. In my naivety, I believed that a confession would lead me to Hope and Hope would eventually lead me to my eternal companion.

The only bishop I felt close enough to at the time was Oliver's bishop—Bishop Clark. I got to know this sweet, kind, elderly gentleman when I would occasionally visit the Danville ward. In his mid-sixties, Bishop Clark had a good, kind heart. Because I believed he would understand my plight, I decided to make the 180-mile round trip to the Bay Area to seek his counsel.

When I arrived at the meeting house, I found myself standing in a mile-long confession line that coiled down the hallway and out the front door. All those young divorcees were members of the ward. A gal standing in line next to me divulged that the long line was typical. I felt better knowing I wasn't the only one battling sexual temptation, although it did get me wondering, *Does Bishop Clark ever have time to eat?*

An hour later, after inching my way up the line, the kind, elderly leader with a full head of snow-white hair finally appeared in his doorway to welcome me. I immediately plopped myself in the chair across from him and blurted out my story. He listened intently while I shared every detail about my intimate sleepover with Oliver—the man I believed to be the ward's notorious philanderer.

I soon learned that mine was not the first confession Bishop Clark had heard about indiscretions with Oliver Huxley. There had been other women in the Danville ward who had either touched him or had been "touched" by him in some way.

Bishop Clark assured me that he planned to have another talk with Oliver. He even mentioned that he was going to ask Oliver to make a public apology in Sacrament Meeting. *Wow. I guess being a strategist didn't pay off after all.* Because my pillow partner and I didn't have sex, this dear leader assured me I had nothing to worry about. And because he was so easy to talk to, I spilled my guts openly, candidly, and perhaps, foolishly. I made sure that he knew I was a highly sexual woman who found it extremely challenging to live the law of chastity.

I let him know how hard it was to find a good man. And, most importantly, I talked about my concerns with missing out on all that sex in the interim. But I didn't stop there. I challenged him with the possibility of a heaven without physical intimacy. "What if I die?" I said, scrunching my little pixie nose, "and I find out there's no sex in heaven? What then?"

As I waited for an answer, I noticed that Bishop Clark could no longer keep a straight face. His thin lips gradually gave way to a smile.

Then he let out a warm sigh and told me I was refreshingly delightful. *Wow. I never had a bishop compliment me before.*

The best part was when he went on to assure me that if I were to remain faithful, the Lord would provide me with a loving companion, and that all my worries of being unfulfilled would dissipate. He even wrapped up our session by praising me for coming in and being honest. And just like that, Guilt and Shame vanished. It felt amazing.

On my way home, I contemplated marriage. Not with Oliver, of course. No way. After talking with his bishop, I no longer believed he was bluefin tuna. *I would find a far worthier catch.*

Back home as I moseyed into my bedroom, I contemplated Bishop Clark's words—that I was worthy of someone. *Where was he?* All I knew was that I could not endure another night without a man beside me. I longed to reach out for something warm, something hard, only to rub up against cold mattress buttons and loose yarn from wear and tear. Closing my eyes in the darkness, I comforted myself with the idea of a husband. I believed the right man would change everything.

Round and round went the insanity. The marriage-manhunt journey was not a straight path at all. I was forever spinning. I guess that's why I ended up with John …

Loneliness can take you to places
You don't really want to go.
Like spending the night with a guy on a whim
When you're feeling incredibly low.
A rest stop might keep you warm for a while
But soon you're left in the cold
In the meantime, your leaders are there to help
Just DON'T CONFESS, and you're gold.

CHAPTER 51

VANILLA JOHN

When I met John at an LDS Modesto dance, my "thrift store shopping" analogy regarding dating after thirty still rang true. He was the only one out of three dozen other singles who didn't look like he belonged on a two-for-one display table. The rest of the guys looked like they had wandered off from an assisted living facility as they aimlessly roamed the dance floor, blocking traffic with a hollow stare while flashing their excessive gingival smiles.

Once I arrived at the dance, it was third-grade dodgeball all over again. I panicked when I noticed a senior with an unusually bulbous nose, sporting a black toupee, heading my way. *Did he purchase it from that same two-for-one display rack?* My only option was to run. The game was afoot. That was, until a more youthful-looking suitor caught up with me and pulled me into the safety of his arms.

As I got to know this rather nice-looking John fellow, I wished I hadn't. My new acquaintance was tall, dark, and boring as hell. But because he was an upgrade from empty space, I endured his never-ending, pathetic monologue. We danced for a while, then agreed to go out to a coffee house for some pie; and somehow, we ended up at my apartment on my living room carpet.

"Do you want to have sex?"

"No thank you," I said, trying to tune out his lifeless drone. Bohemian poetry readings had nothing on John's dry, drawn-out deliveries. I knew if he didn't jumpstart his personality soon, we'd be going nowhere. After about a ten-minute snore-worthy, naked kissing session, I got dressed, told him to do the same, then booted him out the door.

After he left, I felt cheap and dirty all over again. But the reason why I kept repeating this unhealthy pattern was because I didn't know where else to find comfort. I just wanted the loneliness to go away. Therapy would have done wonders for me, but I couldn't afford it. Mostly I felt dead; walking in the shadows of the living.

I felt as though I'd been stranded on a barge in the middle of the ocean waiting to be rescued by a heroic LDS sea captain who happened to be single. I feared I might have missed his boat by falling away from the covenant path. I'd been floating for almost a year, battered and blistered from wind and sun without a sign of any worthy marriage candidate. *Was God punishing me because I strayed?*

Being with Oliver quenched me for a time. But just like the salty sea surrounding me, his kisses and affection only caused more thirst for real love.

I was further discouraged knowing that my ex-husband was already happily married. He too, had attended the Danville dances and found his wife right away. I happened to be the wrong gender.

Women far outnumbered the men in the singles arena, which gave guys a huge advantage.

While I was trying to stay afloat, Gary's new wife stood by his side, carrying on as if she were the mother of my children. Five days out of seven, I was an empty nester. Some weekends, I didn't even get to see my kids. That woman didn't deserve my children. Especially when I learned from my kids that she had cut my head out of their family photo albums and replaced it with hers. *What kind of nutjob was she?*

Yet I was the fool who got cheated out of my custody rights. That mistake would forever haunt me. There was no such thing as a "do-over." The most I could hope for was a "try-to-do-better," and so far that wasn't working out too well.

Sharing intimacy with guys I had just barely met was a welcome distraction from the unrelenting grief of having stupidly lost my children. Even if the relief was for only a few moments—even if it was with Vanilla John. For those ten minutes, I didn't think about my unbearable self-hatred. Ironically, those 600 seconds of escapism resulted in weeks of self-loathing. It was a tyrannical, vicious cycle; and I had neither the insight nor the strength to end it.

On top of the guilt and shame, I was also having to adjust to a new environment. I had recently moved from Atwater to Merced and presently belonged to the Merced Ward. More than happy to leave behind my ruthless shepherd, I had no idea what kind of man my next spin of the Bishop Roulette wheel would produce. I knew I needed compassion, understanding, and guidance. Bishop York, my new bishop, was a wild card. It was one thing to be naked with a stranger, but quite another to talk to a stranger about being naked with a stranger. So I did what any lost, divorced Latter-day Saint would do. I prayed.

Dear Heavenly Father,
Please guide the way,
I want to come clean and confess.
I'm not the type who can hide my sins,
I'm not a good strategist.
Give me the courage to call my bishop
Although I don't know him well.
He's not aware of my sorrow and pain—
I have a sad story to tell.
I hope he'll listen
With true compassion
And understand my plight.
I pray he'll see my genuine heart
And know I want to do right.
In the name of Jesus Christ, Amen

CHAPTER 52

HE WHO SINS AGAINST
THE GREATER LIGHT

A few weeks new to my ward, I hadn't yet been properly introduced to my bishop. I had heard through the grapevine that he was an ultra-conservative, by-the-book, kind of guy. That made me feel uneasy, but what choice did I have? I had to talk to him, so I set up an appointment.

The following Sunday, as Bishop York greeted me at his office door, I guessed him to be in his late forties. He had a full head of hair, stood about five-foot-ten and was in good shape. Appearing far statelier up close than when speaking from the pulpit, his good looks were intimidating. If I could have just thrown a burlap sack over his head while confessing, I would have felt a lot less self-conscious.

Sitting down across from him, I was dying to get the whole nerve-racking thing over with. I started off by sharing the details of my divorce and how I got tricked out of my custody rights. I also shared how lonely I was along with my overwhelming feelings of grief and loss. My leader listened intently with a pained expression, which boosted my confidence, so I continued talking.

Although Bishop York was a stranger, I bore my soul openly and freely, trusting him with my most heart-wrenched feelings—like the aching need to hold my children, my feelings of despair, and how I had been sitting on my lonely raft for almost a year without a lifeline.

"I think I just went a little crazy," I said, as my leader teetered his pen between his index and middle fingers clicking it in and out. *Was I boring him?*

Screw it. I needed to get this painful process over with. So I told him about my naked cuddling session with John, a practical stranger, making sure to let Bishop York know that I didn't have sex. He didn't need to know about Oliver since that sin had been confessed.

I studied my bishop as he took out a handkerchief and mopped the sweat from his forehead, then lowered his gaze as if in deep contemplation. Looking back to that particularly uncomfortable moment with him, I remember feeling so nervous about confessing, that I had completely forgotten why I chose to visit him in the first place. I was hoping that a confession might wipe my slate clean and that I might be given a church calling.

To me the answer was service. I was convinced that if this solemn man felt moved upon to grant me a church calling, it would give me a chance to serve others, and in turn, give me a sense of purpose as I connected with my fellow saints. Being surrounded by loving friends would be the fortress I needed to keep me from falling back into that deep, dark place of loneliness and vulnerability. As it was, I was hanging by a thread.

As I sat across from my designated leader, picking at a hang nail, waiting for him to respond, I was hopeful. I was hopeful because in my childlike faith, I believed that most bishops were divinely appointed and that they had the spirit of discernment. I thought all they had to do was hear my pathetic story, look into the depths of my troubled soul, and share a revelation that would bring back the sunshine.

But that's not what happened. The twitch in Bishop York's eye spoke of uneasiness. It was as if I had dumped an expected pile of garbage in his lap and he was trying to figure out what to do with it. I studied him with angst as he leaned back in his chair and shot a look over the top of his glasses straight out asking me if I was a temple-recommend holder. Right then, I knew I was toast. When I volunteered a weak "yes," he shook his head slowly then told me that because I had made sacred covenants in the temple, I was required to live a higher law. He really didn't have to tell me that. I knew what scripture he was referring to. I referred to it daily to give myself a good whipping.

"To whom much is given, much is required; and he who sins against the greater light shall receive the greater condemnation." (Doctrine & Covenants 82:3). Because I had been endowed in sacred temple underwear, made covenants with God, and received "the greater light," the church required more of me. Instead, I got naked with John. No doubt, I'd be going to hell in a handbag. Yet, none of it made sense.

I was only twenty-two when I entered the temple for the first time. I didn't understand what was going on. The whole ritual ceremony made me feel terribly uncomfortable due to its misogynistic nature. And there wasn't anyone inside or outside God's holy house who was willing to answer my questions. How could I know about "the greater light" when I was constantly kept in the dark?

As Bishop York continued to grill me, his tone guarded and his brow furrowed, he seemed more indignant than compassionate. I wasn't expecting to be grilled. I went to him to share my situation. I needed to break the pattern of getting naked with men I barely knew.

Bishop York had no concept that what I didn't need was his full army of Shame shoving my face down in the mud, taunting me, accusing me, and spitting on me. My own militia had been working overtime to convince me I was a mistake; that I was too vile to walk the earth—that I should have never been born.

I finally drummed up the courage to look across the desk into the eyes of my leader. Then I felt them. Tears. They began to well up in my eyes. I refused to look like a cry-baby in front of him. I fought like hell to keep the tears from falling. I needed to be brave. I wanted that man to see me as stoic.

Perhaps he was looking for tears. Maybe my bishop mistakenly believed that with true remorse, there's tear shedding. *Could that be why he was so displeased with me?* It all made sense now. I hadn't shed a tear when I shared my story with him.

My fears were confirmed when he opened his drawer, pulled out an Ensign magazine, and handed it to me. He had it opened to a conference talk on repentance. "Here. Take this home to read," he said dryly. "True remorse takes wrestling before the Lord. Sometimes for days, even weeks or months." I balanced the magazine over my trembling knees and fully regretted my decision to meet with him. I didn't even know how to respond. How was he to measure the howling winds of my Guilt or the storms of my Sorrow?

I went to him with a broken heart and contrite sprit seeking comfort. More than that, I was a broken woman. My life was shattered. Everyone and everything I lived for had slipped away. I was in quicksand, quietly going under, soon to be covered in mud. I wanted to scream, "Can you read my eyes and see my shattered state?" But I knew it would do no good. I could tell that Bishop York was all about the law.

After handing me the magazine, he said nothing. Aggrieved and still fighting my tears, I immediately grabbed my purse, stood up, and thanked him for his time. The mood couldn't have been more somber as he rose from his desk and escorted me to the door. Then there was—get ready—the blindside ...

"By the way," he said, "you'll be getting a letter in the mail summoning you to a church court to determine your punishment." I knew that meant the possibility of being disfellowshipped or excommunicated. I had already lost my family, home, my stability, and my self-respect. Suddenly I stood the chance of losing my church, my last lifeline, and suffering public humiliation in the process.

Did I really hear him correctly? A church court? This bishop was so far-removed from my suffering that he delivered the news as if he were reporting the weather: "There will be cloudy skies with a good chance for showers, and by the way, you may soon lose your church membership." I reached to rub my aching jaw and fought hard to blink back the tears that had been welling up for almost an hour.

This is the punishment I get for being brave enough to come in and voluntarily confess my sin? Where was his grace? Where was his love? Perhaps I should have never confessed? But I had been programmed all my life to confess when involved in unholy practices. And for me, getting naked with no purpose other than wanting comfort was unholy.

I couldn't believe my ears when he said there might even be a possibility of excommunication. Excommunication was typically reserved for those accused of the most serious offenses, ranging from adultery, sexual abuse and murder to teaching false doctrine. I certainly didn't fit into any of these categories. I was simply a lost sheep seeking a shepherd to help guide me back to the fold.

Still, Bishop York seemed to believe he was being more than gracious by informing me of my options. He said I could choose to bring family members to the hearing if I wanted to. *How kind of him, but no thank you. Like I'm going to get all cozy with mom and dad while they sit in on a confession about the intimate details of my personal love life?*

I received his dreaded letter a few weeks later and read it in disbelief.

CHAPTER 53

HOT TEARS UPON THE HOT SEAT

When the Bishop's dreaded letter arrived, I ripped it open. As my eyes scanned the page, I wasn't sure why I was shaking my head in disbelief. It said everything Bishop York told me it would say—predictable, yet surreal. A church court date was given along with a statement that mentioned the possibility of being disfellowshipped or excommunicated from the church I dearly loved and believed in.

A year earlier, my family had been severed from me, along with the only life I had known for over a decade. Stripped of my parental rights, the church was the only thing I had left for comfort and support. The letter stated that a decision would be made about my membership status whether I was present or not. That sounded scary.

It was important that the other bishopric members hear my story. Perhaps his counselors would have more compassion, and collectively these men might have a solution to help get me back on the right road. Maybe even show a little understanding. Even though I dreaded that my choices would be on trial, I felt impressed that I needed to be there.

My church court date was on a rainy November evening in 1991.

> Rain, Rain, don't go away,
> For God is crying on this day.
> Tears of sorrow for my pain,
> Tears of gladness for my gain.
> For I will trust no one but Him,
> And conquer those who judge my sin.

At 7:00 p.m., I pulled into the church parking lot and spotted Bishop York's Ford Taurus and a handful of other cars. They were all inside waiting. I had come to the meeting house in my Sunday best although it was Tuesday evening. Perhaps following the church's dress code would help them see that I took my membership seriously.

Walking with trepidation down the front walkway, I arrived at the glass door leading into the semi-dark foyer. Entering the building, I noticed a light emanating from under the bishop's office door. With one last deep breath, I headed down the hallway toward his office. When I arrived at his closed door, I stood quietly. *I could always head back home.*

As I raised my hand to knock, I was sorely tempted to run. *No. You vowed to come here. Woman up. You can do this.* My queasy tummy said otherwise. I believed with my whole being that what they were doing was unwarranted. Shaming me was not going to help me figure out my life. I needed guidance not judgement.

Lingering by the door, I assured myself this was the right thing to do, so I knocked timidly.

The door opened. Bishop York kindly welcomed me into the office with a firm grip of my hand. I found his smile disquieting. Directly over his shoulder, I spotted his two counselors and the ward clerk. They extended their hands from their spider-black suits, casting a shadow across my arm as I held it out to greet them.

The four men were all there to hear my story then judge me accordingly. Right then, I regretted not inviting my parents. I could have really used their moral support had I known I'd be this nervous. I wiped my damp bangs from my eyes and clenched my fists, my nails stabbing my palms as the bishop offered me a chair. Then he and his three assistants sat down at a table across from me. All four had the same solemn expression on their faces. The executive secretary reached to scratch his nose, then sat straighter and stiffened his shoulders as if to appear like the others.

I was sure Bishop York had already shared my story with them, but I knew they'd have to hear it from me, and they'd be assessing my humility. Their pending judgment along with superfluous amounts of Old Spice aftershave permeated the room. The smell of male dominance wafted through the air and rendered me dizzy. Fighting a wave of nausea, I silently prayed for strength.

On my far left was my handsome bishop with his perfectly coiffed hair and intense hazel eyes. He broke the silence by suggesting in his usual hushed tone that we begin with prayer. *Good idea.* I needed Heavenly Father on my side more than ever.

After the prayer, the first counselor, who I guessed to be in his mid-fifties, spoke up and inquired about the details of the night John and I disrobed in my front room. As a woman alone facing a panel of men, this suddenly hit me as wildly inappropriate. I shifted in my chair and avoided his eyes. I didn't even know this man. *Why should I tell him anything?*

My story was short and simple. "We removed our clothes, talked, hugged, and kissed each other. We did not have sexual intercourse."

After I finished sharing, my bishop looked unmoved. He'd heard it before. But the other three looked dumbfounded, their eyes popping out of their sockets like a blowfish on the end of a hook. I couldn't help but wonder how they would have reacted to Oliver's stories, which were no doubt far more erotic and colorful.

After I had risked being so vulnerable, a kind word or a friendly nod would have gone a long way, but they looked like they might pick up a stone any minute and throw it at me, despite the fact I had not even committed fornication, let alone adultery.

I was outnumbered four to one; more significantly, I was gender outnumbered. And because they were strangers, the whole circumstance was starting to make me paranoid. Bishop York was in his mid-to late forties. I guessed the rest of them to be in their fifties. *Perhaps they got aroused when interviewing sinners with erotic stories.* I've always had quite an imagination. I could have been totally off base, but how could I know for sure? This abusive situation had me at least considering that these men might be enjoying this escape from the doldrums of their family lives.

"Does John's bishop know about what happened with you two?" asked the second counselor. He ran his tongue across his lower lip and pushed up his wire-rimmed glasses to keep them from sliding off his ski-slope nose. When I didn't answer right away, he pushed up his glasses again. I suddenly didn't feel well. I hated being put on the spot. I wasn't sure how to answer his question, because honestly, I wanted to tell him it was none of his business. This was my church court, not John's. "I don't know," I finally muttered. John lived in Modesto, outside the boundaries of their jurisdiction. *Who did they think they were? The worldwide morality police?* There were limits to how many people they could control.

Then it dawned on me. My leaders were extremely naive. *Could those promptings that encouraged me to come here have been as much about their need to listen as mine to speak up?* Because I was a downtrodden divorcee and knew about others who were struggling, perhaps the Lord wanted me to help enlighten these men about a few things.

I started with the Danville Singles Ward. I told them I had attended the Bay Area Ward a few times and described the weekly confession line, how it snaked down the hallway from the bishop's office, spilling into the parking lot. I bravely let them know that if Bishop Clark decided to take court action every time a lonely divorcee committed some type of transgression, there'd be no one left in the congregation.

I don't think they liked what I had to say. But I didn't regret sharing any of it. I said my piece. It was up to them whether to receive it.

As I looked across the table from them, they remained stiff in their chairs, except for the occasional throat clearing. Still no smiles. Clearly, they were unmoved after learning about the sweet, forgiving bishop in the East Bay.

Moments before their deliberation, I made one last attempt to clear my name by proceeding with my own personal story. I hoped to move them, not necessarily to tears, because these men were quite stoic, but in hopes to touch them in some way. I vividly described the details of my divorce—how the priesthood leader of our family whom I had wholeheartedly trusted, scammed me out of my parental custody rights and would not even allow me to step foot in his new home to see my children.

I confessed that my foolish, bleeding heart for my kids moved me to bypass the filing of court-ordered alimony, resulting in my financial and emotional struggles. I even explained that I had gone to my former bishop and asked for church assisted counseling, only to be turned down.

Four sets of eyes locked onto me as I continued to talk, then blinked in unison. Each of them nodded their heads to appear compassionate. One of them had even shared with me that he understood my pain. Yet, their body language told me a different story as they folded into themselves.

Did they see me as nothing more than a pathetic drama queen? I didn't really know them well enough to judge them. But these men had no special training in the ministry as is required of religious leaders outside the Mormon faith. They seemed completely clueless about how to listen with compassion and flustered about how to handle the information I gave them.

Bishop York took over from there and asked me if I understood the severity of my sin. I said I did, to save peace. Inwardly, I was feeling indignant, but I was gathering my strength. No way was I going to be nailed to a cross without a fight. So I spoke up, my heart beating, a pulsating thump under my blouse.

"I don't mean to disrespect any of you," I asserted, "but in Romans 3:23, the apostle Paul states: 'For all have sinned and fall short of the glory of God." That means we are all sinners." My eyes were glued to theirs and didn't flinch as I spoke with assurance. For once, the entire bishopric was at a loss for words. The ward clerk reached to scratch the folds of his double chin. "Yes, true … we are all sinners, he said. "But we have not sinned to the degree you have."

I beg your pardon? My unspoken reaction burned hot in my mind. My nerves jangled in counterpoint to his sanctimonious words. I immediately threw back my shoulders, and all at once took on a confidence I didn't know I possessed. Looking each one of them in the eye, I boldly reminded them that they had not lost their families, nor had they been tested to the degree I had been tested.

After my projection, the room fell to a hush and the clock ticked louder in the silence. I knew they would have to choose their words carefully or not say anything at all. They decided to choose the latter. Maybe I came across to them as a self-righteous "Miss Defiant," but that wasn't my intent. Beneath the tabletop, my fingers trembled uncontrollably. I was on the edge, about to burst into tears. I could only hope I had been understood.

It was the bishop who finally broke the silence with a practical solution. "I think we need to take this matter to the Lord," he said, his voice gentle, his eyes greener than the plastic fern standing against the back wall.

"Great idea," I murmured under my breath. "The Lord knows my heart far better than you do."

They left me in the room alone so they could deliberate and then pray to determine their next move: to forgive and encourage me, or to discipline me with an appropriate degree of harshness. *Would I be disfellowshipped? Excommunicated?* I had no idea. It was completely out of my control. It was in their hands.

CHAPTER 54

IF CHRIST WERE HERE

With the men in another room praying and deliberating, I felt relieved to finally find myself alone. I dropped my head to the hardwood table and covered it with my hands, letting out a slow, staggered breath. A gazillion thoughts rushed through me as my feverish face rested on the cool wood. *Why did I let Vanilla John in my house?* I wanted and needed to be loved again, but I didn't want to keep making the same mistakes with men who meant nothing to me. I silently prayed that my leaders could sense my genuine remorse and extend understanding and compassion.

Sooner than expected, I heard the slow creak of the door down the hall and the sound of footsteps returning. They'd been deliberating for only fifteen minutes. I nervously fingered my jewelry while bouncing my crossed leg on my knee.

As much as I believed in the Lord and His church, my unmet expectations had left me thoroughly disappointed with its leaders. Why couldn't Bishop York discern that I was a good person who loved my Heavenly Father? I would have had no motivation to confess if this were not so. Couldn't he look into my eyes and see what I'd been through? Extending a calling to me would have been my best chance for healing and moving forward. But he was too busy following the handbook.

While none of the men were mean or cruel, neither did they seem able to empathize sufficiently with my many challenges. *But how could I expect them to?* They were required to follow a one-size-fits-all religious bylaw, a "black-and-white" rulebook for disciplining members without much liberty to delve into "the grays" and allow for a broader perspective.

Still, the question begs to be answered: How can any human being accurately judge another when each is a product of circumstances, experience, personality, past trauma, and so much more? *And what about mercy and grace? Where does that come in?* Perhaps this group of men who'd been appointed to judge me were concerned about being disciplined themselves by those above them in power and authority. These were my thoughts as I sat alone in a cold room waiting for them to deliberate, feeling far too hurt to empathize with their difficult position.

Soon, the gentlemen were settled in their chairs again, their eyes fixed on me, ready to deliver the results of their deliberation. The room's large dark-wood table was about three feet wide. I sat with my arms folded in my lap, my back pressed into my chair, my eyes averted to avoid their stares. They had jotted a few things on their yellow legal-sized pads, and I was curious as to what the Lord had told them about me. I hoped He had helped them remember His words to the woman taken in sin, "Neither do I condemn thee. Go and sin no more."

My heart beat wildly as Bishop York cleared his throat. I was now looking straight into his eyes, forcing myself to focus on the matter at hand. When he proceeded to tell me that none of them felt prompted to disfellowship or communicate me, my entire body went limp. Yet honestly, I wasn't all that surprised. God new my heart. He knew I had suffered enough. He had spoken up for me and answered their prayers.

Instead of being stripped of my membership, they chose to put me on church probation. With great relief and gratitude, I silently thanked the Lord for being my advocate. Church probation was the lightest of the possible discipline measures, but it still meant I was not allowed to say public prayers, nor be assigned a calling, nor partake of the Sacrament. (much like communion). I hated being called upon to say prayers, so that was actually a welcome reprieve, but it didn't make sense that I would be prohibited from serving in my ward. A church calling was exactly what I needed. Having the opportunity to fellowship with other ward members while serving them would have certainly helped me focus on my worth rather than my shame.

The bishop's first counselor spoke up and told me my spiritual progress would be evaluated over the next few months. He said if I needed anything, to just ask. Instinctively, I knew I needed fellowship with the saints to progress spiritually and emotionally. But they had made their decision, according to the church guidelines, and I didn't want to challenge them.

After the church court adjourned, the bishop walked me to the door and asked if I had any other questions or concerns. That was my chance. I told him I had just one. I immediately swung around and fixed my gaze on the two counselors and the clerk sitting across the table, then deliberately turned to look at the bishop. After a slow exhale, I proceeded.

"I just want you gentlemen to understand that if Jesus were in this room tonight, He would have wrapped his arms around me and wept with me and shown me a heckuva lot more compassion." I then blinked to fight back the tears, turned around, and walked out.

IF CHRIST WERE HERE

I strived to live the Gospel,
Shackling the throes of vanity.
Admonished to marry quickly
To a man who stole my sanity.
Was reprimanded and scolded
When presenting my latest sin.
They held a court for my actions
Not knowing my anguish within.
Hot tears upon the hot seat.
Lost, alone, and confused.
They cast their stones and judged me,
Still sinners, yet they accused.
I let them know if Christ were here
He'd set the story straight.
He'd lift the blinders from their eyes
To see my depleted state.
He'd teach that charity comes first—
Compassion conquers all.
He'd do away with courts like these
That judge me for "my fall."
And then He'd take me in His arms,
He'd weep with me and pray.
Without condemning, my dear Lord
Would wash my sins away.

CHAPTER 55

BISHOP ROULETTE

A few days after my humiliating church hearing, while in the shower, I had what I call "a shower rush" —a moment of clarity. All at once, it dawned on me that any decision that had been made to determine the consequences of my sin was largely dependent on one man and his opinion—my bishop.

Think about it. Church members can be deemed worthy or unworthy, innocent or guilty, set free or excommunicated, or get this— not sent to church court at all, depending on what ward or stake they attend. I've since learned that congregates call this kind of randomness, "leadership roulette."

No two bishops are alike. They all have different personalities, experiences, and personal prejudices. Some may be pharisaical—all about law, and others may gravitate to the "go and sin no more" adage. Although they are expected to go by the Handbook, and the great majority do, it blows my mind to think that something as profoundly significant as your membership—which members believe is the same as their eternal salvation, *can be largely* determined by the spin of a wheel, depending on where you live.

At that time of my life, I was too naive to consider that my bishop and his counselors would take so seriously a sin that I deeply regretted. But that's exactly what they did. It all started with a simple confession and ended with an eye-opening, reality check about how the church operates.

There is enormous pressure on local leaders to follow the Handbook. They are counseled to "cut out the cancerous sin" in ways that I felt were more destructive than helpful. I had to come to terms with the truth— that every church leader, including the Prophet, is just a man. All are fallible. After my church court experience, I was ready to take responsibility for myself. Let God be my judge and give no man the power to absolve or condemn me.

Oliver Huxley learned that lesson early on. He was not only a savvy player in the dating arena, but he knew church politics. He never voluntarily confessed his sins. Although he did stand up in Sacrament meeting and publicly apologized as Bishop Clark had requested, his apology was a far cry from direct. How would one publicly confess anyway? Was he supposed to say, "I'm so sorry for all you ladies out there whom I got naked with."?

In the wake of my church probation, I felt stained with sin. Every Sunday, I sat on the center pew imagining that everyone could see my proverbial Scarlet Letter. I was required to refuse the Sacrament when it was passed to me, and I knew some people would be imagining the worst. "Look at Jennifer, everyone. What nasty sins has she committed! Sucks to be her!"

I felt like an outsider looking in on those who were saintlier— those members whose privileges were not revoked. Yet according to the brethren, church hearings are courts of love. I didn't feel loved at all as I sat alone, marked as unworthy.

Despite being at odds with my church, my relationship with the Lord was airtight. I continued to pray diligently and read my scriptures.

I longed for a hiatus from what I saw as pharisaical judgment. Not wanting to feel like a castaway, I eventually filled my Sundays with other activities. Church no longer seemed important to me. Maybe someday I would try again …

CHAPTER 56

HAPPY AT KAPPY'S

As 1992 rolled around, three things were happening all at once—Bill Clinton was elected 42nd President of the US, America was voting for either a young or old Elvis Presley postage stamp, and I was finally moving up in the world. Four months after my deplorable church hearing, I finally had a reason to break out the Martinelli's. I had landed my dream job—a great way to welcome in the new year.

When Errol Kappy hired me to work at Kappy's Music, I was speechless. I just stood there, mouth gaping. *You want me?* Towering over me by at least six inches, he rendered an affectionate smile. That was the affirmation I needed. I knew that hiring an inexperienced worker like me was a big gamble. But in his mid-thirties, Errol was a self-confident, visionary risk-taker. *How could I be so lucky?* I wanted to shower him from head to toe with grateful kisses. But I held back. Errol was married.

It had been over a year since my separation, and I had an around-the-clock yen for the smell and taste of musky, leathery feral maleness. I craved the feel of a man. I craved a man's touch. I loved hearing the sound of a man's deep voice. That gold ring on Errol's finger kept him safe from a sex-crazed fiend like me. If he were single, I'd be flirting up a storm with him. He was everything I loved—tall, good-looking, confident, mysterious, and most of all, a dreamy musician. But I needed a job even more than love.

I was so remarkably ill-equipped to join the workforce. Besides teaching piano, I had few marketable skills to fall back on. That problem was not uncommon among women who grew up in the 60's, but it was especially true of LDS women. I grew up hearing church leaders admonish us often to prioritize marriage over an education. Choosing a career over stay-at-home motherhood was looked down upon. As a believing, obedient Mormon girl, my sole ambition was to be a Homemaker.

Since I stupidly signed away my custody rights thirteen months earlier, I no longer had the daily responsibilities and encumbrances of motherhood. The working world would welcome me, and I was ready to explore new horizons where I would become financially independent and self-sufficient.

I had a lot to learn about being a working girl in the corporate world. I had heard that there were hustlers out there like Dow Jones and Wally Street, men my ex-husband cursed for gambling away his money. *Would I have to watch out for those types?*

Thrust into a world of bulky computer monitors, fax machines, and brick-sized mobile phones, I had no secretarial skills. But about a year prior to Errol hiring me, I had shown some aptitude. I had weeded out my competition by selling parents on the idea that I would offer piano lessons in their home. My marketing strategy and willingness to push myself to leave my apartment and work late into the evenings resulted in a handsome payoff. I had saved enough money to upgrade my living conditions.

I now had a spacious, Merced apartment that shared walls with only one other tenant. There were only a few units like mine that stood in the center of the property. I got lucky, and one was available. Outside my front door was a plush green lawn with a majestic fountain. The sound of peace was strange at first. It replaced the noise of my pinging wall furnace, calmed my riddled anxieties, and assuaged my feelings of hopelessness. At last, everything seemed to be falling into place.

Errol, owner of Kappy's Music not only allowed me to work the sales floor leasing band instruments, he also promised me a decent commission if I could sell a piano or two. In addition, he signed me up as a piano teacher in a nice studio and promoted me through ads to grow my pool of students—all while taking only ten percent of my profits.

Into my third week at Kappy's, things were going so well that I just couldn't wipe the perpetual smile off my face. While dusting a Yamaha grand one afternoon, I couldn't contain my joy as it exploded in a tingling-bell like laughter. Alerted by the unusual sound of merriment in his store, Errol peaked around the corner of his office door. *Uh, oh.* With my hand over my mouth, I sucked in a breath as he shook his head of wavy chestnut hair and rendered an affectionate smile. *Phew!* If I lasted here a month, I might treat myself to a rib eye. Then it happened. One fine day, something far juicier than steak strolled into the store.

CHAPTER 57

UNCAGED & UNCLIPPED

Errol's store, a large, renovated warehouse was spacious and drafty but filled with life. I worked the front register with cute, young Garrison. He and I were leasing band instruments, and because I was fresh on the floor and hyped about my new job, I was eager to sell my first Yamaha grand. It wasn't every day that a customer walked into the store wanting to buy a piano, but I hoped it would happen in the next month or two.

Jayden and Ryder, both Red Bull junkies in their twenties, worked the back register in the demo room. As the pounding, wailing, and whistling sounds reverberated the store walls, I soaked up the cacophony. I felt at home with it. Kappy's Music was my Fairytale Wonderland. Kappy's was my family.

One morning, just when I thought my trick-or-treat bag was so full it might split, a seriously hot-looking Latino strolled into the store in a dark cotton T. He was a ravishing vision with bungee cords falling across his left shoulder and a piano dolly tucked under his right arm. I tried to keep my jaw hinged as he swaggered toward me. For sure he was heading in my direction. That is until he suddenly turned and disappeared into the storeroom. *Who is he?* I had never seen him before. That's when I realized he had to be the store's muscle.

A few days later I saw him again when ringing up some resin for a cello player. This time, he sauntered through the door without a piano dolly. After glancing my way, he flashed his pretty-boy smile. I punched in the sale, the drawer popped open, and the bell rang, "Cha-ching." I grinned back at him with a big, playful smile. I was flirting by way of the cash drawer. But I don't think he caught on. Again, he disappeared into the storeroom. Yet, within moments, he emerged and ambled toward me, his broad shoulders swaying to the rhythm of his walk. He was up-close and personal now. I was far better at long-distance flirting. I tried to stay calm, but my knees were shaking.

"Gonna get some lunch, does anyone want anything?" He looked at me and grinned, then turned his eyes toward my co-worker, Garrison, who was at the register with me. Garrison immediately put in his request for a double cheeseburger. *Why couldn't I speak up?* This Herculean hunk had me tongue-tied. He might have been a regular churchgoer for all I knew, but how could anyone with eyes that pretty be saintly? If he did go to church, he probably lived in a confession booth.

"One double-cheese; any other takers, going ... going." He was looking straight into my eyes. His arms with bulging veins were quite a distraction. Especially since I had never touched a man with arms like that. Not even close. "I'd like a hamburger please," I squeaked. That's all it took. Over a few lunch breaks, Mateo, my new heartthrob, pocketed my number.

One evening on my couch while chatting away about work, Mateo occasionally squeezed that place above my knee—just a friendly little squeeze. No big deal. But it sure sent my heart racing. I found myself patting his thigh when making a point. I just couldn't resist. It had been way too long since I had touched a man. Far too long since I had been kissed. And now this gorgeous young guy was sitting only inches away from me.

The fact that I was no longer married nor active in the Church evoked a sense of naughty excitement in me. But right while I was experiencing long forgotten inner-thigh twinges, Guilt showed up. *Not again.* As I looked beyond my handsome friend, there It was—standing in the shadows, staring at me with sad, haunting eyes. Guilt had surfaced to remind me of past choices and the shame that consumed me after making those choices.

Would I listen to Guilt's warning and kick Delicious Temptation out the door, or would I ignore the warning yet again? More importantly, I needed to determine when and if Guilt deserved a place at the table. I began to believe he was a figment of the purity culture mentality; but at other times, he seemed to sound an important warning that needed to be heard. The longer I was single, the more confusing the whole thing was. I was a divorced, lonely women in my sexual prime. Why should I deny myself such pleasure?

On the sofa across from me, my sexy friend had me dazed and confused. The unknown was before me—a complex, intricate world of question marks, crooked lines, and curves. In that moment, I believed I was ready to dismantle the old purity-obsessed Guilt and no longer pay heed to it. I couldn't wait to be spun into a world beyond the black and white.

In one wild, unexpected moment when things became awkwardly quiet, Mateo leaned in, threaded his hands through my auburn locks and drew me in for a kiss. It was a perfect kiss. It was a kiss that quieted my restless mind—the kind of kiss I had been longing for. I'd been struggling to find my place in the world for months, and with his kiss, I felt grounded. I felt airlifted. I felt all kinds of wonderful things.

My dark eyes, filled with desire, were a dead giveaway. They spoke the unspoken. Too late to act mysterious and coy. My tall, burly friend intuitively picked up on my tacit cues. All he had to do was charm me with his overly confident smile, and I knew that he knew I was smitten. With this ego-stroking affirmation, no doubt Mateo was ready to give me one helluva ride

I felt a hot friction rush through me as Mateo slowly brought his head down to mine for a sloppy, open-mouthed kiss. Wow. Such an unexpected turn on. My heart took off and hammered through my chest as our tongues tangoed like dancing flames.

We sunk into each other on the couch cushion and ended up on my soft, sandy-colored carpet. Straddling over me, Mateo gazed down at me, his dark-brown eyes filled with an intensity that continued to raise my heart rate. I impulsively reached up to brush the curls away from his eyes.

As my friend planted gentle kisses on my lips and nose and nibbled on my ears, he kept calling me "darling" while whimpering moans escaped my lips. There was a lot of below-the-waist pulsing and contorting as my skilled friend planted a trail of wet kisses down my neck and between the erogenous places above my collar bone. Mateo's mouth was warm and soft, and he smelled like the ocean mixed with lavender.

When he broke his rhythm of kisses, he sat up on his knees, clenching his sturdy thighs around my hips, raising a flirtatious brow. I knew what that brow lift meant. I was fully onboard this train, willing to go the full distance.

Lost in my own lust, I forcefully ripped off his cotton-T. Wow. I'd never seen a six-pack close-up before. At least not on someone so … I couldn't find the words. The race was on. We couldn't undress each other fast enough as we fumbled and flailed in the storm of our passion, jaws bumping in midair, tongues desperate to tango. We kissed, nibbled, groaned, and wailed.

I ended up on my back and tossed my last stitch of clothing to the floor. Mateo took one look at me, rolled toward me, and gently wrapped his legs around my hips, scanning my curves. "You're beautiful," he said, his voice a mere whisper, staring at me with tenderness in his eyes. I never once heard that word uttered from Gary's lips. It was the first time I had ever felt seen. I had to catch my breath as his long, slender fingers caressed the sensitive underside of my breasts and lifted them as to offer them up. *Oh, how I needed this.*

Unable to keep my hands off his chest, I finally broke away and leaned back to admire him properly, soaking up every glorious, sculpted inch of him. *So this is what a real man looks like without his clothes?* He was all male from his broad shoulders to his hefty thighs, to his gorgeous six pack, to his, … let's just say he was packing it. We paused to don protection before the fire burned out of control.

For over a decade, I was married to a man who was the complete opposite: dangerously thin, fair skinned, lacking vigor and vim. Yet I would never have left him had he not made life hell for me. And I never would have known this passionate, sun-kissed Latino, the kind of man on the covers of romance novels that some women only dream about. All my life, this is what I had been missing. Finally, in my late thirties, Mateo had walked through the door at Kappy's and into my life.

Out on my front lawn, a majestic fountain peacefully babbled as it arched across the verdant grass. Inside, the sounds were voracious as I adjusted to the feel of him, a slow, steady rhythmic thrust; until without warning, Mateo plowed full speed ahead, his body trembling and his energy surging into me and forcing me to scream out as I reached the top of the summit. A few beats later, he joined me, our wet, entangled bodies shaking and limp.

As I lay next to my lover with shallow breath and a racing heart, I no longer felt guilty or ashamed or unworthy. I felt satiated. I felt gloriously reborn. Why did it take so damn long to let my hair down and live a little? Having sex with Mateo seemed to be far grander than any heaven I had been chasing. *Did I really want to go back to church?* Mateo and I kept up our routine for about a week or two until I woke up from my short-sighted stupor. Even though I was no longer attending church, I still believed the Lord was watching over me. Yet my concerns went well beyond God-based fears. Deep down, not being in love with Mateo was what bothered me most. Although he was hotter than hell and much younger, he lived from day to day. And he wasn't very deep. So I bit the bullet and broke it off.

After hunting for "the one" for over a year and coming up empty-handed, I had finally given up the search. With no promise of a husband, celibacy no longer felt like a healthy option while in my sexual prime. I told myself I would date with the purpose of nurturing a friendship and connection, and if sex resulted from that, so be it. *Was I becoming more enlightened, or was I falling into the outer darkness of no return?*

Guilt never left for good. It would shout at me just for wanting sex. Sunday School lessons about how fornicators would end up in the lowest kingdom without genitals scared the bejeebers out of me. *Who wants to be neutered for all eternity?* This haunting reality put a damper on the peace I was hoping to achieve while exploring my brand-new world of choices. And my most fervent desire to marry never wavered, even though love seemed elusive.

I reasoned that if I couldn't have love, at least, I could be set free from puritanical rules. I just needed to decide what guidelines I would create for myself. The thought that I wasn't getting any younger was bothersome.

When I had met Jizz-in-the-Pants at the Eureka conference, my metaphorical yellow sun had turned to a pale orange. Now with my thirty-seventh birthday around the corner, I still didn't have anyone to call my own. A part of me still wondered if only a Mormon man could lead me toward salvation. Did that part of me still believe in princes and castles and Mormon temples and happily-ever-afters?

CHAPTER 58

A DIFFERENT KIND OF BATTLE

In the valley, it was an unusually hot day for March. And as the California oaks outside Kappy's storefront window kept the downtown strip mall shaded, I too, was playing it cool. I had emerged from a conservative world of no-no's and with my newfound freedom I'd sold three pianos. Not bad for the past three months. My commission checks were proof that I was good at my job, and the extra money boosted my confidence. I was discovering Jennifer all over again—The Jennifer who was no longer attending church.

As I stocked the front display-case with various supplies, my mind wandered, as it often did, to thoughts of my kids. My new place was fifteen minutes from them, farther away than I'd have liked, but things were good. Claire was now coming around. And when the boys visited, they seemed much happier in our improved living environment. No more grunge-yellow walls or funky toilets. Best of all, no roaches.

The display case was now fully stocked, and it was time to fetch a box of reeds from the warehouse and populate the empty hooks on the wall. Such mundane tasks left my brain free to reflect on other things, like how grateful I was for my beautiful apartment and wonderful job. I had come a long way in such a short time. It gave me pause as I considered how much my life had suddenly improved once I abandoned my Sunday pew and my Scarlet A.

My religion had always been my rock. But now as an inactive Mormon, there was one question that weighed heavily on my heart: Had my life-long Mormon beliefs anchored me to doctrines that would save me from life's treacherous seas? Or had my church been the anchor that had been dragging me down to dark waters where I was drowning in ignorance? Perhaps both were true. Since the day of my disciplinary hearing, I had begun questioning everything.

My experience with the church court had me believing I was a despicable sinner for having given into temptation. I had tried to be a good girl and had resisted many temptations and even refused opportunities to date members and non-members alike who had questionable intentions. I was weak and so very lonely, and although that's no excuse for putting myself in harm's way, it didn't seem right that at church I was defined by my weak moments rather than by many years of strong ones.

I was beginning to realize that being an avid rule follower was making me feel powerless. I was letting others take control of my life. I was struggling hard and falling short. Mostly, I was feeling pressured to meet a standard of perfection beyond my reach. All of it was utterly exhausting.

Now that I had left my church and was working at Kappy's, I felt fresh and alive. Yet I was facing a different kind of battle. As I began replenishing the shelves with accessories, I examined my present situation. Since my absence from church, I'd had more time to think about what I wanted and needed, and about the values I would choose to guide my life. It was time to do some thoughtful reprogramming so that Guilt and I could live together in peace and harmony.

Before leaving the fold, I practiced abstinence because I believed God expected me to, but after having experienced a cold-hearted, compassionless church court, I didn't know what to believe anymore. My leaders never once praised me or gave me kudos for showing strength while my life was crumbling around me.

Now I was immersed in a work environment that was teeming with testosterone-filled energy. As Kappy's only female worker, I was surrounded by hot guys, including my boss. Young, cute, musically talented, the entire store was a sex advertisement. If I wanted to maintain my old-fashion values, this was hardly the right place for me, a lonely woman in my prime. I had a feeling that my life was about to get either very exciting or very dangerous. Or both.

I was supposed to be taking my job seriously. I needed to stay focused. I needed to take pride in stocking the shelves. Instead, I kept thinking back to the time when I had sex with Mateo. That hot herculean helped me to discover that talking, laughing, and connecting was the foreplay I'd been missing in my marriage. And it wasn't just because Mateo had the body of a Greek God, although that sure didn't hurt.

Now that I had finally discovered what had been missing in my life, I no longer wanted to deprive myself. Breaking away from the confines of my Mormon bubble challenged me to navigate my new world without religious rules and restrictions. Growing up in a purity culture where I was bombarded with reminders not to partake of "the candy," had me thinking about the candy even more. It wasn't just my loneliness that had propelled me onto my determined path to find "the one," although being alone was a huge part of it. But it was the "candy" I was craving. The longer I denied myself, the more obsessed I became.

Even though Mateo wasn't the right guy for me, our friendship and physical intimacy temporarily relieved my tension and loneliness. I concluded that if I didn't find love soon, perhaps friendship sex would at least help alleviate the emptiness. It was better than nothing. After all, I deserved it. At least that's what I told myself. There was just one problem: I had no idea how dating was done outside the church.

Still lost in reverie, I tossed a box of resin in the display case, when Garrison, my co-worker, interrupted my thoughts. "Hey Jennifer, would you mind grabbing a clarinet in the storeroom for this young lady while I go over her rental contract?" Garrison and I worked the front register together leasing band instruments. He was always proper and cordial. And he could multitask. I depended on him to teach me the ropes.

After I retrieved the encased instrument from the storeroom and placed it on the counter, my cute young coworker stopped what he was doing, looked me square in the eye, and thanked me. Of all the guys in my life, he was at present the one most responsible for setting my loins on fire. When we worked side by side, I couldn't help myself. He smelled like fresh pine and expensive soap. A nerdy polymath with a five o'clock-shadow, Garrison was brilliant like my dad. He was also my hero when it came to balancing the cash drawer.

Over the months, my coworker and I got to know each other quite well. My friend's disheveled bangs looked as though he had forgotten to give them a comb sweep before coming to work. Was his active, preoccupied mind the reason? I liked the way he looked. His fly-away curls and sweet demeanor screamed adorable. But Garrison was unavailable. He had a girlfriend. Still, that didn't stop me from dreaming.

To get my mind off what I couldn't have, I tried to fall back on my church's advice. I counted my blessings and named them one by one, as suggested by Hymn #153 in the Mormon hymnal. My blessings started with Errol's advertising. Thanks to him, my students had grown from five to twenty-five in only four months. I also had been growing a savings account from the commission I earned from selling a few pianos. Yep. I was slowly but surely working my way toward success in the business world. It felt beyond gratifying.

Near the end of April, one more blessing popped up unexpectedly. Garrison and his girlfriend called it quits. Now that he was officially back on the market, it was an opportunity I couldn't let it slide. I wasn't about to let the fact that he was twelve-years younger keep me from making my big move. If I only knew how to make one.

At five-foot-ten, Garrison was beautifully fit. And I was always a sucker for a nerd, especially a cute one. Having worked with him for months, I felt I knew him pretty well. He was grounded with a strong sense of self. He had long-term goals. He knew how to have fun. He even played the cornet in a military marching band. Best of all—he was a deep thinker. I mean, really deep. When it came to relationships, Garrison was not a player. He was a gentleman. A kind, sensitive twenty-four-year-old. Which meant if I married him at age thirty-six, I'd probably never have to be a widow.

I certainly wasn't going to ask him out. That just wasn't my style. Thank God I got a lucky break when our coworker Jayden did something that made me want to hug him. *Who would have ever thought that a twenty-two-year-old Red Bull junkie would be my hero?*

CHAPTER 59

RIGHT GUY, WRONG TIME

Perhaps Jayden was playing cupid. Not wanting to attend his cousin's high school concert alone, he asked Garrison and me if we'd like to tag along. The two of us were single. We both had no night life. Why not?

The coolest thing that happened that evening besides not hearing a single squeak from a flute or clarinet, was that Jayden left directly after the concert. Although ecstatic to be alone with Garrison, I had no idea how to banter with him outside the store. Lucky for me, he took the initiative to suggest going for ice-cream. As we licked our cones, his eyes lit up when he shared his love for astronomy, history and music. While crunching down his cone, he even winked at me a few times. These subtle gestures gave me hope that perhaps my feelings for him were not one-sided. After our impromptu date, Garrison dropped me off at my place. Like I said—a perfect gentleman.

Soon we realized that eating dinner was so much more fun together than alone. Since we were both on a budget, McDonald's, Wendy's, and Domino's Pizza were our favorite go-to places. Sometimes we took the food back to his place and set it on his coffee table which was made from a slab of wood held up by two orange crates. The guy was a broke spring chicken gravid with potential.

After closing time one night, we were the only ones left in the store, when Garrison slapped me on the shoulder and said, "You're it!" The chase was on. After I led him on a high-speed pursuit around several grand pianos, he pushed me into a tall, flimsy music stand. I fell into it backside first and my behind smacked it so hard that the stand cracked in half. As stacks of sheet music went flying across the floor, I lost my footing and fell onto the carpet. Garrison immediately joined me. We were like two high school kids that couldn't contain our laughter.

From that day forward, he gave me a name I proudly wore: "Boney Butt." My caboose was anything but boney, but if he saw that ample part of me as thin, I gladly went along.

Back at his place, we had just finished dinner and were sitting in front of his custom-built coffee table, when he reached across it, cranked the dial on his bubble-gum-machine centerpiece, and popped a candy ball into both our mouths.

As we chewed our gum, he threw me off guard when he spontaneously scooped me up and carried me off to his king-size floor mattress. We were laughing as he dumped me onto the sheets, my limbs in disarray.

When Garrison dropped on his knees beside me, all at once the room fell to a hush, and I let out a nervous giggle. With a slightly raised brow, he graced me with a smile that spoke of safety, comfort, and reassurance. I exhaled slowly, and knew I was in the exact place I had been longing to be for some time.

Eyeing me with deep emotion, Garrison energetically swept me onto his lap as if I were a weightless, precious rag doll. As I rested my head on his shoulder, I felt my heart pounding against my ribcage. Then he leaned over and tugged me closer for a quick kiss that soon turned into a longer one, his bubble-gum breath lingering on my tongue.

This was the most connected I had felt with any man since my divorce. My breath was slow and labored as my friend's soft tongue tickled the shell of my ear, his teeth gently nipping at my lobe; and just like that, all the tension between us that had been bottled up from months of working beside each other suddenly bubbled over.

Garrison pulled me closer for a rough kiss and then another—fierce assaults on my mouth that instigated a succession of vocally expressive wails that I could no longer hold back. I lavished him with more kisses while anchoring my hands in his disheveled hair, then lightly tugged at his lower lip with my teeth while he kissed my mouth, my jaw, and the column of my throat. He nibbled the hollow between my breasts before ripping off my top. That was the night we made love.

It wasn't until that very evening that I learned my coworker had it going on for me, or that he was capable of being so romantic. That night, he revealed his tender side. He revealed his inner animal. I had a yen for both the good boy and the bad boy. I couldn't get enough.

As time passed, I soon developed deep feelings for him. I loved the way his eyes danced when he read a dessert menu. The way he'd raise one brow at me when passing me in the store. And the way he'd grab my hand in public, then let go and walk ahead of me just to see what I'd do. At times when I felt lost and confused, he'd tease me with a cheesy grin and say, "Hey, kiddo, there's always cheeese-cake." His goofiness had a way of easing my anxieties.

By day, my hot coworker and I rented band instruments. By night, we synchronized our rhythm to the backbeat of DeVoe's "Poison." Those were the good times.

In the wee morning hours before work, I'd often pop in to see him. He needed coffee. I needed a Garrison fix. I'd meet him at the door with a hot styrofoam cup and barely have a chance to set it down before he'd whisk me into his arms. With my legs locked around his hips, he'd carry me to his floor mattress and lower me down. Unclothed, our bodies tucked into each other's so perfectly. And as he etched his fingers around the globe of my breasts, he looked at me with affection.

As we pleasured each other, he would call out my name in a way that made it sound holy. Yet I never felt worthy of his praise. Burying my face in his neck, I tried to bury my insecurities as well. I met each steady grind with loud wails, yet a silent cry inside insisted I was undeserving of him.

Through the years, Gary had stomped out every bit of my self-worth. Such were my thoughts as Garrison and I made love. With his repeated thrusts, perhaps my lover could pound self-worth right back into me. As a gold-foiled square lay torn and empty on the carpet, I hung on for the ride, grateful for my friend's stamina, hoping I could pretend to feel worthy just a little longer.

When Garrison told me he was an atheist, I couldn't understand how someone so sweet and kind and good could not believe in Heavenly Father. As an intellectual, he saw supernatural beings as mythical manmade constructs. I saw God as a white-bearded Daddy in the sky who smiled down on me and listened to my every prayer.

With great enthusiasm, I told Garrison about my special moment when singing in the temple-pageant as a teen, how I heard a heavenly choir joining in song as the spirit of God burned within me. Garrison insisted that many people of all faiths have had those same spiritual experiences of visions and feelings of ecstasy and heavenly peace. He sure shot down my moment.

My intellectual friend searched for truth differently than I did. When he told me he needed empirical evidence, I didn't even know what that meant. In my world, truth was confirmed by spiritual feelings. I sang with angels. The Spirit spoke to my soul. At least that's what I'd been taught.

Even though I was an inactive church member and wasn't wearing my sacred underwear, I still believed in the Golden Plates, magic stones, and in an afterlife where I participated in the divine baby-making process of creation with my polygamist husband. No doubt I looked ridiculous to someone as erudite as Garrison.

As much as we liked each other, my lover and I were worlds apart in the way we saw the very foundation of our existence. We decided it wouldn't work for the long haul. How could we make it as a team if our life's philosophies were on opposite ends of the spectrum? We had hit a wall.

If I hadn't been so indoctrinated, who knows? It might have led to something great. Garrison could have been the wild card I'd been looking for all along.

CHAPTER 60

I DIDN'T START THE FIRE

It had only been a month since Garrison and I had broken it off. And now a different man, a taller, broader-shouldered man was now sitting on my couch, whimpering like a child. How could this be happening? I tossed him one tissue after another, as fast as I could pull them out of the box, some landing on his face. Even *I* looked like I was about to burst into tears. "Is there anything I can do?" I asked helplessly, my sing-song chirp almost too chirpy. I couldn't stand to see a grown man cry. Especially someone I admired so much.

I tried to reassure him that he'd be okay, but honestly, I just wanted to throw my arms around him and never let go, but that would have been inappropriate. The man who was flooding my couch with his tears *was Errol, my boss.*

How did he end up on my living room sofa in the first place? It all started in the store after work one day when I asked if I could pay him to help me learn how to run my music software. When he filled in some calendar space for me, I was overjoyed. Technically savvy and musically gifted, that man could make a chainsaw sing.

Only fifteen minutes after his arrival that night, Errol had fixed all my issues and had even given me a crash course on software basics. Now I could start writing music again. How easy my life would be if I was married to the man. The truth was that I had been secretly in love with my boss for some time. His wife, a woman I fiercely envied, worked the payroll at Kappy's. But now, Errol was crying on my couch. My software problems had been fixed. Now I just needed to know how to put my boss back together.

The moment he entered my apartment, our conversation went from music to computer software to a men's weekend retreat from which he had just returned home. Then he burst into tears after mumbling something about his wife. With a pillow over his face, his head shook to the rhythm of his sobs. I finally gently reached over and took the cushion from him. His eyes were glossy-red and swollen. "What about your wife?" I asked, longing to cradle his neck and bury his face in the comfort of my soft bosom.

With my continued encouragement, he eventually let it all out. Through all his blubbering I managed to distinguish most of his words as he attempted to explain his distress. The bottom line—his wife had been cheating on him for years. I just couldn't believe it. I sat there with a gaping jaw then threw another mountain of tissues in his lap.

I couldn't help but notice his dejected look and the misaligned buttons and funky gaps that dipped and rose down the center of his shirt. He was a mess. It broke my heart to see him this way. *How could his wife be so heartless? And why hadn't he left her?* Errol was obviously a broken man, and I felt helpless to do anything but toss him tissues.

When I got up to fetch my boss a glass of water, suddenly a pillow grazed my head. It was Errol's way of trying to lighten the mood. I caught on, grinned, and tossed it right back. After setting the tumbler of water on the end table, he instantly grabbed me and pulled me onto his lap. I immediately froze. "What are you doing, Errol?" I scolded him while scooting a few feet away from him on the couch cushion. "You're married!" I said indignantly.

My boss quickly apologized, but in his confused state, tugged me closer. *Was all his blubbering just a ruse to get sympathy so he could have his way with me?* I knew I didn't belong to him. Still, I didn't pull away either. This moment was something that had happened many times, but only in my dreams.

Although his bloodshot eyes looked like they'd seen the worst the world could offer, my boss was beautiful to me. His shaggy unkempt curls and "lost puppy dog" look made him even more pathetically endearing. In the silence, I tucked my head under his chin, and felt his weight settle into me. No words were needed as we rocked each other in the silence.

On the outside everything was calm. On the inside my mind was spinning in a thousand different directions. *What on earth was I doing?* At that moment, Errol had his nose in my hair, and he dropped his voice and told me how nice it smelled and how good I felt in his arms. I breathed in the scent of his Beech Nut Fruit Stripe gum as my heart accelerated. Before I could even register what was happening, his quivering lips fell to meet mine. In that one moment, the nagging guilt that had been sloshing around in my head immediately dissipated. Everything that felt so wrong, all at once, felt so right.

I looked up at him, my eyes filled with desire, and as I traced my fingers along the outline of his mouth, he nibbled on them. We stayed put for a while, just the two of us simply taking in the silence.

Although Errol was a total wreck, and needed comfort, I felt the guilt creeping up again. *Why couldn't I allow both of us to feel happy, even but for a small moment?* In the same way I felt at home at Kappy's, I felt at home with Errol. Granted, I didn't see my boss as a typical guy. Between us there was more than a physical attraction. Our heart-to-heart connection went back about three years before I started working for him.

When I first ran into Errol, I was still married to Gary. I entered Kappy's one day looking for a guitar capo. Errol happened to be demoing a Yamaha grand, and as I edged my way toward him, he turned his head and spotted me. His eyes were half-closed, his dreamy gaze fixed on me. I never had a man look at me the way he did. It was as though he were saying, "We belong together." *Was this love at first sight?*

In a beat, he became one with the melody again. He wasn't reading a musical score. The song was flowing from his heart to his fingertips, and never in my life had I heard anything so hauntingly beautiful. That was the day I discovered we shared an unspoken language.

Every time I ran into him after that, he would look at me that same way. His eyes, half-closed, dreamy and seductive. He made me feel like the most beautiful woman on earth. We didn't need to say anything. Our connection was cemented by the glow of the same melody within us. Then one day, he hired me to work in his store.

Now here we were huddled on my couch. But I had to get a grip. Errol did not belong to me. He belonged to someone else—an unfaithful wretch who didn't deserve him. At least that's what he led me to believe. And I knew one thing. I may have bedded two of his employees, but I was no adulteress.

I glanced down at the couch pillow, then glanced upward. He was looking at me in that same way when he first laid eyes on me. His "I love you" misty blues sent a hot surge through my cheeks. After years of imagining this scenario, here we were in each other's arms. *If only he didn't have that stupid ring on his finger.*

Somehow, I mustered the strength to send him home before we ended up doing something stupid. After working for Errol for five months, I wasn't about to blow it. We needed to maintain a professional relationship if I wanted to keep my job.

During the few short months I'd been working for Errol (before he ended up on my couch), I would often ask if I could pay him for a one-on-one songwriting course. He kept stalling. Then one evening, when business slowed, he emerged from his office, quietly bidding me to follow him. After lowering himself on the bench of one of his shiny Yamahas, he invited me to join him.

"Close your eyes," he said. "Now let your heart lead." He then began to play. I followed suit as our four hands intertwined in and out and around each other's, giving birth to a glorious tapestry of notes that only moments before, had never breathed life.

As I write this memoir, three decades have passed, but the magic of that moment has not faded. I play my own song now, just the way he once taught me, and blink back the tears as the music swirls from my fingertips, eager to write its own story.

What made Errol different from most men? His energy flowed through me and still does. His melodies are like Debussy's, only more emotional. His music is impressionist art. When I close my eyes and listen, I can still hear his waterfall of notes trailing through pink pastels and soft periwinkles.

On my couch that night, after we had expressed our feelings for each other, working at Kappy's grew more impossible. I didn't start the fire, but no matter how much I tried to extinguish it, the flames would leap and dance around us whenever we passed each other on the sales floor.

Sometimes I'd spot him through his office window and catch him gazing at me in that mesmerized way. And each time, my stomach would leap into my throat. We didn't need words to communicate. His penetrating gaze said it all. But a few days after we bonded on my couch, I sensed a sadness in his eyes. I too, was a mess.

One day, when business in the store slowed, I pulled Errol aside. I couldn't keep up the charade and told him so. Damn him anyway. He was always in my head. I was no longer sleeping or eating. I could no longer think straight or concentrate on my work. I wanted to slap him hard across the face and then smother him with my kisses. I hated him and loved him at the same time. *Why did he grab me on my couch? Why did I pity him when he cried? How dare he make me fall harder for him!*

After having known the joy of being in this man's arms and feeling his love, I didn't know how I could ever live my life without him. I believed we were soul mates. And although I would never allow myself to commit adultery, I was yearning to hold him one last time. *Would he agree to meet somewhere?*

CHAPTER 61

OUT OF THE FIRE INTO THE FRYING PAN

Errol knew he had made a mistake. From the time I first walked into his store to purchase a capo, we both felt that instant, undeniable spark. Considering how broken his marriage was, I was surprised he didn't strike the match sooner. But now that the flame had been lit, I was a mess. So, he agreed to meet me in an obscure parking lot after work. From there, we drove to a touristy, over-glamorized diner off Interstate 5.

When arriving at the noisy diner, we slipped into an empty booth. From there, I wasted no time and jumped at the chance to speak my mind, holding nothing back. With tears in my eyes, I rattled on about my sleep deprivation and how I couldn't stop thinking about him and how I was a big ball of nerves. Of course, I blamed everything on *him*. He sat across from me, a shadow passing over his eyes, taking my hits like a trooper.

I blew my nose into a napkin—a napkin that I managed to slip out from beneath my silverware without flipping my knife, fork or spoon to the floor, which for clutzy me, was a miracle. I guess this was my lucky night—or not—as my napkin pile continued to rise.

Although Errol revealed that he hadn't been on speaking terms with his wife and had been sleeping on the couch, he assured me it had nothing to do with me nor did she know anything about us. He had to be a wreck from the stress of his marriage; if he was, he masked it with a warm, reassuring smile— a look that intensified as I continued to blow my nose—a look of adoration. Perhaps his wife never showed him any kind of emotion. Maybe instead of seeing a napkin pile in front of me, he saw a heap of devotion.

When Errol unexpectedly reached across the table and clutched my trembling hand, all at once, that unrelenting ache to belong to him melted away. The feeling of my hand in his allayed the paralyzing guilt that had been festering inside me for days. After thirty-seven years on the planet, I had finally found this beautiful connection.

Errol seemed to be made for me—as if a witch brewed a love potion using special ingredients creating a fantasy so perfect, that I'd never yearn for anyone other than him. He was the whole package, except for the shiny band on his finger that flashed "not available!" After all those years, to finally discover he had been secretly admiring me, too, made me dizzy. Now his wife just needed to dump him for good so that all my dreams would come true.

If Errol had a solid marriage, Guilt would serve a purpose. But if what he had told me were true—if his wife didn't value him enough to honor her vows, this was no marriage. How could it be wrong for him to leave her and seek happiness with someone who appreciated him? As I sat there with his hand on mine, I prayed he would grasp the reality that I was willing to commit my life to his happiness.

"I can't believe I'm about to ask you this," he said, his fingers caressing my hand. He didn't save to say a thing. That dumb-in-love grin on his face said it all. Could I live with myself if I said yes? ...

CHAPTER 62

MAKING LOVE WITH MY HEART

"Would you spend the night with me?" There was a quiver in Errol's voice as he nervously probed my face. He sounded like a frightened child in urgent need of comfort. The intensity in his eyes made my heart beat a little faster. I loved him, and my bones quivered at the thought of holding him in my arms. I didn't even have to think about my answer.

"Okay," I whispered, hoping the couple in the booth beside us weren't busy bodies. "But one rule. No sex." I was firm about that. Errol's radiant smile confirmed we were on the same page. Sex or no sex, his face immediately softened. He was a Christian man. Because we both knew what we were planning was wrong in the eyes of God, we established a line over which we promised we would not cross, perhaps hoping to make it feel a little "less wrong."

When we entered the hotel suite, Errol asked if I'd like to shower with him. I had never taken a shower with any man before, not even my husband, so I responded with a nervous giggle.

The pianist who played the songs I carried in my heart used those same adroit fingers to gently work the soapsuds into my wet locks. I arched my back, as one gorgeous melody melted into another, his hands softly swirling mounds of warm suds along my head. Soft foam drifted down my neck as he wrapped me in his burley arms. Pulling away just enough to caress my face with both his hands, he lowered his head until his lips met mine in a perfect kiss. This man was a healer.

Now it was my turn to be a healer. As I lathered up his back, the water danced around us like laughing rain. Through the frosted glass, two shadows became one as Errol covered my body with kisses. Could there be a feeling more intimate, more beautiful than this?

After we towel-dried each other's hair, my sexy lover eased me onto the bedsheet and swept the wet mop of dark-red curls from my eyes. I reached to caress his face and couldn't help noticing how happy he looked. He was glowing. Gently placing my hands on both sides of his face, I guided him down to me, kissing him again and again.

We didn't go all the way. I know. Sounds hard to believe, but I believed that having intercourse with a man who was married to someone else was the defining step that would make me an adulteress, and that was not who I wanted to be. Errol never pushed the matter. He told me he was elated just being with me.

We were probably the oddest couple on the planet. We honestly didn't need intercourse to feel satisfied. Don't get me wrong. We were both wildly attracted to each other. My sexy boss told me I was the most beautiful thing he ever laid eyes on, and I was physically enamored with him as well. He looked like that dreamy guy who sang to me from the windblown curtain in the 60's Wind Song perfume commercials. But even better, we had an attraction that went beyond the physical. Our emotional connection ran deep—so deep that it felt as though we were making love with our hearts and not with our bodies. I had never experienced that kind of connection with any man.

Errol and I had almost too much to say as we cuddled and talked till the wee hours of the morning. I barely slept, yet I felt so high I was almost in tears. For the first time in my life, I had made love to a man with my heart, mind, and soul without him physically entering my body; yet I had never felt so satisfied.

At around 4:00 a. m. I finally drifted off to sleep only to awaken two hours later to find "my soulmate" sipping his coffee and reading the front-page news of the Gustine Press. He pulled the paper down just long enough to wink at me. When he offered me coffee and I refused, he learned that good little Mormon girls don't drink coffee or tea. They just sleep with their bosses if they get lonely enough.

Squinting my eyes, I examined him in the shadows as the sun sliced through the cracks in the blinds and lay in bright lines on the floor. Donned in a white shirt, gray slacks, and polished penny loafers, this dedicated entrepreneur had a store to open. Everything about him, his dusty brown untamed curls, his quiet stance, the way his one leg rested on his knee as he sipped from his cup, made me want to eat him up. He was married, but I was too head-over-heels in love to walk away, especially knowing that his wife had been unfaithful throughout their entire fifteen-year marriage. I convinced myself that he never really belonged to her in the first place. Not really.

As we jumped into his Dodge Viper and headed for CA-140 E, one of my most indelible memories was now in the rearview mirror. I warmed my hands against the low, rumbling heater and watched my boss go into his mental man cave. A few miles later, he looked over at me and told me that he had always dreamed of opening a music store in Florida and wanted to know if I would build that dream with him.

"Really? Are you serious?" That was my response. I saw him as more of a rational planner. He was the kind of guy who would schedule a visit to the DMV a year in advance, making sure he carried a hearty supply of water and high-calorie food bars in preparation for a long wait.

"So, what do you think?" he asked again. I wasn't convinced he was serious. I reasoned that he was acting irrationally—that he'd been swept up in the emotion of the night. We needed to live in the real world, not in some fairyland-romance novel. "It sounds too good to be true." I stammered.

Then I saw it. A tear trickled down his cheek. A memory of the night he pulled me onto his lap and kissed me for the very first time came flooding back. I admired his ability to show emotion. To me, he was more of a man because he *could* cry. And I knew why he was crying. Florida wasn't going to happen. His life was far too complicated.

CHAPTER 63

JET PLANE TOWARD REDEMPTION

Reality is a bitch sometimes. And I was feeling it. Just because I knew Florida would never happen, didn't mean I couldn't dream. By the time my boss and I met in secret again, this time at my place, Guilt had caught up with me once again, and I knew we couldn't go on this way. It wasn't right. But this was the night that would change everything. He shared with me that he was planning to leave his wife. My relief was palpable. I was absolutely giddy.

He also revealed that Kappy's was having some money problems, and he planned to announce an employee meeting to discuss how to save the store. Wow. I had no idea. And since he and his wife worked side by side, he felt it would be appropriate to give everyone a heads up regarding the coming dissolution of his marriage. Inside I was doing a little jig.

Two days later, the meeting took place. As the employees gathered, he announced that a separation was in the works. I was secretly thrilled. I knew this was a big step for him, and I honestly thought he might chicken out at the last minute. His public announcement reassured me that he was dead serious about moving forward. One day we would both be free to share a life together.

How does one describe such unspeakable joy? Sometimes there are no words for it. I walked around with a smile so full of song, I thought my grin might dance right off my face. I finally had a purpose and a destiny. As I pictured our life together, I felt warm and calm, and filled with light and hope. I had been restored to a perfect balance of peace. At last, everything was falling into place.

I never thought I would have to admit this, but the day came when I made love to a married man. The "chirping flute" and "bellowing oboe" danced around each other quite happily. It was a beautiful moment. But the mental pain and anguish of Shame haunted me, destroying all my joy.

Now I was as unworthy as his wife. Before we made love, although I knew that being with a married man was not okay, I found it easy to rationalize our trysts. After all, his wife's affairs involved sex and ours did not. Errol and I had a real friendship and connection that went beyond sex. But now we had crossed the very line that we had drawn and agreed upon. Errol was a cheater. I was a cheater. I saw the faint image of a Scarlet A across my chest each time I looked in the mirror. I was being eaten alive with so many conflicting feelings.

At times when I stuffed down the feelings of shame, I felt incredible happiness; but an underlying sense of dread would eventually surface to remind me that punishment would come later, after my death.

Mormon beliefs about Heaven and Hell differ from mainstream Christianity. I'd been taught that Hell, which we called "the Telestial Kingdom" was the lowest of the three Mormon heavens. There was no fire and brimstone; but if I were to go there, I'd remain single, separate, and sexless forever. That didn't sound like heaven to me.

Later that evening, on the floor in front of the TV, Errol laid his head in my lap as I gently combed my fingers through his hair. I never had a guy sit in my lap before. It felt unique and connecting. I also loved the way he would sometimes stand against the wall and spin me outward, then wrap his arms around my chest and gently rock me. He was so romantic that he gave me goosebumps.

As we sat in the quiet, I prayed for time to stand still. There was nowhere else on earth I wanted to be. Yet Guilt would not stop nagging. I couldn't ignore it any longer. I had to tell Errol my devised plan. So I grabbed the remote, flipped off the TV, and had him sit beside me. "Errol," I said, "We need to stop seeing each other."

He looked at me with a shocked expression, then quickly averted his gaze, staring blankly at the TV screen. I was hurting too, yet I knew I wouldn't be able to live with myself if I had a part in his breakup, and I told him so. I was no home wrecker. I knew that if we were to have a fighting chance, we had to do it right.

I told him about my plan to take a temporary leave from work and move to Utah to stay with my sister for the summer. In the meantime, he could take over my lease while working on the legal requirements of his divorce. Then once everything was finalized, I'd move back to California, and we'd be married in no time. Sounded good in theory.

Today as I look back at this situation, I admit that my quantum-leap logic from sleeping with my boss a few times to being his wife may seem a little crazy. But this was my typical method of operation. As a hopeless romantic, I fell in love quite easily, yet at the same time, this felt different. Although Errol was not Mormon, for once, this didn't matter. I was convinced I had found my soulmate.

If he thought my plan to move away then return to marry him sounded psychotic, he didn't really say. I had just assumed his only reason for telling me privately that he was leaving his wife would have been that he wanted to marry me. On top of that, my daughter and his son, who were both musicians, hung out together and she already knew Errol as a dad. Why not join in holy matrimony and be one very happy musical family?

When Errol winced, I felt more helpless than ever. "Don't go," he pleaded, "I'm not that strong." I didn't want to hear that. I deserved better than these clandestine meetings. I didn't want to keep our love a secret. I needed to temporarily exit the scene so he could move forward with his divorce, free from my direct influence. I needed to feel better about what we were doing. If there was ever a time I needed him to be strong, it was at that moment.

After much persuasion, Errol finally agreed that he'd move into my place and take over my lease after I moved out. I took leave of my job at Kappy's, packed my bags, and left everything behind—my amazing job, my beautiful apartment, and craziest of all, my kids. This sacrifice was necessary to protect his honor and mine. That's how much I loved him.

My mom, who had been visiting my sister in Utah, had crossed two state lines to rescue me from my affair. After loading up the car, we headed back to my sister's the next day. As we drove the long desert strip, I talked non-stop about Errol the whole way, yapping like a lovestruck schoolgirl. She listened attentively, but I could see the worry in her eyes. *Why wasn't she happy for me?*

I was too dumb in love to be a Debbie Downer. As in Shakespeare's "Romeo and Juliet," I knew that in the larger scheme of things, "parting with such sweet sorrow" would be but a moment and ultimately add timeless romance to our love story.

CHAPTER 64

THE LETTER

In my sister's colonial-style Utah home, my basement apartment accessed the main floor by way of a narrow spiral staircase. I slowly climbed the angular steps to the opening where daylight peaked through. A day or two had passed since I had last left my bed and headed up toward the morning light. Consumed by Grief, I hadn't been able to eat. Food had lost its appeal.

My sister's basement kept me cool through the hot, dry summer, and I had plenty of space and privacy. Yet in my grief, I wasn't aware of the advantages of my surrounding conditions. As I lay on my floor-mattress unable to control my tears, I wondered how the human eye could be capable of producing so much water. I'd been bawling so much, my head hurt, and in my fog of mental anguish, everything around me was spinning.

My sister's shadow appeared by my bed one night as she waited and listened for air to fill my lungs. I hated worrying her like that. I can't say how many days it took me to emerge from the depths of my despair to the top of her staircase, yet I'm sure she was relieved when I did.

Eventually, after a few dark days, I was standing vertically, then eating, then talking. From the time my sister welcomed me into her home to the day I emerged from her basement, I went from ecstatic, to grief-stricken, to a partially functioning zombie.

When I first arrived, I was full of hopes and dreams. I was counting the days when I'd be back in California and married to the love of my life. After a few encouraging phone calls and hearing Errol assure me that he had moved into my apartment as planned and that everything was going well, he had suddenly ghosted me.

A few weeks earlier, he had informed me that his teenage son had moved into my place with him. That was okay by me, but the downside was that my cozy apartment rarely allowed him the opportunity to talk freely. Trying to stay positive, I convinced myself that a once-a-week call was better than none. Until he stopped calling altogether.

Then I received "the letter." I'd been living with my sister for about five weeks when it arrived. Paradoxically, I could not have been in a more gorgeous setting when receiving the worst news ever. Nestled along the beautiful Wasatch mountains, Mapleton, Utah was the perfect environment for healing and rejuvenation. But no dose of natural beauty and fresh air could put the pieces of my shattered heart back together.

The letter in my sister's mailbox was from Kappy's Music. I couldn't understand why Errol would be writing me from the store. My fingers trembled and my heart palpitated as I nervously ripped open the envelope. As I began reading the words across the page, my eyes stung in disbelief and a wrenching pain filled my gut. The letter informed me that I would no longer be employed at Kappy's. It also stated that I was no longer welcome in the store. It was signed by both Errol and his wife. I dropped the stationary to the floor, my hand cupping my mouth. *This couldn't be happening. It just couldn't be!*

Trying to wrap my brain around this unexpected blow, I lumbered into the living room and collapsed in front of the large bay window that photo-framed a picturesque view of breathtaking Maple Mountain. As sobs overtook my body, I wondered how the world could be so bold as to slap me in the face with so much beauty when my insides were folding in on each other.

I had celebrated my thirty-seventh birthday about a month before Errol and I got together. When I was with him, I didn't care that I was a year older or that my metaphorical sun had turned from pale orange to a deep, vibrant orange. But after receiving the baffling letter, the promise of a love everlasting was replaced by visions of my life being hauled away to the city dump. In my mind's eye, I watched bitterly as it disintegrated into a huge landfill.

Pouring into my thoughts were questions I could not answer. Everything was going so well between us. *How could Errol go from loving me, to exposing our secret to his wife, to firing me, all while keeping me in the dark?* It made no sense. I had not only been fired, but I had been banished from his life.

A few weeks later, I finally got through to Errol on his personal phone. I barely recognized his "hello." He was hesitant at first. When I finally got him talking, he reported to me in a flat, phlegmatic tone that he had sprained his ankle in a waterskiing accident and had moved back home so his wife could take care of him. I couldn't believe what I was hearing. Errol was cold, disconnected, and aloof. This was not the same fervid musician who had wept in my arms. His impassive nature made me want to punch him right through the phone. *Where was his emotion? Where was his soul?*

"My son spilled the beans," he muttered. "He told my wife that you and I had been together." Errol ended the call by telling me that he had no choice but to sign the horrid letter so he could keep peace at home. Then there was a pause … a "but" coming. After a beat of silence, he told me I could sue him for sexual harassment. *Is that how he saw me? A bimbo employee who foolishly fell for him at a weak moment?*

I was so livid, I wanted to fly to Merced and scream at him until I was bloody hoarse. Then I wanted to shoot him in the head and toss him over a bridge. Not really. But I had never felt so betrayed, so hurt and so angry. The thought of Errol running back to his wife the second he needed her was the heaviest blow that had been dealt to me since the loss of my family.

I didn't bother hanging up the phone. I just let the receiver slip through my fingers and dangle in the air. I kept eyeing the cord, tempted to use it as a hangman's rope so I could end my suffering once and for all.

A dark space enveloped me nearly to insanity. To stay afloat emotionally, I eventually forced myself to get out of the house and look for a job. Soon, I found a parttime gig selling emergency supplies in an outdoor marketing tent in front of a supermarket. While there, I ended up having protected sex with two of my customers, yet I never considered the risks involved in not knowing these guys. It was not a good time. I really couldn't have cared less if I lived or died.

After weeks of wallowing in self-pity, I finally came to my senses. Maybe Errol's suggestion to sue him came from a place of guilt for turning my life upside down. Perhaps he still truly loved me, and his only way of coping was to shut down his feelings for me. Maybe he signed the letter because his wife gave him an ultimatum. "Fire that homewrecker or …" Errol might have been caught in a dilemma. Perhaps my former boss was a broken-hearted man. I guess I would never know.

The whole crazy situation was out of my hands now. I couldn't sue him. I wasn't the suing type. Besides, I still loved him. For the present moment, I needed to figure out a way to get back on my feet.

As July turned to August, and as my sister and I strolled her neighborhood in the summer heat, I became more rational in my thinking. I couldn't blame Errol for doing what he did. Before I left for Utah, he begged me not to leave. He had warned me again and again that he was weak and wouldn't be able to follow through with our plans if I left. He was upfront and honest. But I didn't listen. Instead, I closed my ears to what he was trying to tell me. I left my entire life behind, believing this was the only way God would bless our eventual marriage.

I thought about how Errol would have come to me after his accident if I hadn't moved away, because after all, he had already moved into my apartment. That very thought filled me with regret. I could have been the one nursing him back to health instead of his wife. I hated myself for leaving my kids and the only job I truly loved, one that not only brought me financial security, but allowed me to thrive emotionally. Kappy's was my life.

Had this entire experience been a fantasy? It had seemed more real than life. It would take time for me to realize my leaving had only hastened the inevitable ending to the most extraordinary love song my imagination could possibly have composed. Now I slept on an old, worn mattress in my sister's basement.

How was I supposed to move back to California now? My sister was gracious enough to allow me to stay with her rent-free until I got on my feet, but what I hated more than loneliness was being dependent on family.

Eventually I got a job as a checker at Allen's Market about two miles down the street, but it really did nothing to relieve my misery.

I was so depressed that I cried at the drop of a hat over anything and everything. To escape the reality of my wretched circumstances, I found myself purchasing a Harlequin-romance novel at the checkout stand every Friday evening after clocking out. For some masochistic reason, I believed that fantasizing about other peoples' juicy love stories would help get me through my pathetic, non-existent one.

To get Errol out of my head, I finally convinced myself that we were not meant to be. It was my only coping strategy. I convinced myself that being stuck in Utah was all part of God's plan. *How else would the Lord help me find an LDS man?* I was convinced that Utah's sixty-two percent Mormon population would increase my odds for a temple marriage over California's measly 1.97 percent. It was time to put an end to my pity party.

As soon as I got hold of an LDS singles calendar, I circled the upcoming activities in the Springville/Mapleton vicinity. I had already experienced the bottom-of-the-barrel singles bunch in the San Joaquin Valley. Any singles group had to be better than that one.

My kids were the world to me. I called them as often as I could; but sometimes I would end up breaking down over the phone, and that's something a mother should never do. I had to be strong for them. All the more reason why I needed to find a man. I figured that if I could just get married, we could be a family again. I would give myself until the end of the summer. If I didn't find Mr. Right by then, I would return home and look for a job. For now, working at Allen's Market kept me focused on my goal to reclaim my independence.

The first singles activity I attended was a game night at one of the member's homes. There, I met my first new Utah friend, Izzy. The second activity was a Sunday devotional at a nearby meeting house. After the meeting ended, I was standing at the refreshment table in the cultural hall with Izzy, when a ruggedly handsome fellow in his early to mid-forties leisurely strolled toward me. I happened to be nibbling on a sugar cookie and barely had time to lick the crumbs from the corners of my mouth when he extended his hand.

"Hi. I'm Dave" he said, showcasing his big, dazzling smile. His grip was so powerful, I had to massage my crunched fingers. Izzy, who was standing next to me, immediately leaned in and cupped my ear. She was trying to warn me about him. *What did she know that I didn't?*

CHAPTER 65

DANGEROUS DAVE

"That's "Dangerous Dave," she whispered, making sure to hold out the long 'a' in "dangerous" while adding theatrics to her delivery. "Watch out. He's a player." Because I couldn't afford to waste my time with a player, I chose to play it cool with Dangerous Dave; maybe catch him off guard, then extend my foot and "innocently" trip him. Or maybe, just maybe, I'd give him one chance.

We talked for about a minute. I sensed a little cockiness, so I went into aloof mode. Dangerous Dave didn't seem offended in the least. He just dialed up his charm, hoping I'd engage. When I didn't, he smiled confidently—even told me that it was a pleasure to meet me. Then he was gone. He left me befuddled.

Another week passed. By then I had lost another pant size. I learned quite by accident that depression was the most effective weight-loss diet. I showed up at a singles picnic the following Saturday wearing skinny jeans and a sassy new haircut ready to take on the world.

As my lady friends and I were munching on our sandwiches, I saw a tall, broad-shouldered fellow with a full head of wavy dark hair strolling toward us from across the lawn. *Is that Dave?* I pulled down my Burberry shades and blinked him into focus ... *Son of a motherless goat!* The scoundrel was strutting toward our table with that same slap-happy grin across his smug mug. Before I had a chance to say anything, he was already making himself comfortable on the bench beside me, casting his shadow over the potato chip bowl. I leaned in to grab a handful of Wavy Lay's when I felt his warm breath skate across my shoulder.

Why was there a sudden pulsing in my groin? I wished Errol were sitting beside me.

To think I could have been living my dreamlife back in sunny CA. Now I was stuck at a Utah singles picnic figuring out how to unhitch this happy camper.

Yet, there was no denying that this perfectly put together, pertinacious man was getting into my head. I needed to get a grip. I refused to allow his seductive brown eyes to dazzle me, nor his glowing tan, nor his superbly aligned bridal-gown-white teeth. When push came to shove, he was still Dangerous Dave.

After tossing a six-pack of ginger ale onto the table, he shot me a prized wink. None of the men at the picnic were in his ballpark as far as looks, class, or charm, but he was still wasting my time.

He smiled at me. I smirk-smiled at him. He tried to make light conversation. I shrugged him off and avoided eye contact. But I quickly learned that my strategy to get him to lose interest wasn't working. *How could I ditch this guy?* The more I ignored him, the more he channeled in. That's not how it was supposed to work. As I continued to smirk, sneer and snub, my stalker remained upbeat, his pleasant, persistent nature throwing me off course. He wasn't giving up. I eventually caved. He won. He had me curious.

Who was this man? Was Dangerous Dave really all that dangerous? Or was he someone like me, just trying to find his way in this crazy world of LDS midlife spouse-hunting? Whoever he was, dangerous or otherwise, I decided I needed to judge that for myself. Entranced by his tenacity, he was slowly but surely worming his way into my affections.

It was only a matter of time before Dave and I became best buds. Soon, I was introducing him to my sister. If she were single, he might have gone for her instead. At forty-three, she was a lot more chic and socially sophisticated. I wore my heart on my sleeve and often came across as wide-eyed and unstudied. Yet Dave seemed to admire us both for our differences. We grew to love him too. He cast a spell on us with his engaging intellect. He was an out-of-the-box thinker, but even with his intellectual style, he put people at ease.

Shame on those girls in the singles arena for judging him as "dangerous" simply because he was a touchy-feely kinda guy who was not in a space to get married. And shame on me for believing them. He had just gone through a horrible divorce and couldn't even think about marriage. The more I got to know Dave, the more I saw how downright honest he was. He was hardly a phony and certainly wasn't shallow. Anything but dangerous, Dave made me feel safe and happy at a time when I really needed a friend.

The "Dangerous Dave" rumor that spread around the local LDS community got me seriously thinking how religious rhetoric can condition our minds to focus on a tiny piece of the puzzle and miss the big, beautiful picture. When we're taught to believe that there is only one right and true way and that we should all cram ourselves into the same mold, we tend to reject instead of embrace our differences. More dangerous than any "Dangerous Dave" is the type of mind-control that blinds us to judge others unfairly.

As a programmed Latter-day Saint, I too have been guilty of judging others. Instead of considering someone's personal path, I condemned them for not walking mine. Like I was so much holier and saintlier. *Who gave me the right to judge?* Well, The Church, I thought. Their cookie-cutter standard for how to look, dress, act, feel, think—what we are allowed to read, eat, or drink gets into our heads. We see people who don't fit the standard mold, so we put our blinders on and judge them, missing opportunities for connection and growth.

One afternoon, when I was feeling more down in the dumps than usual, I unloaded on poor Dave. I shared all about Errol, how I lost my job, my life, my kids, the whole bit. He listened without judgment as I whined about my internal clock and worried about becoming an old spinster. Without a word, my caring friend reached over and caressed my shoulder as I continued to grouse about my stupid life. Then, out of the blue, he told me to get in his car. That was the moment Dave taught me that ice-cream with a friend was the best antidepressant.

My fun pal with his thoughtful gestures always rescued me from a stark situation to help me feel a little lighter. If he saw me standing on the sidelines at the LDS single clubs, he'd grab me for a slow dance. While dancing, I took the opportunity to lift my skirt a few inches above the knee as I flashed a smile at those girls who gossiped about my "dangerous" dance partner. I know. *Scandalous!* "Dangerous Dave," my ass, I thought. I'll show them who's dangerous. Wrapping my arms around my friend's neck, I griped to him about my forever empty dance card. After he candidly told me that perhaps the problem was my outdated wardrobe, we got right to work.

The next day, Dave came over to check out my closet. Soon we were both pulling out my clothes and examining them. I showed him a few racy skirts where the hemlines hit an inch or two above the knee.

Then I introduced him to the rest of my wardrobe, mainly full-length prairie dresses. Some had bibbed collars, others had gathered bodices, high-necklines, and long, puffy sleeves. I treasured their simple elegance and modest fashion statement. After all, I needed to attract a humble, modest guy.

The following afternoon, Dave escorted me to a variety of boutique shops and brought me up to speed on what women were wearing in the 90s. He insisted it wouldn't hurt me to show a little leg and cleavage. "If you want to catch carp, wear a prairie dress," he teased. "If you want to catch salmon or bass, wear one of these," he quipped, pointing to the more modern, chic-looking dresses. You can display your wares with class," he added with his extra-large Cheshire grin.

My new dresses worked wonders. At the dances, I was no longer ignored. I met a lot of nice guys, and socializing with them helped build my confidence. I came to life that summer. I still cried easily the second I thought about my kids. It was a struggle to lose everything twice within a couple of years. But Dave kept me afloat during a time I couldn't afford to see a therapist. He was my confidence booster. He was my bright orange party balloon when the world looked morose.

In mid-September, as the Utah sun wilted the flowers and brought in the locusts, I knew the time had come for me to reach out to Ellie, my one and only true Mormon friend back home. It was time to return to sunny California.

After I talked to Ellie about my homeless living situation, she contacted a widow in the Atwater ward. Roberta was in her mid-forties and lived alone in a lovely two-bedroom home off highway 99. Although Roberta didn't know anything about me, this sweet lady took me in like a stray cat. She even had milk and cookies waiting for my arrival …

CHAPTER 66

OLD HABITS DIE HARD

After my crazy summer in Mapleton Utah, I moved into my rent-free Atwater, CA home. Roberta, a woman whom I had never met, knew I was jobless and didn't expect me to pay rent until I was employed. I wasn't about to take advantage of a widow with a kind heart. So I worked my butt off trying to put my life back together.

I thought about returning to college, but my dire financial situation needed immediate attention. It didn't take long before I landed a job at the Merced Mall selling autostereograms—two-dimensional images that create the illusion of three-dimensional depth if you stare into them long enough. In the nineties it was quite the trend as artists worked hard to outdo each other.

I also worked as a temporary office worker answering phones, filing, and typing. I even catered elaborate weddings with outdoor fountains and everything romantic and glamorous. You can only imagine how dross I felt in my little black apron serving caviar and cocktails to highfalutin' guests in extravagant attire.

Near the end of the year, I left my flyers on every porch in upscale neighborhoods, advertising my availability as a pianist for Christmas parties. When I got my first gig at a multimillion-dollar estate, I was hyped. Nestled in the back corner near a bar, my renditions of up-beat tunes added to the festivities where decked-out merry couples laughed and sang amid red tinsel and bright chandeliers. Unbeknownst to anyone else, I was having my own personal pity party. Always an observer, but never part of the action, I felt unseen and irrelevant.

It never once occurred to me that a perfect LDS prince didn't really exist. If this guy were real, he certainly would have no interest in me, who at age thirty-seven, continually made poor choices due to my hyperfocus on marriage. A lifetime of Mormon programming as to the disastrous, eternal consequences of singledom didn't help me any. My faith was so blind that I couldn't get out of my own way.

I was proud of my entrepreneurship. I had gumption. I had drive. But even through this lens, I was still ruminating about Errol. Oh, how I missed the taste of his Beech Nut kiss when he pocketed his fruity gum in his cheeks, adding sweetness to our passion. Baffled at how he could possibly go back to his cheating wife, I dreamt about basking in the comfort of his arms. After what he did, my heart should have been stone-cold. But it was the holidays—the most wonderful time of the year. And I still loved him. To get him off my mind, I tried to focus on the glitter and gold and cheer of the season. Yet nothing could bring me joy. I was having a blue, blue Christmas.

In April of 1993, two months after the World Trade Center bombing, I started attending church again. Without Errol in my life, I had no sense of direction. I felt hopelessly lost. I yearned to belong. To fit in somewhere. Attending Sunday meetings was better than spending the day alone. After being forced to leave my job at Kappy's, church was once again the only "family" I could turn to besides my precious children. I had also been in regular contact with my friend, Ellie, since I returned to California, and she recently shared the exciting news that her husband had just been called to be the bishop.

Unlike Bishop York of the Merced Ward, who summoned me to church court and put me on probation after my voluntary confession, Ellie's husband, Bishop Snyder, was the kind of leader who I could not imagine judging me in my time of loss. Because he knew I had been stuck behind the piano in Primary for decades, he asked if I would like to direct the ward choir. I watched my mom do it for years and always wanted to try my hand at it. My ear-to-ear smile gave him the answer he anticipated.

The following month, on the day I turned 38, I pursed my lips as I examined my bare ring finger. My internal clock—the burnt orange sun had turned red. My heart pounded furiously with panic as it slowly edged toward the horizon.

For a full year, I worked madly gluing back together the pieces of my life. Since Roberta, my guardian angel, knew I couldn't afford to pay rent, I stayed busy with household chores while continuing to work for various temp agencies.

With the financial help of my parents, I eventually moved further south into an apartment located only a few blocks from my children. When 12-year-old Zach and 9-year-old Drew came to visit me in my new place, I greeted them with giant hugs, not wanting to ever let go. They were both so happy to see me and extremely helpful around the house. Because I couldn't be with them every day, I would often fall into despair. Tears of joy spilled down my cheeks with every affectionate gesture, and tears of grief followed every time they'd leave. But I carried on.

Soon, I obtained a free spinet piano through the give-away section of the Dollar Saver ads and built up my piano students through street flyers and newspaper advertisements. Although I missed my upscale Merced apartment with verdant lawns and springing fountains, I was grateful for people in my life like Roberta and my parents, and for my entrepreneurial skills, all of which helped me become independent again.

The following year in April, when I least expected it, a new friend in the ward said she wanted to set me up with her 33-year-old bachelor brother, Mortimer. She bragged about his fetching speaking voice. I was piqued. Then she showed me his picture. Not so piqued. But then I remembered my mom's words: "You can't have everything."

Our first date was at the Sno-White Drive In, a little stand that served burgers, fries, and ice-cream. As he approached me in the parking lot, my first thought was maybe a guy *could* have everything. Or perhaps I could lower my expectations? ...

CHAPTER 67

JAW-DROPPERS, SHOCKERS & THUNDERCLAPS

I worked hard to adjust my wish list as I sat across from Mortimer eating my burger and toying with my straw while he talked about the latest novel he'd been working on. Gazing into his smallish gray eyes, I wanted to like him, but my Butterfinger-malt had far more going on than he did. It was to die for. Yet I had to give Mortimer credit for something. He had a deep, virile voice and he was artistic, single, *and* LDS. All qualities I thought were important. At my age, I couldn't afford to be picky. *But could I afford to not be picky?*

Then there was his name. I could not help that his name had no symphonic quality to my ears. Rather, it was more reminiscent of a band of kazoos and combs covered with wax paper. *Could a Mortimer really lead me down the road to marital bliss?*

On our first date, he predicted with almost a little too much fervor that his soon-to-be-published science fiction novel would become a multi-million-dollar box office hit. Had I held my breath waiting for that to happen, I would have been buried long ago.

From the beginning, Morty (I refused to call him Mortimer), was the quintessential geek. Although I wasn't particularly attracted to him, it would be safe to conclude that it was my desperate need to be loved that kept me open-minded. Besides, he seemed genuine when expressing himself, and I really liked that about him. In a world of so much pretense, his down to earth demeanor was refreshing. And he was ready for marriage. *So why not make it work?* When there are scant choices, you just go with what's available. And if it did work out, I would have a cozy family again. My kids would have a male role model in their lives. At church, we'd sit all in a row like all the other families. And Monday night Family Home Evenings would be filled with laughter around the backyard picnic table.

Morty, the potential stepfather for my kids, seemed spiritual enough. Yet I often wondered whom I was fooling when I kept telling myself that physical attraction would develop over time. My nerdy friend had knitted brows that arched pensively above his dark-rimmed coke-bottle glasses. His wispy strands of hair whisked across his head in all directions as though he had a hair explosion in the barber shop. Even more discouraging, he was only five-six—two inches shorter than I was and a little thick around the middle. Normally, I preferred handsome men who were taller and in better shape. But the following year I'd be hitting the big 4-O. I intuitively knew that the fiery sun would be dipping over the horizon. That would be it—no more chances to find my prince.

Shallow girls would never marry a guy like Morty. Only foolish, hard-up women like me would grab a shovel and dig deep to find his redeeming qualities. After intensive digging, I discovered we had a common love for dipped marshmallows. *But can a marriage survive on marshmallows alone?*

His sister thought we would be perfect together because he was in the artist/music industry. He was a radio personality (DJ) for a local country music station. So I accepted another date, then another after that. After three months of dating, he took me to the station and proposed to me live on the air. Because I love surprises and adored his deep, sexy voice, I told him, "Of course I'll marry you." I was far too ecstatic to even think about the fact that we had been dating for only ninety days. *How often does a girl get proposed to on a radio broadcast?*

After we were sealed in the temple for time and eternity, I beamed with pride as I extended my ring finger to show off to my friend, Ellie. Then there was the honeymoon—an unexpected "burst-your-bubble" kind of surprise. It was so bad, I don't even remember where we went. *LA? San Diego?*

When we settled into our hotel room, I slipped into the bathroom and threw on my yummy pink negligee. I couldn't wait to be ravished after all the pain I experienced with Errol. Prancing toward the bed, I practiced the most seductive and inviting smile I could muster. I was hoping for a gaping jaw or mesmerized look. But Morty was sitting on the bed engrossed in a nature movie on TV, totally distracted.

Was learning about how lions prey on giraffes more fascinating than his new wife? I was a titillating strawberry dessert waiting to be consumed. You'd think he would want to dive right in and devour me. But his eyes were far too glued to the small screen to even notice me. My new husband found a new love the moment we stepped foot into our hotel room. And it certainly wasn't me.

After I plopped down beside him in defeat, he finally rolled his eyes my way and forced a weak smile, then turned back to the screen again. Not even a "You look great, Wow." I might as well have thrown on a gunny sack. I felt cheated. My chest felt heavy, my breath went shallow, and my throat felt constricted. As the lion, Morty's new feline mistress, roared loudly from the seductive box on the wall, tears streamed down my face unnoticed. I wanted to die. I guess it was plain asking too much for someone to love me.

I had a feeling something was up before we married. When we made out, my fiancée seemed almost too staid. He never demonstrated a wanting, or gave even a hint that he couldn't keep his hands off me. I shrugged it off, convincing myself that his lack of passion had to do with self-restraint. After all, we needed to remain pure so we could enter the temple. Why would I consider a "death do us part" civil ceremony when I could be married to a man forever and have endless amounts of sex in heaven? It was a no brainer for me.

But all this changed in a flash when I discovered that Morty preferred a nineteen-inch television on our hotel wall to anything I could offer him. *Why did I rush in again? When would I ever learn?* Being stuck with this passionless nerd was a fate worse than death. Yet there was no going back.

Perhaps he was just nervous? Maybe he hadn't had sex in eons? But couldn't he at least react? *Say something. Say anything!* Because I tend to speak my mind without thinking of the consequences, all at once, I blurted it out:

"Are you gay?" I asked with an expressed mix of annoyance and hurt. I huddled a little closer on the sheet hoping he would hear the quiver in my voice.

I guess he heard me too well. My new groom suddenly switched off the TV without saying a word and coiled himself into a ball on the sheet. *Uh-oh.* I guess to him, that was an insult, while to me, it was simply a logical question. I adored gay men, but I wouldn't choose to marry one. I really wanted to know if this could explain his indifference. The damage had now been done. The gay accusation built a fortress between us. Nothing was spoken after that. Our first night was a disaster as we lay on a double bed facing away from each other, weeping into our pillows.

The next morning after breakfast, I had a chance to apologize, but I didn't. I was too busy being hurt myself. The two of us had settled on the front-room sofa watching TV when Morty propped his head on the arm of the couch and eased his knees toward his chest. His dark mood was reflected in his eyes as he woefully turned toward me. "Please tell my dad I love him very much."

How did I ever get mixed up with this sad little man? I wasn't about to fall for his theatrics.

Instead of taking the lead and deciding the two of us needed to have a healthy discussion about our disastrous first night together, Morty chose the passive-aggressive route. He was punishing me by feigning a death wish. His intent was to make me look cruel and heartless. Well, I wasn't going to fall for it. If he would rather choose death over strawberry desert, there wasn't much I could do about it.

Over the next few days, our honeymoon was anything but romantic. In fact, it was so dreary that we ended up cutting it short. A few days after arriving home, Morty warmed up to me and admitted that he was inexperienced and fearful about sex. He said he felt he was out of his element on our honeymoon, and that I looked so intimating, that he just froze. In the weeks following, there was progress in the bedroom. But admittedly, I wasn't near as happy as I had hoped to be.

Morty won my heart by his impromptu proposal on the air. But as soon as we settled in to married life, the ensuing surprises stunk. Each jaw-dropper was more jolting than the last.

The first thunderclap occurred when I learned he had accrued quite a bit of debt before we married. Yet he insisted we get cable TV.

I didn't want cable TV or debt. I wasn't a couch potato, but I quickly learned my new husband was. One thing I hated more than couch spuds were interest payments. Debt wasn't about to accrue on my watch if I could help it. Spud Guy didn't mind debt.

I was hit between the eyes with a second bolt-from-the-blue on a Friday evening, about two weeks into our marriage—the night I had planned a candlelight dinner. At the very last minute, Morty told me he had to head for Sacramento. Out of the blue, I learned he was a jet mechanic in the National Guard. He would be gone all weekend. I never pictured him as a military guy. *Did he even have a uniform?* I ended up eating alone when he suddenly appeared before me in his camouflage wear. He actually looked kind a cute. All he needed was a rifle and his daffy duck sidekick and he could pass for Elmer Fudd. After a quick kiss, Morty headed north on 99 toward the base.

The third lightning bolt hit a month after he returned home from his weekend reserve duty. I fetched the mail one morning and received our phone bill. In 1994, we were still using landlines and cordless brick-sized Motorolas and paying surcharges, out-of-area charges, and long-distance charges. When I unfolded the bill, I received my third shocker. The bill was not one page or two. I counted three, then four, then five full pages as I furrowed my brows and felt my stomach twisting in knots. There was no white space. Just an endless column of black phone numbers.

I couldn't believe what I was seeing. Who were these people my spouse had called? My typical bill was $20. My eyes bulged in disbelief when I saw the number of total charges on the bottom of page five in bolded black: $483.24. *Was Mortimer having an affair?*

My breaths came in short gasps as I grappled with the idea of Morty being a cheater. *Maybe he wasn't even in the reserves? Perhaps he had a lover in another city.* As I closed my eyes willing this nightmare to disappear, all my energy centers went dark, like when you witness a whole city shutting down from an emergency blackout. Before I let my imagination totally run away with me, I sucked in a deep breath and dialed my friend Ellie.

Thank God she answered. She told me to come right over. Because I was hyperventilating, Ellie took control and dialed one of the numbers on the bill. We soon learned that this endless list of 900 numbers were sex-talk lines—the kind where anyone could be on the other end, even a guy in girls' lingerie. That's when we both conjectured that my new spouse carried around more sexual insecurities than he dared tell. The thought of him jerking off to a stranger's suggestions over the phone when he could have the real thing with me anytime was beyond my comprehension.

"At least he's into girls and not guys," my friend piped. I wasn't too sure. But that upbeat lilt in Ellie's voice always conveyed positivity. She was the kind of woman who was determined to find a silver lining in a billion-volt thunderstorm. Thank God she was there when I needed her.

When Morty returned home from work that day, I tried to get him to open up to me about the reasons why he felt he needed to make those calls. But he really couldn't give me a logical explanation. I didn't know who my husband was. This was far more disturbing than the bill itself. But since he wouldn't talk, I expressed anger another way.

"How are we going to pay this?" I screamed, thrusting the bill in his face. He stood there, totally unresponsive. The astronomical bill overshadowed any compassion. As much as I wanted to understand his issues, how could I if he refused to talk about them?

As months passed without much activity on the mattress, I was so sexually frustrated that one morning I blew up at him. "Why don't you want me?" I wailed. Morty just sat there with a blank expression—his eyes, two flat, tiny pebbles. *Was he gay after all? Asexual? Greysexual, Demisexual?* I began to realize I should have stayed single, but there seemed to be no reprogramming the indoctrinated chip that had been embedded in my brain that insisted *I had to be married.*

Since my new spouse spent his reserve-duty weekend debasing himself by listening to smutty sex talk and had nothing left for me, I worked off my sexual tension by canvasing the neighborhoods and promoting my flyers to acquire more piano students.

Soon, we were able to afford a nicer apartment that would create an atmosphere more conducive to learning for my students. I received my fourth clincher when Morty refused to help me box up the apartment in preparation for our move. As his clothes lay untouched in his dresser, his excuse was that he was low on energy. After working hard to pack for the both of us, I was a little low on energy too, but was I complaining? I ended up packing the entire apartment singlehandedly.

After we moved into our new place, I also did most of the unpacking and a lot of yelling. Getting the listless whiner to do anything took an act of Congress, ten Hail Mary's, and a Mormon prayer. Somehow, his last four boxes choking in duct tape and bursting at the seams, were still holding up the bedroom wall after three months. Three months!

I'd been begging Morty for ninety days with a pretty please in the sweetest singsong voice I had if he would kindly unpack his four damn boxes so our bedroom wouldn't look like a warehouse. But all my pretty pleases fell on deaf ears. That's when I put my foot down. I threatened him in a nice sorta way.

Right before I took off to the grocery store one morning, I told him that I'd give him an hour to get his things unpacked. Then I'd be back with his favorite treat if the job was done. Looking back on that crazy time, it would've been far easier training a dog to sit and rollover.

When I arrived through the door an hour later, my troubled husband opened my eyes to bombshell number five. Things were always a little weird with him. But this was beyond … well, … this is what happened …

I find him sitting on the kitchen floor crying, obviously feeling daunted by this minor task. I think I'm feeling more overwhelmed than he is just looking at him. He suddenly goes from crying to yelling. He's so full of rage, his whole body is shaking, and the blood vessels near his temple are about to burst. He even uses the "f" word, which I hate, and heads for the bedroom and locks himself in.

It's awfully quiet on the other side of the door and I don't know what's happening and I'm getting worried. I call Brother Richards, the bishop's first counselor since I'm unable to reach the bishop. I've always adored Brother Richards. He's cool, calm, and collected and the perfect man for this job. If anyone can handle my man-child, it's Brother Richards. I feel humiliated having to explain to such a spiritual man as Brother Richards that my supposed-adult spouse has been weeping like a baby behind a locked door for an hour because I asked him to unpack four boxes.

I still remember Brother Richard's persistent knocking, commanding in his kind, but stern fashion, "Morty, please open the door! Morty, do you hear me?" We pause and wait in the silence. Then we hear a big crash. Sounds like glass. *What's going on?*

CHAPTER 68

DYSFUNCTION COMES
IN MANY FORMS

Brother Richards finally succeeds in wedging the door open. My husband is sitting on the floor cross-legged at the edge of the bed staring sightlessly at the wall. One box is open, and the smell of musty old books fills the room. In his lap is our wedding photo, exposed and gouged with pockmarks and shards of glass. My jaw drops when I glance around at a pile of broken glass littering the carpet.

Decades later, I still haven't been able to expel his image from my mind—the dried patch of blood in his thin matted hair, his mind that seemed to be detached from his body, his quivering, tearstained cheeks. He had cracked the beautiful picture of the two of us over his head. Was this his childish, passive aggressive way of saying he wanted out? If he wanted a divorce, why didn't he just say so?

He simply had to unpack four boxes. Four. *How did I manage to get hooked up with such a troubled soul?* I don't know why I didn't call it quits right then. Well, actually I do. We had been married in the temple. There's no easy way out of a temple marriage, or so I believed. The voice in my head assured me that backing out of a second eternal marriage would be the damning nail in my coffin. The church's tentacles had a chokehold on my very soul.

Surprise number six, the biggest deathblow of all was when Morty confessed that when he was eleven, he had molested his six-year-old sister. This might have explained those 900 number-calls, and why he didn't enjoy sex all that much with me. Maybe he was a pedophile. Mighty brave of him to lay it all out like that. But I felt sick to my stomach and couldn't even look at him. This was serious shit. I suggested that a confession to the bishop might lighten his burden and propel him on a path toward emotional healing.

My traumatic experience confessing to the wrong bishop didn't mean that Bishop Snyder lacked special powers from God that could miraculously cure my poor husband. Yes, his offence was horrific, but maybe two decades of being haunted by Guilt and Shame was enough.

In the bishop's office that day, I did most of the talking. I told him about Morty's wild emotional swings from crying to sudden rage and how his behavior frightened me. Then my husband bravely confessed his crimes against his sister. Our gentle leader listened with compassion. He was just as lovely as his wife. Then he said something that completely caught us off guard.

As we sat across from him, Bishop Snyder told us he was convinced that my husband was possessed by a demon and insisted on casting out the evil spirit. *Come again?* I never heard of any bishop doing this sort of thing and found it rather weird, but I kept my mouth shut. I really loved Bishop Snyder, and I didn't want to make waves. I also rationalized that a blessing couldn't hurt. Ultimately, Morty did need help.

After our kind shepherd cast out Satan, my troubled husband said he felt a lot better. I'm not sure if he really did, but his other option would have been to defy the bishop and tell him the stinker was still lurking around in there somewhere. In any case, the blessing's placebo effect worked for a while. *Or maybe it was the lithium?* After Morty's supposed demon had been cast out by our exorcist bishop, I managed to get my husband to see a psychiatrist who gave him a script.

A few weeks later, I celebrated my big 4-0. I closed my eyes and in my mind's eye, I saw the sun dipping below the horizon. Yet I didn't mind the passage of time, because I was married for "time and all eternity." But gradually, Morty's lithium had morphed him into the most lethargic version of his laziest couch-spud self.

On a windy October day in 1995, Morty came home and told me he was on the verge of a mental breakdown. He was no longer working at the radio station due to cutbacks but had a different job at a paper mill factory. I'm not sure how he managed to stay awake anywhere and surprised he hadn't come home covered in paper cuts.

When he tried to convince me that most of his anxiety sprang from my unwillingness to upgrade to cable TV, I almost burst out laughing. *Like I was the one making him nuts because going into debt and wearing out the couch cushions weren't my priorities?*

I chose to marry Morty because I foolishly believed I was getting a man who was emotionally, sexually, and spiritually healthy. Instead, I ended up with a dysfunctional, mentally unstable manchild with a poor credit score. Because Morty couldn't have his cable television, he checked himself into a mental institution, faking a breakdown to escape a "prison marriage." But that was my lucky break. I was finally set free.

I would be remiss if I chose to turn a blind eye to my own deficits. Just like Morty, my dysfunction came in many forms. It came in the form of impulsiveness, allowing my libido to lead and rush into marriage twice, while blindly following a manmade construct without question. How long does it take to overcome dysfunction? *A lifetime? Maybe more?* I'm not sure about Morty. But as for me, I'm still dysfunctional in many ways.

CHAPTER 69

BEDAZZLED BY BEELZEBUB

A year after Morty and I divorced, although I was 41, the red, fiery sun was still peeking over the skyline. I bit off the nail of my bare ring finger, willing the scarlet crescent to share its illumination a little longer. If there was light, there was hope.

That hope came when I met Sebastian on a warm spring day in 1996. Twelve weeks later, we were married. I get it. I still rushed in after two failed marriages. but this time I had some good reasons to believe Sebastian and I would do well together. He had been a family friend for years. My oldest sister and he were high-school buds and together they were voted the school's most talented. How could I go wrong with a man who was both musically gifted and a long-time family friend?

Still, I hadn't yet learned to take my time before marriage to know for myself if the guy I had hooked was one of those fish that needed to be thrown back into the water. I was dying to be loved and wanted to end my fishing expedition once and for all.

I may not have been the wisest of fisherwomen, but I sure was an easy catch when it came to mind-conditioning. I bought it all hook, line, and sinker that marriage, in and of itself, was the ultimate goal of this life. Although I did take one step in the right direction by not marrying husband number three in the temple, Sebastian was LDS, and this meant we could be sealed in the future if things went well.

I hoped it would work out with Sebastian, because if we did eventually get sealed, our temple wedding would automatically cancel out my sealing with Mortimer. I couldn't conceive of being stuck with Couch Potato Morty for eternity. And I desperately wanted a wonderful, fulfilling marriage here on earth—one I could be excited about for eternity. But if I got it wrong again, at least the good Lord will have had a lot of practice undoing what we couldn't get right on earth by the time I get to heaven.

My new spouse was Portuguese and was shall we say, vertically challenged? The top of his head came to the top of my ear when he wore his elevator shoes. When standing beside him, I felt like Dubai's Burj Khalifa. My embarrassment about being seen with a shorter man was admittedly *my* problem, but I didn't know how to make the problem go away. I mean, my husbands were getting smaller with each marriage, and if I kept on marrying, there would be nothing left of them.

Before we married, I played by the rules. When kissing, I saw Sebastian's wandering hands as a good thing. I assumed his libido was at least as strong as mine. It's not good to assume.

After we married, I met *Lowell Libido and Noah Interest*, my husband's alter personalities. In my forties, my daily aerobics kept me trim and fit. I still had a washboard tummy and curves that didn't quit. *Did shorter men have less room for testosterone storage?*

I tried to put sex out of my mind by concentrating on my husband's abundance of talent. When I was asked to sing in church, I didn't need to hunt down an accompanist. I had a built-in one with Sebastian. He didn't need big hands to play the piano. His short, stubby fingers danced up and down the ivories so fast you couldn't see them. Jazz, classical, ragtime, boogie-woogie, you name it, he could play it while shaking the life out of any baby grand.

My gifted hubby would often perform at the Oakland Interstate Center, a huge concert hall, and oh, what a charmer he was to those who drove miles to watch him. Right before lifting his hands above the keyboard, he'd shake his thick dark bangs from his penny-brown eyes and brush his tuxedo tails behind him with Liberace flair. He perfected the art of seduction with his songs; but at home, I had a hunch that this man behind the mask was far more of a mess than Morty the Manchild himself.

Other than his talent, I think he knew deep down he didn't have a lot to offer me, so he wormed his way into my affections with his charm. A truck driver gets plenty of practice on the road. "Forty dollars on pump two, baby doll," he'd say with a twinkle in his eye. My new husband could charm the socks off a man-eating chimp. Flirting came naturally for him. And this worried me. *When he winked at me, was he creating the illusion that all was well?*

Before we married, he confessed he once had a cocaine and alcohol addiction but assured me it was all in the past. He'd been to AA, had his five-year chip, and was as good as gold. If you can't trust the man you're going to marry, who can you trust? About three months in, I found a bottle of booze in the garbage bin. He told me he had one slip up and promised to never drink again, but his alcohol problem was the least of my worries.

Only weeks after our marriage, creditors came knocking on our door, as well as the IRS—and that was after he had filed for bankruptcy *twice*. I learned he not only owed tons of money in back child-support from a previous marriage, but he also owed his boss money. His monthly paychecks were a joke—about enough to pay a couple of utility bills.

Sebastian worked his tail off hauling milk ten hours a day, six days a week; yet what did he have to show for it? As a traveling piano teacher, I was bringing home almost five times as much as he was. If I had known this was going to be my new world, I never would have signed up for it. But I was the fool who consistently rushed in. At least I could have asked him more questions. Yet even if I had, what chance was there that he would have been completely honest with me? Sometimes the most damning lies are the truths that go unspoken.

Neither of us were big spenders, but we ended up having to borrow money to pay our bills. Since Sebastian filed for bankruptcy before we met, guess whose credit card we used? Soon, we were thousands of dollars in debt, all of which was on my personal card. I had always been taught that in marriage: what was mine was his, including my credit card; and what was his was mine, which was nothing but liability.

To save the failing enterprise, I abandoned ship and returned to college to pursue a teaching degree. I guess I never believed I was capable enough or had it in me, but going back to school was the smartest thing I had done in years. Hitting the books and working toward a goal helped me to gain a sense of control over my life. That is, until Sebastian injured his back and became an internet junkie while collecting workman's comp and guzzling down three to four giant-size bottles of Mountain Dew daily. *Was he spiking them with alcohol?*

Returning home from class every day to a stinky-breath, salami-eating slug whose stomach was expanding by the hour was wearing on me. But I could smell more stink around the corner. I glared at him suspiciously as he huddled behind his computer screen, all shifty-eyed. Something was up. If he was into porn, he could have at least invited me into his world. Especially since the spice had disappeared from our bedroom. But when he confessed that he had contacted an old flame, I smacked my palm against my forehead and stumbled backward. What an idiot. I didn't see any of it coming.

The only thing that kept our marriage afloat for a while was our new and exciting music endeavor. One day, Sandy, a seminary teacher in our ward called me and asked if I'd like to write songs for the church's "seminary scripture masteries." The LDS General Authorities had selected one-hundred scriptures for teenage students to memorize in order to graduate from the seminary program. The seminary scripture mastery program was a worldwide project.

Because Sandy was communicating with seminary teachers across the globe on an LDS forum, she learned that they were desperate to get their hands on some music—songs with snappy beats that would help their students memorize long passages. Sandy predicted this worthwhile project could have potential earning power. Enthusiastically I took her up on it. I was a songwriting junkie. I would have done it for free.

I ended up writing a total of fifty scripture mastery songs, twenty-five for the Old Testament and twenty-five for the New Testament, all while attending my last two years of college from 1998-2000. Sebastian fancied up my written chord charts and put dazzle into my songs. He was quite good, but just like husbands one and two, he had a hot temper. Yet for him, anger looked more like a tapping Savion Glover in triple speed only without the smile.

If I even gave a hint of a suggestion for a note change, he'd sit ramrod straight on the edge of the piano bench, nostrils flaring, his whole face contorting, as he hit the piano keys with his fists. He couldn't handle the competition, yet I wasn't competing. I wanted to work as a team. That had always been my dream. But Sebastian made sure to tell me it was his way or the highway. I would often have to leave the room until he calmed down.

Through it all, we managed to record two albums without murdering each other. We sold hundreds our first year. Pulling out of the red would be a hard task, but at least this project gave us hope. Because I was a full-time college student, I had no choice but to leave Sebastian in charge of the business and to pay the bills.

Between classes I would intermittently ask him how the bills were going. He would smile and give me a thumbs up. But it didn't take long for me to discover a pile of unpaid bills hidden in the back of the filing cabinet. Foolishly, I gave him another chance.

Summer arrived, and while I was in Utah selling our CDs at a seminary conference, Sebastian called and told me he was heading north to look for a job. He had contacts up there who were willing to train him in a different line of work.

When I returned to California, I called him and asked when he would be home. With the phone cupped to my ear, I couldn't quite make out his words, so I asked him to clarify: "Did you just say you wanted to "please" me or "leave" me?"

CHAPTER 70

I'LL GIVE YOU REAL

Don't you just hate those yearly newsletters that come in the mail every year around Christmas time? You know what I'm talking about. Just when you're finally feeling good about yourself and believe you have made some worthwhile contributions to the world … BAP! Just like that, you're suddenly pounded to the ground and squashed like a bug. The thing is: people brag so they can feel better about themselves. None of its real. If you want real, I'll give you real.

Dear Friends and Family,

It's Christmas 2000, and even though this year was filled with a blindside of deception, abandonment and loss, I'm still vertical and breathing. While finishing up my last year of college, with one semester to go, my husband decided to take off up north to look for a job and never came back. So this year I have reluctantly but graciously accepted the "Abandoned Wife Award" and am quite pleased, because it has helped me to become a stronger, more independent woman. At first, it was hard to manage without the man I thought loved me, but after sobbing myself to sleep for a solid week, I decided to put an end to my pity party.

That's when I received my "Parting with Pity Parties Award" and am quite proud of it. Yet shortly afterward, my pledge to be strong weakened when I discovered that my so-called loving spouse had packed up my synthesiser, took my custom speakers that my dad built for me, and cleaned out my bank account. Even worse, "the Portuguese Grinch" borrowed thousands of dollars against my account, so I had no money to pay the bills, and the bank wanted their money that my husband stole. But I didn't have it. So I was red tagged in bank systems, which means I wouldn't be allowed to open an account in any bank for a decade. As a busy college student, I trusted Sebastian with the finances. Bad choice. He also neglected to pay the phone bill. That surprise came when I went to use the phone and the line was dead.

The day I discovered Sebastian's wizardry, I glared at the teller with a wrinkled brow but didn't throw a public tantrum. No way would I part with my "Parting with Pity Parties Award." Back at home, I scrounged for loose change inside the couch cushions and shook a handful of coins from my piggy bank, then sorted them in envelopes.

After parking at the bank, I grabbed all the envelopes that I hadn't taken the time to seal, and in my haste, lost my grip on them. It happened so fast that I just stood there with my mouth agape and helplessly watched all my coins spill from their envelopes, clinking, scattering, and spinning across not one parking space, but two. Crouching down, I moved full tilt, scooping up every last penny before anyone had a chance to appear on this embarrassing scene.

Although I could feel tears welling in my eyes, I kept saying, "Be strong, woman. You don't want to lose your "Parting with Pity Parties

Award." After collecting the last coin along with my composure, I strolled nonchalantly into the bank again.

Flashing my big, fake, fetching smile, I handed the teller all my precious envelopes. "We have no time to count or roll these," she said flatly.

"I thought that's what banks were for!" I exclaimed.

"No, we don't do that," she drawled, "but they have a little machine at the grocery store where you can ..." I walked away before she could finish. I was having a low-blood-sugar moment.

By the time I entered the grocery store, my head was spinning. The smell of fresh baked goods awakened my palette, and it dawned on me how little I had eaten in the last three days. But I needed to focus on one thing—how much money I didn't have.

A few days later, without any coins left and needing to see a doctor, I had to start borrowing. Fortunately, a friend lent me the money. "Give me drugs," I said. My doctor took my blood pressure and quickly wrote a script for Trazodone—a prescription I couldn't pay for, so my friend came to my rescue again. I popped the pills like candy and woke up three days later. How grateful I was for her loan. Since then, I've become quite the expert at borrowing from others and keeping track of my debts. In that same month, I received my third honor—the "I.O. U. Award". I was on a roll.

When fall semester began, I didn't have to pay a dime to enroll. I allowed the school to pay instead. I became quite popular on campus, and at the financial aid office, everyone knew me on a first name basis.

Anything that could have gone wrong this year *did,* but I'm still hanging on like a trooper. For this noted accomplishment, I gave myself the "Embracing Murphy's Law Award."

In between classes and schoolwork, I had to hire and fire not one but two paralegals. Since Sebastian was too lazy to divorce me, I had to take charge. I camped out at the courthouse and obtained copies of records that I didn't have a chance to even read or sign—records that had been carelessly skimmed over and filed. Some documents even had incorrect information.

Murphy's Law continued to shadow me when a popular local Mormon vocalist who'd been acquainted with my music, stole one of my songs and put it on her album without my permission. Then she had the audacity to title her album after my song. *Really?* When her ex-husband asked me for a date a month later, I saw a song-trade for a hot guy as a pretty good deal. But the long-distance dating soon fizzled along with my junk truck.

So many things went wrong this year that I can't brag about all of them. I will say, however, that I still managed to maintain my grades, make the dean's list, win a scholarship, sell my music, keep track of bills I had yet to pay, magnify my church callings, and most important of all, graduate from CSU Stanislaus—my greatest accomplishment in years.

So, here's a message to all the June Cleavers out there: The only way people truly grow is through adversity. And if life is as perfect as you say it is, and all your ten kids are as wonderful as you say they are, you simply don't have enough challenges to fill your life.

Don't forget: This is not the age of stay-at-home moms. It is the age of diversity, divorce, single-parenting, careers, (writing newsletters doesn't count), hard economic times, and real people. If you can't check any of these boxes, then please cross me off your Christmas Newsletter List because I probably don't have a clue who you are anyway.

Love, Jennifer

CHAPTER 71

WHAT'S YOUR EMERGENCY?

College Graduation, Summer of 2001

With a cap and gown and Hawaiian lei around my neck, my ear-to-ear smile can be seen from the top bleachers. I toss my cap in the air as my siblings and children huddle around me and shower me with congrats. What a blessed day. At age 46, I now have a bachelor's degree in liberal studies. It is one of the biggest accomplishments of my life. Now I just have another year in the credential program, and I'll be a certified elementary school teacher.

As much as I didn't want a day so special to end, eventually the clouds roll in. Soon after graduation, I learned that my oldest son, Zach at age 20, was diagnosed with Hodgkin's Disease. Even though this disease has excellent treatment success, Zach didn't have health insurance, so his treatment went on hold. Although my emotionally tormented son continued to challenge me with his issues, I loved him dearly, and I found the waiting and feelings of helplessness to be distressing.

At age 23, my daughter was attending UC Santa Cruz, and Drew at age seventeen lived with his dad in Utah. I tried to fight the move in court but lost. It was devastating. Since Sebastian had emptied my account and put me in the red, my bishop finally agreed to pay a portion of my bills, and I felt and expressed tremendous gratitude, yet even with his assistance, life was daunting.

Because I thrived on the energy of others, being alone again didn't serve me well. I felt like I went back in time and was reliving the nightmare of my first divorce. All my friends were busy with their spouses and their church callings. I had just entered the credential program and had very little time to socialize anyway. Without even a dog to keep me company, I tried to embrace solitude.

When it's quiet, I can write music. I can meditate and be still. But when there's too much quiet, it can be deafening. I struggled with too much quiet through the first half of the credential program, yet I still managed to get straight A's. When I began my student teaching in the fall, everything started going south. The facilitator who was assigned to work with me was controlling and detached. My son's disease was worsening. I was overwhelmed with mounds of debt despite the church's assistance. I had no support system except for my bishop who, thank God, was helping me with my bills. And there was no one to cheer me toward the finish line except for Carly, my visiting teacher.

WE ARE ALL BUMPING AROUND

Slowly but surely, I was losing my grip. When Sebastian and I were married, we enjoyed the camaraderie of our friends from the Turlock Ward. Once he left, it seemed as if my married girlfriends wanted me to stay away. Sandy, the seminary teacher who encouraged me to write scripture mastery music, suddenly gave me the cold shoulder. I know she admired Sebastian's talent, but it wasn't my fault that he left without telling her goodbye. Then there was my other friend who clung to her husband for dear life whenever I would pass the two of them in the church foyer. *Did she really see me as a husband snatcher?* Little did she know that I moved two states away from the one man I truly loved because he was married.

However, there was one person in the ward who *didn't* want me to stay away. In fact, he said, "Come hither." He was the one I needed to stay clear of. But Satan had a way of ushering temptation to my door when I least expected it. Brother Santiago, a hot, sharp-dressed Latino, was the delicious devil who came knocking. Informally known as Javier, I actually got to know him through his daughter when I coached her on a few songs she sang for a ward talent show.

Impulsively, I invited Javier in and offered him a place beside me on the couch. When I asked him the reason for his visit, he kind of hummed around. It had been ages since I last had sex, and now this hot hunk was here in my living room. I'm talking about tall, swarthy, gourmet eye-candy—a See's Cafe Au Lait Truffle wonderfully invading my space, so close, I could smell the very pheromones of his body, and his smell was as yummy as he was.

My tall, broad-shouldered visitor hand-combed his thick curls and massaged one of his brows, appearing to be distraught. He told me he was considering a divorce and needed some consolation. *Trouble on the home front?* I highly doubted it. I wasn't stupid. I had a hunch it was a sham, a way to get into my pants. It was working a little.

Javier had the most beautiful smile I had ever seen, and his dark Latino eyes were calling. I could already taste him on my tongue. I longed to kiss his eyes, his nose, his lips, then pull his tongue into my mouth, so at least one part of us was intertwined.

We somehow got on the topic of his daughter, and he began flattering me with his words, his silver tongue rolling out the compliments about my teaching skills. Hearing someone talk to me like this, especially someone as hunky as Javier, breathed life back into my lungs again.

Then, unexpectedly, this beautiful man pulled me in and kissed me in just the way I had imagined. On impulse, I eagerly braced the back of Javier's neck and basked in the feeling of his tongue gently folding into mine.

Our groans and pants became louder as he pulled me into him, his kisses soft and plentiful, as he danced his yummy Latino lips down my neck reviving my lifeless spirit. "Oh, my God! … my God, this is … so" *Wait! What on earth am I doing?* All at once, I came to my senses and peeled myself away. In doing so, I rolled off the couch. *Shame on you,* I told myself. I should have scolded him too, but instead, I just told him to leave. The guy was married and had four kids. I sure didn't want to give him a fifth.

What was going on with the people in my ward? And why didn't my home teacher speak up when his wife … well, let me start from the beginning …

As I was walking across the college campus on my way to class near the end of last semester after Sebastian dumped me, I lost my footing in a pothole in the grass and sprained my ankle. When my home teacher, Brother Jones and his wife came to visit me that month, my ankle, which was propped up on ice, had swollen to the size of a grapefruit and was mottled with blotches of black, blue, pink, and green.

"Do you need anything?" asked Brother Jones. *Wasn't it obvious?* Not wanting to appear bothersome, I chose a passive aggressive response. "No, I'll be fine," I said. "I think I can make dinner if I balance myself against the counter and hobble." Secretly hoping he'd get the hint, I thought perhaps he'd offer a home-cooked meal. But when he didn't respond, I looked over at Sister Jones. She was glaring at my grapefruit. She loathed my grapefruit. It meant more compassionate service. She had far too much on her plate, so she finally spoke up and said, "I think you'll be just fine. Just give it time."

All the dysfunction in our ward gradually got to me. Sundays became paralyzing. I couldn't get myself to attend church although I was supposed to be playing the piano for primary. One morning, I felt so numb, I couldn't even get dressed. I just sat on my living room carpet and stared blankly into space.

Later that day, I received a call from the primary chorister. She was upset. She was expecting a pianist, and I was a no-show. I understood why she was mad. I'd be mad too if I were her. But all I could think about was how much better off I'd be if I hung myself in my closet. And even if I went to hell for killing myself, I was sure it would be a lot sweeter than my present state. *Why not now?* I was ready. *Besides, who would miss me? The chorister sure wouldn't.*

I began thinking about how we all served in the church, but where was the true spirit of service? Were we as Mormons so caught up in obligatory duties and a quest for an imagined kingdom in the sky that Hymn #223 "Have I Done Any Good in the World Today?" meant nothing?

How often had I attended to someone simply out of obligation? The church can sometimes overwhelm us with too much responsibility. Giving our all and beyond can sometimes sour our love for service. If our hearts are no longer in it, why serve if serving becomes a burden and a source of stress?

Carly, my visiting teacher, was a woman I admired and respected. She was an angel. Sweet, bubbly, and always wearing a smile, I lived for her monthly visits. In a moment of desperation, I called her one Sunday. I needed to hear her voice. I needed more than the mailman to talk to although he was pretty cute. Carly suggested an ice-cream date on Friday.

It couldn't happen fast enough. Her invitation was just what I needed to pull me out of my funk. Every day, as I prepared my classroom lessons for the student teaching program, I imagined our upcoming ice cream date. I counted the days until we would finally meet. They were a slow grind. Friday couldn't come fast enough.

When Thursday evening arrived, I started my countdown. In twenty-four hours, I'd be connecting with a warm-bodied person. Then the phone rang. I picked it up. It was Carly. She said she had to cancel our date because her husband wanted to attend the temple with her that Friday night. I understood that temple attendance with her spouse would be more important than a date with her friend. Still, it was hard to describe the kind of anguish that washed over me. I felt abandoned and alone.

My sweet visiting teacher had no idea how serious my depression was, nor did she know that she was my only lifeline. Just the thought of another empty Friday had me spiraling to the floor. The kitchen tile was cold, but the truth of my situation was colder and harder. I was completely and utterly alone.

Hours later I was still in the same place. Praying didn't help because I would start crying as soon as my knees hit the floor. I had been crying so much, it felt as if my head would explode. It was around ll:00 p.m. when I got brave enough to pick up the phone and dial 9-1-1.

"Hello. What's your emergency?"

"I don't want to live anymore." I mumbled. I waited in darkness until a calm, reassuring voice pulled me through. The kind man on the other end asked me if I had a favorite TV program. I nodded in the affirmative as if I expected him to see the nod. It wasn't his question that was my saving grace, but his gentle, empathetic tone that drew me in. I could tell he was genuine. I could tell he truly wanted to help me although I was a mere stranger. That beautiful, kind man kept me alive for another day.

CHAPTER 72

A MUCH BETTER HELL

Not long after a stranger on a 911 call rescued me, another stranger entered my life. I met him at an unexpected time and place, and what he offered knocked me for a loop. *Was the Lord trying to test me further?*

After three failed marriages, I no longer felt I fit in with the Mormon culture. I could no longer paint myself into the picture of the Mormon "happily ever after." I felt invisible amid the family togetherness as I slipped quietly away in the middle of Sacrament meeting, trying to suppress tears. A married gentleman was giving a talk about "The Sin of Divorce." Didn't he know that Sebastian's abandonment caused me enough grief?

Yet, even amid the sadness, leaving the only church I had known my entire life was unfathomable. I had been taught to make sacrifices— to selflessly give my all, to endure to the end. *Where was my strength to hang in there during the rough times? Where was my pioneer spirit?*

Amid my turmoil, I reached out to my siblings in hopes for some answers. I tried to let them know about the huge disparity between my desire to please the Lord through my church callings and the emotional connection I was lacking with my ward family. My siblings advised me to press forward—to faithfully attend my meetings despite my misery. Sooner or later, I would be rewarded, they said. *Yet how much longer could I hold on?*

Occasionally, I'd muster the strength to make the long, dreary monthly drives to the one and only place I thought would save me—the LDS Danville dances. There, I futilely hunted for a spouse. *Geez woman, when is enough, enough?* I ignored the devil when he talked to me like that. I assumed it was the devil. *Could it have been God?*

On the way there, I was always muttering one last desperate plea, hoping the Lord would help me accomplish this most impossible mission. I'm sure He was rolling his weary eyes every time He heard the word "Danville" or "husband." I would never let Him rest until I had a wedding ring on my finger, hoping my fourth catch would be the charm.

One evening, as my old rattletrap rumbled through the Altamont Pass, I knew I wouldn't be able to handle another night of disappointment. So I got vocal with Heavenly Father. I demanded that He give me a husband or else. I didn't know what the "or else" was. I mean, *who threatens God?* I guess I had hit my breaking point. I was tired of asking nicely. *Hadn't I put in the work? Was I not deserving?*

Doing the same thing repeatedly and expecting different results would soon have me in a straitjacket. Yet I didn't consider myself insane. Trying to be faithful with every ounce of my being, it felt completely wrong and morally dangerous to look outside the church for a man. But the day finally came when even *I* had had enough. *A new venue perhaps?*

Finding an LDS man, especially a temple-worthy one, was a long shot. So when I decided to search for my husband at a local night club, I knew my chances would be next to nil. Still, I didn't know of any other place within a thirty-mile radius from home that had more divorcees than Modesto's popular downtown nightclub, which catered to the middle-aged single crowd.

Soon I began making regular weekend trips to Crocodile's. It was there that I met Fynn, a tall, attractive Swede with a full head of honey-blonde hair. I had always been a sucker for a sexy accent.

Fynn was refreshingly not into playing games like most guys. He was a straight shooter and point blank asked if I'd be interested in a casual hookup. Of course, I said no. It's one thing to have sex with a coworker or friend, but to have sex with a stranger? No way was this girl going to engage in such a sin. It was one thing to want to die after deciding that hell might be a happier place, but quite another to commit fornication and end up there. I had come too far to lose points with the Lord and throw away my salvation. *But would it hurt to exchange phone numbers?*

This light-hearted, clean-cut, nicely dressed Swede and I soon developed a friendship over the phone and danced whenever we bumped into each other at the club. He seemed like a decent, respectable man by the world's standards. But his main intent was to bed me, not wed me. In my sanctimonious judgment, his lustful desires were iniquitous.

One night, when I was feeling extra needy for company, I called my carnally minded friend. Because it had been far too long since I felt loved and touched, or even had a friend to talk to, I knew there was a possibility of losing control with him. After he travelled twenty miles to my house, I sat next to him on the couch and watched with wide-eyed wonder as he pried the cork from a fancy wine bottle and poured two glasses of Zinfandel. I had never tasted wine before, and it sure was nasty. Other than the wine, everything was going well until I accidently knocked over my goblet. As wine flooded the coffee table and dripped down into the carpet fibers, I panicked and took it as a bad omen. I told him I just couldn't do it. Although Fynn was ready for a good time, he didn't push the situation and graciously bowed out.

At the time I met Fynn, I was attending the post-graduate program and was trapped in a classroom all day with a bunch of uppity, suburban housewives who seemed to try to "one-up" each other as they bragged about their perfect marriages—how their husbands gave them nightly foot rubs and would show up with a new sports car in the driveway for no damn good reason. How would it be to have any kind of man, let alone a foot-rubbing, rich one. My ex-husband's generosity went as far as handing over a junker pick-up that was on the brink of falling into a thousand little pieces on the highway.

That evening, as I sat reading The Book of Mormon, I thought about my new Swedish friend. Right there and then, I decided I wouldn't turn down sex the next time he offered it. My life was already one very long, drawn out hell anyway.

When Fynn called me a week later, I was up for it. We met at his place, had a nice conversation, and engaged in responsible, protected sex. Then something unexpected happened. Immediately afterward, I burst into tears, not because of Guilt or fear that I'd be cast down to Hell, but because of a sweet sense of calm—a place where Guilt and Shame did not reside. *How could I possibly feel calm after committing such a so-called sin?* I didn't know what to make of it.

After all my insurmountable challenges along with the stress of working toward a degree while picking up the pieces of what was left of my life, I finally made a choice contrary to the principles and standards which I had been taught. I slept with a practical stranger. According to church leaders, this choice should have led me to pain and misery, but it didn't. Instead, it led me to a place of self-acceptance and calm.

Some people take it for granted if they have it, but I can't overstate the importance of being touched and feeling connected to another human being, even if enduring love is elusive. Being with Fynn released endorphins in my brain that lowered my anxieties and fears. Sadly, I didn't know of anyone I could embrace except for my visiting teacher; but what was I supposed to do? She was busy raising five kids. *Was she just supposed to drop everything and come over to my house every time I needed a hug?*

As Fynn and I laughed, talked and snuggled, the impenetrable darkness that once surrounded me had finally dissipated. Our emotional and physical connection seemed to be the remedy to carry me through that dark period of my life.

Ten years prior to meeting Fynn after Gary and I divorced, I naively believed God would bless me with a Mormon prince if I resisted all manner of temptation. But that never happened. Now my life was a far cry from what it used to be and far too complicated and crazy to put together the puzzle as to how The Lord operated. *Maybe this was the kind of Hell Heavenly Father approved of if it helped me to stay above water?*

Although I knew Fynn's visa would expire and he'd be returning home someday, I simply enjoyed the moments we had together. This gentle foreigner who I met on a cold, lonely night in a crowded hedonistic bar rescued me from my devastating loneliness. Even after he left for home, the memories of his gentle warmth stayed with me and bring a smile even today.

CHAPTER 73

STANDING AT THE CROSSROADS

At age 46, I stood at the crossroads re-examining my life. My dismal resume had nothing to show but three divorces, loss of my custodial rights, and a string of impulsive decisions that created a continuum of financial distress, massive debt, judgment, condemnation, and heartache.

There was no question that I could have made far better choices. But because I'd been taught and believed that a temple marriage was everything, my LDS Marriage Manhunt had become a vicious cycle of failed efforts and self-condemnation. At mid-life I needed to face the reality that I was damaged, both emotionally and spiritually. I had nothing to show for my life. I had been masterfully programmed to become a good little Mormon robot.

In coming to this realization, for the first time, I seriously questioned my lifelong belief in the Church's First Presidency and Quorum of the Twelve and their "divine inspiration" to guide the Church. I'd always believed these men to be warm, fuzzy grandpa-types, humble, yet powerful oracles of God. But now I no longer knew what to think.

Since I pledged my life to the Lord at age fifteen, I tried with everything in me to follow the standards and values the church set for me, believing with childlike faith that this would lead to happiness, exaltation, and eternal life. And there, I stood, a broken soul. *Where should I go from here?* At the crossroads, do I stay on course, or do I take a left or a right? Having leaned so long on being told what to do, I couldn't even trust my own intuition.

Deciding to leave the faith would require independent thinking. Because the church had outlined nearly every detail of my daily existence, I had not become skilled at thinking for myself. But one thing I did have was a big, fat bank account of suffering. I knew that if I were to continue on this emotionally treacherous road, I was due for more heartache.

But how would I get off the road? I was too depressed to have any kind of clarity. Before making any life-alternating decision, I realized I needed to see a doctor. I was far too sad. Every day, I fought hard to suppress my tears and cling to life.

At his office, my internist showed interest and compassion as I explained the trail of losses I had experienced within the past decade including my recent divorce. Due to my weight loss and obvious anguish and distress, he put me on Lexapro to treat my clinical depression. I then took advantage of a quiet moment to ask him if he knew of any churches that catered to divorced singles. To my surprise and delight, this kind, sweet man told me the exact location of a Christian community church in downtown Modesto that was brimming with singles.

I went home that day feeling excited. A tiny voice in the back of my head had been urging me for some time to find a church that would help me heal. At first, I was sure that my doctor was the vehicle leading me in a new direction. But my noisy brain was beginning to have doubts. Each time, I thought about that new church, I heard a Primary children's choir in my frontal lobe belting out the song, "Follow the Prophet." In my confusion, I immediately took the matter to the Lord; and on my knees, I wrestled with Him for weeks, letting Him know how much I needed His approval of this life-altering decision. I would not survive a journey down a different path if it would anger my Heavenly Father and cause him to turn His back on me.

After weeks of praying, I never received that heartwarming confirmation or a burning in the bosom which our founding prophet claimed any earnest saint would feel after they made the right decision. That was the moment I finally decided for myself to use my brain and common sense. *Did I want to simply survive? Or did I want to take a chance on an unknown path, and possibly thrive for the 40 or 50 years I had left?*

Still on the fence when the following Sunday arrived, I decided I'd give this new church a test run. Heading north on Hwy 99, I prayed the whole way there, hoping this new group of people would be my unicorn.

Thirty minutes later, I spotted the sign: "The Christian Community Church" stenciled in black across the front of a white-framed, brown-bricked building. It looked like it was a part of a community of buildings that were scattered across a large corner lot. There were no glass-stained windows or steeples or fancy architecture—just plain brick rectangular structures with simple windows. I hoped the people inside were just as unpretentious.

I parked near the entrance and entered the front lobby and inquired about the singles group. With map in hand, I headed east to the old, ivory-brick building, then climbed the outside switchback staircase to the second story. After pushing open the glass door, my eyes grew wide at first glance. I was looking at a twenty-five by thirty-foot room overflowing with singles; some younger than me, some older, but most looked about my age. Best of all, there were tons of guys—cute ones too.

As I studied my surroundings, I couldn't help but be drawn to the wall-to-wall, rich, dark walnut floor. Colorful throw rugs throughout the room added warmth and style to earthtone couches and pillows. There was a counter on the side wall where drinks, juice, and hot beverages were served. I was expecting something much different. It didn't look like the inside of a church at all. It was more like a barista coffee bar with comfy sofas and bistro tables.

Feeling a little out of my comfort zone, I forced myself to walk over and introduce myself to a few girls who were chatting on a nearby couch. They had a relaxed, light energy about them as they welcomed me to this main hangout, which they explained was for both Sunday Bible class and Friday game-night. It all sounded so cozy and fun. Even more fun was that most of the women wore jeans. No strict dress code. Praise the Lord! With the casual, relaxed atmosphere, I already felt like one of them.

Twice a week, I found myself driving down Hwy 99 for Bible class and Friday game night. I started bonding with people who shared my same struggles. It felt amazing. I had finally found connection. And connection was my lifeline. Carly, my visiting teacher, knew there was no support system for me in our ward due to the sparse amount of single people, so I couldn't wait to share my excitement with her about this new group.

I was bubbling over with perhaps too much enthusiasm when I called her one day and told her about my new friends. Her less-than-enthusiastic response took me aback. "I'm not sure about this new group," she offered flatly. "Why can't you get involved in the ward singles program?"

She must have forgotten our conversation about the motley group. The singles program in our ward consisted of six senior citizens and a couple of guys my age that seemed to be teetering on the spectrum of mental illness. Typically, Carly always had my back. She even seemed empathetic when she once suggested that if I wanted to find love, I would need to date non-members and convert them.

Now I was telling her about a church that was brimming with singles. It's like I had entered heaven. But she was not impressed. Carly was more concerned about her duty to keep me in the fold than seeing me happy. I guess she cared in the only way she knew how—in the way the Church taught her to care—to ensure that I remained an active member. And if I wasn't happy as a member, that was my problem. As long as she kept me coming back—as long as she did her duty, that's all that really mattered.

A few weeks later, while I was still attending both churches, my hunk-a-junk on wheels broke down. It had a lot of problems. This time, it was the alternator. Carly was the one and only person I felt comfortable calling when I needed help. The last break down was just three months prior. As usual, I called Triple A, but I needed a ride home from the auto shop.

When I explained my situation to her on the phone, she let it all out. Her tone was edgy and harsh, "Jennifer, do you think that perhaps you're having all of these car troubles because you're attending another church?"

I hadn't even left the church yet. I was still fence-sitting, ready to swing my leg to the other side. After that judgy remark, there was no more contemplation.

I tried to gather my composure after her shocking remark. I needed to remain calm yet convicted. "Have you ever heard of Job?" I said, pausing for a bit so my words could sink in. I didn't expect her to answer. Another very long pause. "Well, that's my life." I quipped, my voice falling flat. At that moment, everything went quiet. She apparently had no response. So I gave her a proper goodbye.

Looking back, I now see this episode with Carly with enhanced perspective. Could she have been more sensitive to my dire situation and rendered compassion instead of choosing to judge me? Absolutely. Yet as I've matured through the years, I can now see the importance of not judging her as well. With her husband in the bishopric, she probably felt more pressure to steer her fellow church members in the right direction without even realizing she was judging.

From my standpoint, Carly was simply a victim of a monolithic mind-programming system. As my visiting teacher, she had a genuine concern for my salvation. In her heart, she truly believed the Lord was punishing me. Protected in a happy bubble, she was blessed with a kind, loving husband, great kids, and a lovely home. She couldn't possibly put herself in my shoes, so it would have been futile to try defending myself.

Carly and I rarely talked after that. I wondered if there was another fold that didn't shame people for "church hopping." I had never received that burning in the bosom that I had prayed for—that feeling of confirmation the Holy Ghost was supposed to give me if the decision to stay in the church was right.

I became even more confused and despondent as I continued to attend my required meetings each Sunday. I was much more at peace when attending morning Bible study with my new group of non-Mormon friends.

As clarity began to pierce the fog of my confusion, I allowed myself to admit that LDS doctrine no longer set well with me. It was like an instruction manual written for someone else. Many sermons such as those on marriage and divorce were painful to sit through. I began to see the church as a one-size-fits-all exclusive club with rules that no longer served me. So one Sunday morning, with very little hesitation, I turned right at the fork in the road, away from the LDS church toward the congregation that enjoyed caffeine and casual blue jeans.

CHAPTER 74

BEING SAVED BY GRACE TAKES WORK

Although I had left the church and had no desire to return, it's never a clean getaway when leaving any high-demand religion. All I knew was that my Mormon ghosts refused to leave as I battled to clear them from my thoughts.

Sitting across the desk from my new pastor, I wondered if this impassioned man could trap my Mormon ghosts and suck these tormentors into a containment unit. I needed to learn how to move on without Confusion or Shame.

At five-foot-nine, with a middle-age bulge, Pastor Brown seemed quite comfortable in his casual 49ers footfall jersey as he welcomed me to the fold and pointed to the chair across from him. He appeared easy-going and relaxed. So far so good. Hopefully he was the kind of man who had the enduring capacity to answer my flood of questions and give me some badly needed direction.

Since leaving the church, I was more confused than ever about truth. I didn't know what it looked like anymore. As I told the pastor all about my Mormon departure and the guilt that edged deep into my neuro pathways over the span of four decades, his warm smile and kind, attentive coffee-brown eyes made me feel he was truly interested as he encouraged me to continue.

Sitting straighter in my chair, I noticed an enthusiastic twinkle as I fired a volley of questions his way without taking a breath. When I finally came up for air, this saint-of-a-man let out a sigh and reclined in his seat, clasping his hands behind his head. After a moment of silence, he advised me to practice living moment to moment. And with that, he promised that through time, the answers to all my questions would be revealed. I didn't like that answer. I didn't have much patience. I knew I'd be back. I was the nightmare of nightmares for any good-hearted shepherd. The poor man was never going to get rid of me.

As I left his office and walked toward my truck, I found myself smiling. The smile was still there when I stepped inside the truck and turned the ignition key. Then all at once, my smile disappeared. I groaned. The engine wasn't turning over. I didn't need a jump—I needed a few thousand dollars to fix the electrical problem that had been going on for years.

When I quickly ran back to Pastor Brown's office and explained my situation, he immediately picked up the phone and got things rolling. Using church funds to tow my truck to a shop, he didn't stop there. He paid to have it diagnosed and fixed. He also delegated someone from the singles group to oversee driving me to and from my student-teaching job every day while my car was being worked on. And all along I thought Mormons were well-organized.

What I found most refreshing about these particular Christians was the way they served. Mormons pay their tithing so they can have temple privileges. Although a lot of good Latter-day Saints serve for the right reasons, many serve because they feel it's the only way to insure their slot in the top tier of the Celestial Kingdom. They believe they are saved by their works first, and then by grace. Growing up, I had been convinced that "being saved by grace only" is the easy way out.

I witnessed firsthand how hard my new friends worked—how their combined efforts got my truck back on the road again. Learning to be unselfish takes work. It's human nature to turn inward and become self-absorbed. It takes discipline to pull away from consuming projects and hobbies to go help someone in need. Serving when no one is holding you accountable, when no one is observing or taking notes—serving without expecting anything in return was something I had been taught but had never seen in action as I was seeing in this small congregation. That was the kind of altruism I admired and wanted to cultivate in myself.

The following year I learned how to volunteer my time and talents to help others without being accountable to anyone but myself; nor was my desire to serve motivated by wanting a heavenly reward. Looking back, some of my very best memories of my single years were those shared with dear friends I met at the old ivory-brick building.

Although I was much happier in this new church than as a Mormon, the longing to find a man to complete my life never left me. There were a lot more pickings here than there were LDS single men in the entire Valley. *Would I find a husband among these good people?*

CHAPTER 75

MY DIVINE MATCHMAKER

Since I joined my new group of church friends, I had my eye on one of the guys for a while. Jack was a former drug dealer. He said he was handed a Bible in prison one day, and overnight he turned from Saul, a wicked man, to Paul, the apostle. Charismatic, captivating, and hunkalicious, Jack was on fire for Jesus. His love for the Lord was contagious. I wanted what he had, and I told him so. "Let's get together," he said. So we did.

Jack looked at me in that way—you know the way guys look at you when they like you? My stomach fluttered every time his eyes met mine. He was hot and spiritual, but not a whacko like Manford, my fanatical date who flooded his walls with temples and church talks. I couldn't wait to get together with Jack. That warm, tingling feeling in my gut told me this was it. The Lord was finally going to deliver my husband. My life was about to change in a major way.

Sometimes I gave too much credit to the Lord for what was happening in my life. I believed Him to be my Divine Matchmaker. It wasn't His fault I didn't listen to Him and chose to marry three strangers.

But I believed God knew I had struggled enough. My reward? ...
Ex-Con Jack.

Our first meeting was at my place. Instead of taking out his Bible,
Jack asked me if I wanted to check out the goods under his hood. In my
naivete, I assumed he was referring to his Honda Accord. I had no idea
he was referring to his "junk." I guess he was trying to make up for all
the fun he missed out on when incarcerated. I wasn't about to engage
in his shallow escapades. I had sorely mistaken him for a man who had
purpose and drive and self-control. Knowing those wedding bells would
not be ringing anytime soon really shook me up. *When would I ever learn
it takes time to get to know someone?*

I became hopeful when I got to know Sam. Tall and good-looking
with the whitest teeth I'd ever seen, I wondered if he used peroxide-gel
whitening strips or if he was just blessed with great genetics. Sam was a
48-year-old divorced father of two and a recent convert to Christianity.
Neither showy nor pretentious, he was easily readable, open, and honest,
yet still had enough mystique to be intriguing. He was the kind of guy
who enjoyed country living, fast cars, baseball, and special alone time
with his Bible.

I was drawn to Sam for many reasons. A natural born leader, he
was usually the first person to offer a prayer at the start of every Sunday
worship service. Even when our group met at restaurants for lunch, Sam
was the one who would remind us to stop eating and offer a blessing
on the food. He wasn't complicated, but he was smart. If God didn't
choose him for me, then I'd have to try to work around His Divine
plan. Of all the women there, I felt blessed that Sam started to show an
interest in me.

On our fourth date, Sam and I decided on popcorn and a movie
at his place. When we started making out, I was all in. Sam was a great

kisser. We were spiritually compatible and kiss compatible. *How perfect was that?* Our hearts were aligned. My future looked bright.

When he dropped me off at home, he lingered at my door. The kiss lasted a few minutes until we were both breathless. It all felt so magical. If that kiss wasn't a sign he was falling for me, I don't know what was. The Lord had His hand in this. There was no doubt in my mind. My Heavenly Father had finally come through.

All those agonizing years of driving miles to Danville hoping I'd find my eternal companion, when all along, Sam was only thirty miles away. It was finally happening. The Lord was simply waiting for me to leave that straight and narrow path so I could meet a guy who loved Chevy Camaros, baseball, and bluegrass country music—three things I hated. But a girl can't have everything.

After that mesmerizing kiss at my door, I barley slept a wink that night. I was so giddy in love, I couldn't wait to call my girlfriend and tell her all about Sam. The following morning, I rattled excitedly on the phone about our budding romance. "Congratulations, he's a great catch," my friend said. I agreed.

At church the next Sunday, Sam and I sat next to each other at the same table, our usual routine. He still looked happy to see me. Nothing had changed since the prior evening, yet I felt insecurity rising from the pit of my gut. My stomach was in knots. I needed to know where I stood with him, and if I didn't ask soon, the anxiety would soon cause heart palpitations and God knows what else. Unlike my female peers, I was not coy, or mysterious, nor was I good at playing hard to get. But I knew I was falling fast, even though we'd only had four dates.

After class we went for a stroll. As we circled the block, I unflinchingly asked Sam where the relationship was heading. His reply knocked me sideways. I nearly fell flat on my nose. "What relationship?" he said. "I just like kissing on you, that's all."

I assumed because he was approaching fifty, he was looking for a wife. But I was wrong. It seemed like all the men I ever dated fit into one of two categories: hand-me-down rejects or wandering-hand hotties with no serious intentions. To me, Sam was just another wandering-hand hottie.

As I look back on my vulnerability during that time, it pains me to see how I continually let unrealistic expectations lead me to deep disappointment. I put my whole heart and energy into hunting down love without knowing or learning how to play the dating game. I certainly didn't know how to take it slow.

Ultimately, I saw the Lord as my personal slave. It was like, "God, forget about world peace and hunger, just get me my husband." My perpetual begging was far from normative behavior. The thing I struggled with the most as a hopeless romantic was that I was convinced I had no control over my situation. I thought I could do nothing about changing my single status to married. It was up to the guy to do that, and that sucked; because even though the men my age were old enough to be grandpas, they seemed completely uninterested in tying the knot.

Because I quit taking my anti-depressants to avoid the side effects, my sadness ran deep. In my lonely state, living life without ever experiencing true, reciprocated love, was a fate worse than going to the grave itself. If I wanted a happy ending, it seemed I would have to manufacture a story with a fairy tale happily-ever-after script and be done with it. Truth be damned.

It pained me that Sam couldn't see me as a great catch; probably because I wasn't. He was playful, fun, smart, had goals, loved God, wasn't in debt, didn't molest his sister, nor did he abuse me or have a rage problem. Compared to my three ex-husbands, he was a prime catch. Then there was me—clinically depressed and in denial about my neediness.

After Sam let me down, I went into a deep funk and believed I would never find love again. The mere thought of growing old with no one to share my life flowed through my head like river channels rushing toward the edge of a fifty-foot drop. That's how fast I saw my life going by. I could already see the writing on my epitaph, "She Died Trying To Catch a Man, But At Least She Died Trying." My metaphorical sun had set years ago. Was there still a chance for love when the sky was black, and the moonlight was dimming?

Sometimes we do crazy things when we feel utterly lost and hopeless. If I had never dated Sam, I might have been better off, because with the possibility for love there's also the chance for hurt. When it didn't work out, I crashed hard. I had found a wonderful community of people, yet I allowed one man to sink me. It was time to get back on my anti-depressants. Being drug-dependent wasn't fun, but better to deal with the side effects than to constantly entertain thoughts of death.

Depression usually causes people to lose all rationality and let emotions take over. We don't always think things through. And when our emotions intensify, the ability to make intelligent choices diminishes. The strength to stay happy becomes virtually impossible. I just wanted someone to hold me, cherish me, and to convince me everything would be okay. Knowing that was not going to happen anytime soon, I did something dumb. I said, "Screw it," and slept with a complete stranger—at his home. I even gave him the address to my church in case he wanted to join our group on Sunday. Dumb da dumb dumb.

The next morning, after I slept with him, I was hunting madly for my car keys, and while I fretted and mumbled to myself, he went into a sudden rage—a side of him I hadn't seen since we had only been acquainted for a few hours. While he called me every name in the book, I quickly uttered a silent prayer. "Heavenly Father, help me find my keys." I looked under the coffee table and spotted them. Snatching them from the floor, I fled as if the devil himself were after me. When I finally reached my car, my whole body was shaking.

The following Tuesday, I spotted this same stranger sitting in his car watching my apartment. On Friday, he showed up at our singles game night, briefly skulking around the alcove. The next week, he showed up there again. I was playing Mille Bornes with friends when I glanced up to see him lurking in the shadows. Cold chills ran down my spine as his coal-black eyes met mine, studying me with a predator's unwavering stare. I whispered to Kelli, the pastor's assistant, that I had a stalker, and he was here. I asked her if she would walk me to my car. She quizzed me as we headed to the parking lot, obviously suspecting there was a reason this creep was targeting me.

The next day, Pastor Brown called to ask me to come to his office. His tone wasn't concerned or friendly. *Was I in trouble?*

CHAPTER 76

OH, THOSE SWEET, SWEET LIES

When I sat down across from Pastor Brown, the deep look of disappointment on his face told me I was in trouble. I wondered exactly what Kelli had told him about me and about my stalker. I rubbed my sweaty palms along my jeans then nervously fiddled with my hair.

After my nerve-wracking experience of being judged by past leaders, I was beginning to rebel against the whole idea of male dominance behind a desk which to me seemed more like an opportunity to interrogate without seeking true understanding about my situation.

When I finally managed to look up at my leader, he asked me in a pious tone if I had sex with my stalker. I stiffened in my chair. My fears were confirmed. Either he or Kelli assumed that because a guy was stalking me, I had done something to lure him in.

After becoming involved with a different religious community, which at first promised to fill my need for a church family, it suddenly seemed as though my sins were out on a display table for anyone to inspect, even though I had never confessed them.

In the silence, Pastor Brown's question hung in the air waiting to be answered. Because I have always had a habit of being blatantly honest, I blurted out a firm yes. "Yes, I slept with my stalker." Shifting in my seat, I tapped my fingers on the chair's metal arms as he leaned forward, clenching his mouth, his eyes narrowing with intensity.

"Jennifer, do you know that every time you have sex with someone out of wedlock, you are driving another nail into Jesus's wrist?" I watched the crease between my leader's brows grow deeper as I slumped in my chair, unable to hold his gaze. Hurting Jesus was the last thing I wanted to do. I couldn't have felt sadder or more confused. If Pastor Brown believed scare tactics were the best motivator, he was preaching to the wrong woman. Especially when I knew his little secret.

About a month prior to that day, while his wife and I were chatting, I was surprised to learn that she was engaged to Pastor Brown for six years. I had never known any couple that had been engaged that long. In the Latter-day Saint culture, most partners married within a few months of meeting each other. Naturally I was curious to know how she had managed to stay abstinent for that long with a man she loved. That's when she leaned in and whispered, "Well you know, Jennifer, there's always repentance."

That tidbit of information helped me understand that Pastor Brown and his wife were human like the rest of us. It appeared that he had nailed a stake in the Lord's wrist himself. To respect his wife, I didn't reveal what she had shared with me. Instead, I just asked him outright if he had ever had a weak moment and crossed some lines when he was single and dating. It was a fair question. No one's sinless. Not even Pastor Brown.

When he offered a flat no, he lost all credibility with me. Everything he said after that was nothing but oratory piffle, and I didn't want him wasting my time. But I sure had a lot to say to him.

I told him that there had been a discussion within the singles group about sexual intimacy after divorce. A few couples had admitted to being sexually active. If Pastor Brown wasn't squirming in his chair while lecturing me, he sure was squirming right then while turning fifty shades of red. I guess it was a hard blow to learn that his lectures on virtuous dating were falling on deaf ears, and that some of his sheep had gone astray.

I sat across from him in the silence as he let out an irritated huff. I bet he regretted calling me into his office now that the work to save his flock had just multiplied tenfold. As he lowered his gaze, he appeared to be struggling with the reality of more sinners like me running loose out there. This was probably not how he had pictured our visit going at all.

After a quiet pause, Pastor Brown looked up at me and said something that almost knocked me off my cushioned seat. "Sometimes, it's not a good idea to be so blatantly honest."

What? His first attempt to save me was by trying to convince me that I played a part in my Lord's crucifixion. Now he wanted me to put a gag order on my childlike candor. I was flummoxed. It seemed as though he was determined to cure me of something.

"It's kind of like an 'in your face' honesty that is getting you into trouble," he said, hoping to teach a 46-year-old guileless woman how to be more subtle and crafty. This was his idea of "fixing" me?

I'm the type of person who vocalizes my issues in order to resolve them. This is how my brain operates. *If I couldn't share my sexual struggles with my leaders, then who could I trust?* Certainly not Kelli or Pastor Brown. Maybe they'd rather have such things fester inside and multiply like a tumorous cancer. Would that make them go away? Was that their solution to saving my soul?

At that point, I realized that I had wasted an entire hour with him. What a shame. Because when I first met Pastor Brown, he seemed to be so understanding and compassionate. Once I turned his scare tactics back at him, it appeared he was looking for flimflam excuses to reprimand me. I knew I had done a dumb thing, but I didn't need his fearmongering tactics. What I needed was a good anti-depressant.

While Pastor Brown continued his lecture, all I heard was the sound of "blekety bleck" in my head as I turned and looked up at the mural of Christ on the wall. *It looks like we both put a few nails in your wrists, Lord,* I mumbled. I turned my gaze from the mural and fixed a big frown on my pastor. I think he got the message because he stopped his lecture. I got up from my chair and bid him goodbye for the very last time.

On my way home, I wondered if there was a greener pasture out there with a leader who celebrated the uniqueness of his parishioners rather than trying to create human replicas of his version of perfection. Perhaps there was a pastor who could be a little more humble about his own indiscretions as in "all have sinned" *(Romans 3:23)*. Maybe it was time to go church-hopping again. *Wait? Was that a sin?*

CHAPTER 77

MY DEFINING MOMENT

I found Grace and Mercy Christian Community shortly after experiencing Pastor Brown's unusual methods of "sin interrogation." Honestly, I really liked the man. Perhaps he was just having a rough day, and I know I didn't help. Even so, after that not-so-pleasant chastising experience, I felt prompted to explore elsewhere. It wasn't like I couldn't go back and visit my friends at the old-ivory brick building. And I would be making more friends in the meantime.

Yet as I continued my spiritual journey as a non-denominational Christian, or born-again, or whatever the heck I was, I became disillusioned. At first it was the little things, like churchy people who claimed to have all the answers as they sat on the pew judging others. I get it. We all succumb to our weaknesses and occasionally act like idiots. But over time, I found that going to church took a lot of effort. I wasn't having fun anymore. Even worse—I was beginning to feel like a Mormon again.

Then one day, I received a phone call from a friend from "Grace and Mercy" who sang with me in their church choir. I had a lot on my plate and was taking a break from choir practice when she asked when I'd be returning. I told her I wasn't sure. All at once, I heard a deafening shrill on the other end. "I think Satan has a hold on you," she said. *Wow. Could she be the devil herself?* I couldn't believe what I was hearing. *Were there others in the church who were possessed with this dark-age mentality?*

I never believed in giving too much credit to the devil. To me it's an excuse to not hold yourself accountable for your raunchy behavior. You're irritable with your friends. It's the devil. You're impatient in traffic. It's the devil. You skip out on choir practice. Of course, we know it's the devil.

After that phone call, I lost my appetite for church. It wasn't the one phone call that did me in. There were a lot of little things about organized religion that began to get under my skin. *Who else in my circle of friends had the same ignorant mentality? Who could I go to for consolation without getting accused of being possessed? Was this God's church? And if so, why was that joy in my heart slowly dwindling?*

When it comes right down to it, it's that human condition again. Mormon, Catholic, Baptist, Hindu—we're all humans having human experiences. Some wacko believes we're possessed and makes us feel like crap. We react. Perhaps we're too sensitive. We stop trusting. We haven't yet learned to turn inward and revel in the love we have for ourselves. Or we're just sick and tired of the hypocrisy. The Bible thumpers, the egoic judgment, the thrashing of God's Holy Scriptures of Love—all propelled me to dig deeper within myself for answers.

A few weeks into playing hooky from church, I was reading a book by Wayne Dyer—a self-help author, motivational speaker, and therapist. I can't recall which book it was or his exact words, but I will never forget the impact of his message which implicated *that if we rely on an outside source for forgiveness, we are not empowered.* That golden nugget of truth was the force that changed me. It was my defining moment.

Dyer's message brought me back to my teenage years when I bathed myself in Guilt for pleasuring myself behind closed doors. I wasted hours on my knees feeling wretched and unworthy, pleading for God's mercy. What about John 14:20? ".... On that day you will realize that I am in my Father, and you are in me, and I am in you." If I had only known I already had the power to forgive myself!

For decades, I believed the answers were in religion—that the only way to happiness was knowing God. But when I thought about it, I didn't really know *Him.* I knew the Mormon god. I knew the Fundamentalist god. *But did I know the God who dwells within me?*

Wayne Dyer helped me to know the God who dwells within all of us. He lives within me and lives within you. We're never powerless or left alone. I can commune with this Infinite Wisdom wherever I go.

CHAPTER 78

LIFE AFTER ORGANIZED RELIGION

After almost fifty-years of striving to be a faithful Mormon, I assumed if I withdrew from a religious world, I would be a wandering nomad with no purpose or direction. I was pleasantly surprised to discover that I had it backwards. Stepping away from organized religion toward empowerment helped me define a clear path for myself. My new journey has presented me with limitless opportunities to grow as I am gradually discovering who I am and my hidden potential.

I had left religion around the same time I became disenchanted with the public school system. After a semester of struggling to teach 40 second graders with their endless range of learning abilities— from the gifted child to the learning-challenged, I seriously questioned what I formerly assumed would be my life-long calling. How could the government expect one teacher to meet the individual learning needs of a small army of children whose range of abilities was as wide and diverse as their cultures? I found it an impossible absurdity. Teachers have my utmost respect as they strive to educate our children under such challenging conditions

Walking away from a high-demand religion only to find that I had been immersed in another tightly controlled environment in the school system was the one-two punch I needed to remind myself about my dream. I was born to be an entrepreneur, and the time had come to pursue this quest.

I was no longer unseasoned. I had overcome many challenges and survived. I had earned a college degree, which prepared me with a variety of skills and broadened my perspective of the world. These achievements assured me I had the ability to accomplish whatever I set my mind to. And with that confidence, I made a life-changing decision. I left my teaching position. I knew intuitively the only way I would thrive was by turning to my gifts and talents and doing what I loved the most. I was ready. I trusted myself and my new plan, having faith that the money would follow. And I was not disappointed.

After I quit teaching, I began to build my income creatively, writing and selling songs, teaching piano lessons, and occasionally subbing for the school district. "Sing the Scriptures," the business I created with Sebastian had been slowly expanding since we sold our first CD in 1999. Between 2001-2010, I was crushing it with my sales. While selling my music to seminary teachers in all parts of the world, I formed a tight bond with a handful of them. I wanted to be completely open and honest with the teachers I grew to love, and so I informed them I was no longer attending church. These lovely "sisters" told me they couldn't care less about my church attendance. They just wanted my CDs. (smile).

For a full decade, my scripture mastery CDs were a hot commodity in the LDS market throughout every part of the US, England, Africa, Australia, New Zealand, and in some places in South America. With my success, I expanded my song collection, writing and selling music for children's education, Primary songs, piano solos, and inspirational songs.

During this time, my personal dating life also improved. I found and fell in love with my best friend, Chris, a blue-collar worker whose vitality, support, and light humor made my life a little sweeter. We became friends first and then lovers. But not all romantic relationships are made to last. This one didn't, but we are still friends to this day.

When my romance with Chris ended, I dated dozens of men and enjoyed a host of opportunities that helped me to grow and learn about myself as a person. This personal growth experience has been golden.

In 2010, at age 55, I would be found either at a little country bar or stomping my boots on the Crocodiles dance floor as I successfully mastered with enthusiasm, over a hundred country line dances as well as hip hop. I spent nine hours a weekend enjoying this aerobic activity with my friends and rightfully earned my nickname: "The Dancing Fool."

My friend, Darlene, another bubbly clubber would often meet me on a Friday night before the doors opened so we could hog the spotlight on the dance floor as we'd tap our sequined heels to the rhythm of our moves. Spectators whistled and cheered, and some would even try to join us, mimicking our moves, but no one could ever keep up. Those were the good old days.

Can I please go back to that time when I had knees of steel?

CHAPTER 79

A UNIVERSAL RELIGION

After leaving organized religion, I no longer felt guilty about delving into religious studies that have included many philosophies, mythologies, and spiritual paths. This has been an adventure and an awakening. My world, which was once finite, now has no bounds.

The longer I've been on the planet, the more I see the fallacy in a religion that professes to be the only true one. I've learned from a beloved yogi, Swami Vivekananda, in his essay, "The Ideal of a Universal Religion," that "abstract" humanity is common to us all—"abstract" in that no two humans are alike in personality, physicality, race, sexual orientation, experience, etc. Yet we are all one in humanity. We are all spiritual beings; therefore, we are all different but the same.

Our individual personalities will be drawn to particular paths for guidance and direction. Various religious sects are like pearls on a necklace and God, the common thread, runs through them all. The universe would cease to exist without diversity. The concept of universal balance can be found in many belief systems, including philosophy, science, and religion. Universal balance is the idea that the universe is in a state of equilibrium, and without a balance between opposing forces it cannot sustain itself. It is therefore absurd to believe that every human on the earth should adhere to one belief system. If every living person thought, acted, and believed in the same way, there would be no thoughts to think. We would be like Vivekananda said, "mummies at a museum staring at each other." The exquisite textures and tapestries of our human existence would devolve into a grey fog.

I have learned from the readings of wise men that the concept of a universal religion is one that celebrates rather than suppresses individual uniqueness and reminds us that each of us has different gifts, insights, and experiences to bring to the table as we learn and grow from one another. A universal religion is the idea of rejoicing in the diversity of our humanity and seeing God in everyone.

Its opposite is a religion that claims to be the only true or right path. Such an organization is centered on ego and pride, rather than the God of universal love and divine uniqueness. A religion claiming to speak for God confuses believers into thinking that devotion to church doctrine and leadership is the same as honoring God. If any religion discourages questioning or limits truth-seeking to an approved library, it is oppressive. And when obedience is encouraged over conscience and choice, the divine potential of each individual is suppressed. That type of sanctimony takes a universal God right out of the picture.

I recall my active married-Mormon days and how I so easily judged others, even someone of my own faith. One example was when a young lady in our ward shared that she felt inspired to leave her husband. Because I'd been taught all my life that God never sanctions divorce, I immediately judged that her so-called inspiration came from Satan himself. My judgment prevented me from reaching out to her with love and compassion at a time when she needed my friendship the most.

A church that preempts independent thinking contributes to universal imbalance. A world of unique individuals must also be a world of many paths. Dogmatic doctrine turns our focus away from our spiritual commonality and creates division among friends, families, and communities. Its perceived solution is a conversion of the entire world to the "true church," one lost soul at a time. This arrogance underlines the great divide, the separateness that prevails over common sense and Godly love.

In our world today, increasingly, spiritually-minded people are understanding that church or religious membership cannot by itself help them to know God. It is our own individual responsibility to develop a relationship with Him and learn to love as He loves.

My escape from organized religion has allowed me to concentrate on living in congruence with the infinite wisdom that exists within me. *Who is this girl beyond the veil of mind-conditioning?* After years of being programmed to fit into a repressed, small, shameful, version of myself, I now have the rest of my life to embrace Jennifer Empowered.

CHAPTER 80

FREE AT LAST

From my earliest years, I was raised in a culture of unquestioning obedience. My church chose a path and laid out for me how I should act, dress, think and feel, whom I should befriend and whom to reject, what books I should read or not read, which movies I should watch or not watch, and what I should eat and drink or not eat and drink. The list goes on and on.

Stepping away from all that control has blessed me with the freedom to reject Shame and welcome the gentle voice of Guilt when I stray from the values I've chosen for myself. I am firmly on the path toward self-love, and this has become my definition of "worthy."

With freedom comes empowerment as well as responsibility. It's now up to me to evaluate my own thoughts and actions. I'm the one who decides what choices to make—not because of some rule or commandment, but because I have discovered that my own conscience is a powerful guiding light that I can trust to illuminate my way.

Today, that still, small voice speaks kindly and inspires me to make decisions that are conducive to my health and well-being, and that of others—choices that keep me safe from mental and physical harm. And if I sometimes lose my way, I learn from my mistakes and grow from them, unfettered by the cruel judgement or condemnation of an institution or its authorities.

For a half-century, I whiled away my time frantically searching for that one elusive man. In blind obedience, I continued to believe that following the covenant path would lead to eternal marriage and joy so great that it surpassed any earthly experience.

At the crossroads, I thoughtfully chose a new road, and it has made all the difference. It led me to a vibrant world of endless choices and possibilities. I found my husband after I found me. Of all things, he was on a dating site—an awful place to find a man. I know because I had tried them all from E-harmony to Match.com over many years.

When I turned 60, I joined a free online site just for kicks, thinking it might be fun to exchange a few laughs and interact with a stranger behind a screen. But then I quickly forgot all about the site. Until one day, I remembered and decided to check my messages.

I opened a message from a real hot-looking guy. He had to be a cad. In my experience, all handsome men were problematic in one way or another. "Hi," he said. "Do you wanna meet a really great guy?" With trepidation, I wrote back. There had to be something wrong with him, otherwise he would have been taken already.

But this time I struck gold. Although my metaphorical sun had dipped below the horizon a decade earlier, the cool thing about life is that it's full of surprises.

Charlie, my husband, and I have shared a wonderful life for nine years. Half Italian, and fit at five-eleven, his dark hair has silvered as we approach the golden years. But his inner reflection and self-knowledge has become more refined. He is good, kind, wise, patient, supportive, and my best advocate. Through his spiritual journey of daily meditation, he has taught me by example how natural and easy love is.

In this beautiful place where we reside, Charlie and I and the God that lives within us have the power to create exquisite joy. Together, we find it everywhere as we navigate the ups and downs of life. The journey that ultimately brought me to this place was a wild ride, indeed, and that is my next story ...

THANK YOU FOR READING MY BOOK!

I really appreciate all your feedback and
I would love hearing what you have to say.
I need your input to make my next book
(my continued story) better.

Please take two minutes now to leave a helpful review on
Amazon letting me know what you thought of the book.

Thanks so much!
- *Jennifer Joy Wilson*
jennifer@goodmormongirl.com
youtube handle: crazymusiclady

EPILOGUE

My children's names have been changed.

Today my daughter Claire is successful and happy. She and I are closer than we have been in years. She has earned a Ph.D. in Cognitive Psychology, is an impressive lecturer, and the incredible mother of my adorable sixteen-year-old grandson. Claire sustains her singing/songwriting career by contracting with public educational systems in Third World countries, helping to better educate students living under poor economic conditions.

Zach, like his mom and siblings, has excelled since his youth as a singer/songwriter, and is an amazing pianist and guitarist. He has a brilliant mind which he applies in his career as a website developer. From his first stressful job in New York City, he eventually found peace working remotely from the Philippines. His break from the family has been painful, but we cherish the sweet moments we have had together and hope the future will bring resolve.

My last-born, Drew, is still adorably easy going and laid-back. As a singer/songwriter, pianist and guitarist, he is drawn to unusual lyrics and chord progressions to create untraditional music. He has a BA in Computer Science and a Master's degree in Creative Writing. More importantly, he is a great husband and the proud father of my artistically talented eight-year-old granddaughter.

I'm very proud of all three of my children and their many successes, despite the challenges of a broken home and emotionally troubled father who never got to know them for the marvelous human beings they are.

A GLIMPSE INTO THE AUTHOR

Jennifer Joy Wilson has been writing poetry and stories since she was eight-years old. In her Mormon days, she enjoyed writing musicals for her church and acting goofy on stage. From 1999 to 2010, she sold thousands of her "Sing the Scriptures" mastery songs for LDS Seminary and won the grateful hearts of countless seminary teachers around the globe.

Today, a handful of Jennifer's inspirational songs have radio and interent airtime in five different western states. As an author, singer/songwriter, and classical pianist, Jennifer uses a variety of mediums to bring joy to the hearts of many.

www.ingramcontent.com/pod-product-compliance
Lightning Source LLC
Chambersburg PA
CBHW030350130626
46549CB00004B/1440